COGNTIVE 2020

The Twelfth International Conference on Advanced Cognitive Technologies and Applications

October 25 - 29, 2020

COGNITIVE 2020 Editors

Charlotte Sennersten, CSIRO Mineral Resources, Australia
Oana Dini, IARIA, EU/USA

Printed from e-media with permission by:

Curran Associates, Inc.
57 Morehouse Lane
Red Hook, NY 12571

Some format issues inherent in the e-media version may also appear in this print version.

International Academy, Research, and Industry Association (IARIA)
412 Derby Way
Wilmington, DE 19810

Phone: (408) 893-6407
Fax: (408) 527-6351

petre@iaria.org

Additional copies of this publication are available from:

Curran Associates, Inc.
57 Morehouse Lane
Red Hook, NY 12571 USA
Phone: 845-758-0400
Fax: 845-758-2633
Email: curran@proceedings.com
Web: www.proceedings.com

Table of Contents

The Dictionary Game: Toward a Characterization of Lexical Primitives Using Graph Theory and Relational Concept Analysis 84

Mickael Wajnberg, Jean-Marie Poulin, Alexandre Blondin Masse, and Petko Valtchev

COGNITIVE 2020

Forward

The Twelfth International Conference on Advanced Cognitive Technologies and Applications (COGNITIVE 2020), held on October 25 - 29, 2020, targeted advanced concepts, solutions and applications of artificial intelligence, knowledge processing, agents, as key-players, and autonomy as manifestation of self-organized entities and systems. The advances in applying ontology and semantics concepts, web-oriented agents, ambient intelligence, and coordination between autonomous entities led to different solutions on knowledge discovery, learning, and social solutions.

The conference had the following tracks:

- Brain information processing and informatics
- Artificial intelligence and cognition
- Agent-based adaptive systems
- Applications

Similar to the previous edition, this event attracted excellent contributions and active participation from all over the world. We were very pleased to receive top quality contributions.

We take here the opportunity to warmly thank all the members of the COGNITIVE 2020 technical program committee, as well as the numerous reviewers. The creation of such a high quality conference program would not have been possible without their involvement. We also kindly thank all the authors that dedicated much of their time and effort to contribute to COGNITIVE 2020. We truly believe that, thanks to all these efforts, the final conference program consisted of top quality contributions.

Also, this event could not have been a reality without the support of many individuals, organizations and sponsors. We also gratefully thank the members of the COGNITIVE 2020 organizing committee for their help in handling the logistics and for their work that made this professional meeting a success.

We hope COGNITIVE 2020 was a successful international forum for the exchange of ideas and results between academia and industry and to promote further progress in the area of cognitive technologies and applications.

COGNITIVE 2020 General Chair

Jaime Lloret Mauri, Universitat Politecnica de Valencia, Spain

COGNITIVE 2020 Steering Committee

Charlotte Sennersten, CSIRO Mineral Resources, Australia
Jayfus Tucker Doswell, The Juxtopia Group, Inc., USA

COGNITIVE 2020 Publicity Chair

Javier Rocher, Universitat Politecnica de Valencia, Spain

COGNITIVE 2020 Industry/Research Advisory Committee

Tiago Thompsen Primo, Samsung Research Institute, Brazil
Kazuhisa Miwa, Nagoya University, Japan
Olga Chernavskaya, Lebeved Physical Institute, Moscow, Russia
Paul Smart, University of Southampton, UK

COGNITIVE 2020

Committee

COGNITIVE 2020 General Chair

Jaime Lloret Mauri, Universitat Politecnica de Valencia, Spain

COGNITIVE 2020 Steering Committee

Charlotte Sennersten, CSIRO Mineral Resources, Australia
Jayfus Tucker Doswell, The Juxtopia Group, Inc., USA

COGNITIVE 2020 Publicity Chair

Javier Rocher, Universitat Politecnica de Valencia, Spain

COGNITIVE 2020 Industry/Research Advisory Committee

Tiago Thompsen Primo, Samsung Research Institute, Brazil
Kazuhisa Miwa, Nagoya University, Japan
Olga Chernavskaya, Lebeved Physical Institute, Moscow, Russia
Paul Smart, University of Southampton, UK

COGNITIVE 2020 Technical Program Committee

Witold Abramowicz, University of Economics and Business, Poland
Thomas Agotnes, University of Bergen, Norway
Vered Aharonson, University of the Witwatersrand, Johannesburg, South Africa
Sadam Al-Azani, King Fahd University of Petroleum & Minerals, Saudi Arabia
Piotr Artiemjew, University of Warmia and Masuria in Olsztyn, Poland
Petr Berka, University of Economics, Prague, Czech Republic
Ateet Bhalla, Independent Consultant, India
Mahdi Bidar, University of Regina, Canada
Guy Andre Boy, CentraleSupélec, LGI,Paris Saclay University /ESTIA Institute of Technology, France
Dilyana Budakova, Technical University of Sofia - Branch Plovdiv, Bulgaria
Minghao Cai, University of Alberta, Canada
Valerie Camps, Paul Sabatier University - IRIT, Toulouse, France
Yaser Chaaban, Leibniz University of Hanover, Germany
Olga Chernavskaya, P. N. Lebeved Physical Institute, Moscow, Russia
Helder Coelho, Universidade de Lisboa, Portugal
Geert de Haan, Wittenborg University of Applied Research Apeldoorn/Amsterdam, Netherlands
Angel P. del Pobil, Jaume I University, Spain
Soumyabrata Dev, University College Dublin, Ireland

Jayfus Tucker Doswell, The Juxtopia Group, Inc., USA
António Dourado, University of Coimbra, Portugal
Birgitta Dresp-Langley, Centre National de la Recherche Scientifique (CNRS) | ICube Lab, CNRS - University of Strasbourg, France
Mounîm A. El Yacoubi, Telecom SudParis, France
Mauro Gaggero, National Research Council of Italy, Italy
Foteini Grivokostopoulou, University of Patras, Greece
Grace Grothaus, University of California San Diego, USA
Davide Andrea Guastella, Institut de Recherche en Informatique de Toulouse (IRIT)| Université de Toulouse III - Paul Sabatier, France
Fikret Gürgen, Bogazici University, Turkey
Ioannis Hatzilygeroudis, University of Patras, Greece
Tzung-Pei Hong, National University of Kaohsiung, Taiwan
Xinghua Jia, ULC Robotics, USA
Yasushi Kambayashi. Nippon Institute of Technology, Japan
Jozef Kelemen, Silesian University, Czech Republic
Joao E. Kogler Jr., Polytechnic School of Engineering of University of Sao Paulo, Brazil
Miroslav Kulich, Czech Technical University in Prague, Czech Republic
Leonardo Lana de Carvalho, Universidade Federal dos Vales do Jequitinhonha e Mucuri - UFVJM, Brazil
Nathan Lau, Virginia Tech, USA
Hakim Lounis, UQAM, Canada
Prabhat Mahanti, University of New Brunswick, Canada
Wajahat Mahmood Qazi, COMSATS University Islamabad, Lahore, Pakistan
Giuseppe Mangioni, DIEEI - University of Catania, Italy
Franova Marta, CNRS, LRI & INRIA, France
Kazuhisa Miwa, Nagoya University, Japan
Fernanda Monteiro Eliott, Vanderbilt University, USA
Ardavan S. Nobandegani, McGill University, Montreal, Canada
Yoshimasa Ohmoto, Shizuoka University, Japan
Andrew J. Parkes, University of Nottingham, UK
Alfredo Pereira Jr., São Paulo State University, Brazil
Elaheh Pourabbas, National Research Council of Italy (CNR), Italy
J. Javier Rainer Granados, Universidad Internacional de la Rioja, Spain
Om Prakash Rishi, University of Kota, India
Paul Rosero, Universidad de Salamanca, Spain / Universidad Técnica del Norte, Ecuador
Alexandr Ryjov, Lomonosov Moscow State University | Russian Presidential Academy of National Economy and Public Administration, Russia
Abdel-Badeeh M. Salem, Ain Shams University, Cairo, Egypt
José Santos Reyes, University of A Coruña, Spain
Charlotte Sennersten, CSIRO Mineral Resources, Australia
Paul Smart, University of Southampton, UK
Priyanka Srivastava, International Institute of Information Technology, Hyderabad (IIIT-H), India
Stanimir Stoyanov, Plovdiv University "Paisii Hilendarski", Bulgaria
Tiago Thompsen Primo, Samsung Research Institute, Brazil
Gary Ushaw, Newcastle University, UK
Jaap van den Herik, Leiden Centre of Data Science (LCDS) | Leiden University, Leiden, The Netherlands
Emilio Vivancos, Valencian Research Institute for Artificial Intelligence (VRAIN) | Universitat Politecnica de Valencia, Spain

Xianzhi Wang, University of Technology Sydney, Australia
Ye Yang, Stevens Institute of Technology, USA
Sule Yildirim Yayilgan, NTNU, Norway
Besma Zeddini, EISTI, France

Social Interaction in Knowledge Acquisition: Advanced Curriculum

Critical Review of Studies Relevant to Social Behavior of Infants

Igor Val. Danilov
Academic center for coherent intelligence
ACCI
Riga, Latvia
email: igor_val.danilov@acci.center

***Abstract*— The question of the acquisition of the first social phenomena by newborns is a crucial issue both in understanding the mental development and the ontogenesis of social interaction. The review attempts to investigate other researches that observe social behavior in studies with no communication between subjects. This current analysis reviews several studies on social phenomena – categorization of words, preference of faces and even race – in newborns and 3- to 4-months-old infants and complements their findings. The review states that newborns and young infants are not able to independently classify phenomena from social reality and perceptually interact with adults effectively enough to understand the meanings of social phenomena on their own. The review concludes that the social behavior of infants is driven by adult social learning through non-perceptual social interaction between them. This thesis is supported by the recent review on social behavior of infants and the experiments on language acquisition of adults, where it is also shown the increase of group performance provided by such unconscious mental collaboration. The long-term study of non-perceptual social interaction could form the basis of the advanced curriculum that can efficiently introduce new knowledge into the long-term memory domain of students to facilitate and accelerate their learning.**

Keywords- Interpersonal perception; Socialization; Coherent Intelligence; Non-perceptual social interaction; Mirror system; Theory of mind; Social synchronization; Visual-spatial perspective taking; Problem-Based Learning.

I. INTRODUCTION

Comprehension and interaction with social reality are key issues for the cognitive development. They form many social skills such as language and knowledge acquisition, manifesting themselves practically in social behavior. The question of how and when the meanings of first phenomena of reality are acquired by an empty mind can reveal the ontogenesis of social interaction (i.e., the question of how and when human beings begin behaving socially). The overarching goal of this study is to explore the essence of social interaction by studying social behavior of newborns and infants. Numerous researches were aimed on studying when human beings start behaving socially [1]; other studies explore categorization of social phenomena – words, faces and even race – in newborns and 3- to 4-month-olds infants. This review in particular is designed to investigate more specific questions of what helps newborns and infants behaving socially during experiments, where these human beings do not yet know enough meanings of social phenomena to socially behave and with no communication between subjects. Section II explains the modern knowledge about acquisition of first social phenomena in infants. The Section III reviews articles which studied social behavior among infants through facial recognition. Section IV presents the finding about word categorization in infants. Section V elaborates all findings from Section III and Section IV, describing their meaning. Sections VI and VII present some ideas on advanced curriculum, based on the non-perceptual interaction.

II. ACQUISITION OF SOCIAL PHENOMENA

Key issues in selecting studies for this review were behavioral parameters belonging to the division between physiological reactions and social behavior of newborns and infants (i.e., differences between innate or learned from the environment actions.) Developmental psychologists consider that initial learning occurs within a shared referential context through repetitive multimodal routines, which allow infants to utilize current knowledge to predict and acquire new meanings [2]. Danilov and Mihailova [3] argued that acquisition of knowledge is mainly based on discovery of new key relationships between cause and effect within prior knowledge, and/or on the opening links between elements of prior knowledge and new information domain. 'This means that the acquisition of initial words also requires infants to be able to also demonstrate some basic knowledge on the social reality around – specific basic knowledge of their particular group, considering the existence of about 6,000 languages in even more groups and communities, all with their unique social reality – as well as needs efficient communication, which is a reciprocal exchange of mutually intended meanings [3, p. 147].' That is the issue of 'current knowledge' (i.e., assimilation of the first or initial meanings of social phenomena) is still a focus of discussions. Initial learning theories are developed within the framework of two core approaches: the innate knowledge and the acquired knowledge from the environment. Some recent studies attempted to address the problem of acquiring the initial social phenomena; they suggest that infants exhibit some general sensitivities and expectations at the onset of language acquisition (this later could be adjusted to the particular language environment that the young infants find around) [4] and/or expect to learn reference information through ostensive cues [5]. For instance, Waxman and Leddon [4] have proposed that infants begin the task of word learning equipped with an initially general and universal expectation. The expectation is then formed by the structure of the particular language. They then grow sensitivity to these perceptual cues. This allows them to separate two classes of words: open class words (nouns, adjectives, verbs) and closed class words, including determiners and prepositions [4]. According to Csibra and Gergely [5], infants are sensitive to certain ostensive cues. Their theory of natural pedagogy suggests that infants expect to learn reference information through signals that relatives direct to them. For example in case of young infants these ostensive cues manifest themselves following the gaze [5]. Danilov and Mihailova [3] have questioned these theories above following recent researches and concluding that: The perceptual sensitivities and expectations that Waxman and Leddon [4] proposed, and/or ostensive cues Csibra and Gergely [5] are not able alone to fill infants' personal reality with a sufficient number of phenomena in order to start categorization [3]. The latest study of Silverstein in 2019 [6] supports the above conclusions of Danilov and Mihailova [3], also refuting the idea of core role of ostensive signals in initial learning of infants. The approach to explain the acquisition of initial social phenomena by imitation is also unconvincing. Newborns and 3- to 4-month-olds infants are not able to imitate social behavior, since 'infants do not imitate others until their second year, and that imitation of different kinds of behaviour emerges at different ages [7].'

Another approach, the one from innate knowledge to the problem of acquiring initial social phenomena, is based on the idea of sound–to–meaning correspondences [8][9]. Rizzini introduced an idea of 'visible-expressive code that precedes the use of phonetic codes [8]'. In his study of the sense of articulate-oral gestures people use phonetic sounds to convey meaning. Sounds correspond to oral gestures that create them, which in turn substitute behavioral responses to internal and external events. This means practically that articulate-oral gestures have universal meanings through innate visible-expressive code. This theory also suggests a mechanism for collecting social phenomena by newborns: actual physiological responses of the newborns to internal and external events are superimposed in their neural circuits on the innate visible-expressive codes. If they coincide, then they are filled with meanings and stored. These meaningful gestures remain in their operative disposal, as a library of the same events. The set of articulate-oral gestures, created in such a manner, becomes an adequate response to the actual needs of their social reality. This means that newborns arrive in social life with neurological tools suitable for behavioral responses, and are able to use them carefully and efficiently depending on the occurrence. This process leads to neurological growth of newborns with the help of more and more effective symbolization through the visible-expressive codes [8]. This very well-developed theory explains part of the social interaction that occurs via unconscious communication throughout life. However the acquisition of initial social phenomena by newborns can be explained limitedly within the framework of above noted innate visible-expressive code and/or any other embodied cognition approach, because this approach contains of difficulties:

(i) lack of empirical evidence and, probably, the impossibility of ever proving the standpoint of innate knowledge on social phenomena.

(ii) absence of mechanism that can explain such innate transfer of knowledge based on biology and/or laws of physics. Social behavior is influenced by many environmental factors and also by psychological traits of individual, the heritability of which is caused by many genes of small effect [10]. Obviously, genes impact individuals' traits, which certainly have some influence on social behavior. The genetic mechanism contributes to social behavior but not with a substantial contribution. Psychological traits impact too on behavior of individual but they are one of many other factors that guide a person to make a decision. Another big component that we should not forget is the freewill. People's attitudes toward innate differences in human appearance – such as skin and hair color, shape and color of eyes, and facial attractiveness – evolve in history and differ between cultures. The semiotician Umberto Eco [11] argued about the concept on how these phenomena are construct together: the notions of beautiful and ugly are defined in relation to a particular historical period or a particular culture [11]. Many social phenomena are based on attitudes toward innate physical features of individuals, such as facial attractiveness, skin color, hair color, congenital physical differences and race. The innate nature of these particularities does not change their essence as social phenomena, and it also does not mean that the innate mechanism of social behavior can exist. For example, race is not an inherited social phenomenon. Racial discrimination is a modern social construct, for until the sixteenth century there was practically nothing in the life and thought of the West that could be characterized as racism [12]. Race does not even have a physical or biological meaning. Geneticists note that 'the proportion of human genetic variation due to differences between populations is modest, and individuals from different populations can be genetically more similar than individuals from the same population [13].'

(iii) the conflict with the generally accepted neo-Darwinian evolutionary principles. Even if one assumes that genes impact on traits more than above indicated (in point ii), and therefore the relationship between genes and social behavior is closer than it is, even so, genes can provide inheritance for a very limited number of social phenomena. The cultural development is too fast for natural selection through the genetic mechanism. Social phenomena change faster than genes change through natural selection, so this means that genes encoding the reflection of certain social conventions will be eliminated before being expressed. In a rapidly changing environment, phenotypic flexibility in dealing with different environments is usually preferable to genes that shift the phenotype narrowly toward a particular environment [14]. For instance, the 'young' 'genetic tolerance in adults for lactose probably arose and spread to high frequencies within the last 6,000 years in some populations of this same language family [14]', compared to the 'old' social phenomenon of racial discrimination, which is no more than 600 years old [12].

Taking into account the above arguments, the author believes that the acquisition of first social phenomena is still a subject of discussion. The author also believes that any theory of knowledge and/or mind, in order to become acceptable to the academic community, must comply with the laws of physics and be supported by mathematical models. This means that having a deeper understanding of the physical processes of information transfer that underlies initial learning is the goal of current and future researches. The above reflection noted that the attitude of men to some physical features of other individuals is social phenomena acquired in the process of social learning. Therefore, the current review examined social interaction of newborns and infants, studying what can help newborns behave socially in different social tasks – (a) recognition of faces: Other Race Effect (ORE), Other Species Effect (OSE), facial attractiveness, and (b) categorization of words – until infants understand enough meanings of phenomena from social reality to initiate social behavior their own.

III. Newborns and Infants Behave Socially: Facial Recognition

Over the past 50 years, numerous studies have begun to examine the social behavior of infants through facial recognition. Most of them support results of their identification of parents, women, perception of multiracial faces ORE, other species faces OSE, as well as preference of facial attractiveness. Their findings are crucial for the present review:

(1) Goren et al. [15] showed that newborn tracked a moving schematic face with a strong preference for the face patterns over the other stimuli [15][16].

(2) Newborns demonstrated preference for their mother's face over a stranger's face [17]-[20].

(3) Newborns prefer faces from their own-ethnic group, ORE [21][22].

(4) Preferences of infants depend on their caregivers. Tasting 3- to 4-month-olds infants, Quinn et al. [23] suggested that 'representation of information about human faces by young infants may be influenced by the gender of the primary caregiver.'

(5) 3-month-old infants prefer the natural composition of inner features of faces rather than the same features, but in an unnatural position. Turati et al. [24] observed reactions of infants on women pictures. Black-and-white photographs of women's faces have been digitally modified altering the position of internal facial features. Infants saw both normal and modified faces. This study suggested 'that the face arrangement of the inner features in the natural face affects infants' performance, attracting infants' gaze even when face configurations are paired for stimuli equated with up–down asymmetry in the distribution of inner features [24, p. 268]'.

(6) Newborns recognize familiar faces even presented partly. Simion et al. [25] eliminated one by one inner and internal features from photographs of women's faces found that: '1- to 3-day-old infants are capable of recognizing a familiar face based on either the inner or outer features, and on either featural or configural perceptual properties.'

(7) Newborns prefer attractive faces. 'Human infants prefer to look at physically attractive human faces when they are paired with physically less attractive human faces. Infant preference for attractive faces has been observed for a range of human faces, including Caucasian and African American adult female faces, adult male faces, and infant faces [26]'. 'The attractiveness effect can be demonstrated even in newborn infants, is orientation dependent, occurring for upright but not inverted faces, and is driven by the internal features of faces [26]'.

(8) The 3- to 4-month-olds infants prefer attractive faces of cats. The results of Quinn et al. [26] demonstrated that 'the preference for attractive faces by infants that has previously been observed for human faces can also be observed for domestic cat faces [26, p. 80]'.

(9) The 6- to 9-months-old infants recognize race even through observing grayscale faces in black-and-white photographs. 'Results for the grayscale stimuli showed that even when a salient perceptual cue to race, such as skin color information, is minimized, 6- to 9-month-olds, nonetheless, show an ORE in their face recognition memory. Infants' use of shape-based and configural cues for face recognition is discussed [27, p.641]'.

(10) The 3-month-olds infants from cross-race environment did not show ORE. 'African Israeli infants (who by virtue of being a very small ethnic minority experience considerable cross-race exposure) do not develop a preference for own-race faces [28, p. 162].' 'Biracial infants, however, showed the opposite effect: An 'own-race' novelty preference was associated with reduced scanning between eye and mouth regions of 'own-race' habituation stimuli, suggesting that biracial infants use a distinct approach to processing frequently encountered faces [29, p. 1].'

IV. Newborns and Infants Behave Socially: Words Categorization

Categorization of social phenomena is the skill that allows for social interaction. Adequate interaction with objects depends fundamentally on a person's ability to categorize [30]. How infants bring order into their world by categorizing objects is a core issue for the research in cognitive and language development. Ferry et al. [31] and then Perszyk and Waxman [32] found that 3- to 4-month-olds infants already can categorize words – fishes and dinosaurs from different classes – that do not fit into their personal reality. According I. Val. Danilov and Mihailova [3]: it is necessary to note several circumstances to assess their results:

(i) infants participated at the experiments always with adults: with their caregivers in pair, infants sat on a caregivers' lap facing the stage as well as a supervisor of the experiment, who was there in the contact with infants;

(ii) infants did not perceptually interact with anyone during experiments;

(iii) all persons involved in the experiment – both participants of the pairs infant-caregiver as well as the supervisor – received tasks simultaneously;

(iv) infants improved performance during the experiments when objects were marked vocally that present adult also listened to;

(v) the chosen visual stimuli are fishes and dinosaurs from different classes, that do not fit into the personal reality of 3- to 4-months-old infants [3, p. 151].

V. Discussion

The review evidently shows a discrepancy between the complexity of tasks and ability of infants to solve them. Ten facts from studies on facial recognition and the contradiction from studies on word categorization show infants' social behavior that does not fit with their ability to understand social reality. The beginning of independent assimilation of social phenomena by infants is possible only when a lot of knowledge is already in place: (i) the meaning of 'I', distinct from the environment; (ii) separation of the environment on immovable and movable objects, the retrieval familiar objects from others; (iii) understanding of truth and false, (iv) understanding of the meanings of initial social phenomena, to rely on in order to begin acquiring the meanings of objects from social reality. The analysis of the above noted 11 facts (Sections III and IV) enlightened in the following statements:

– Newborns have very limited knowledge of social reality to behave socially on their own, since their mind does not maintain any communication. Even if one ignores the necessary effectiveness of communication skills to maintain the acquiring social meaning mechanism and assumes that one of the existing hypotheses (or all together) promotes the mechanism of initial learning, then newborns would not have the time to acquire the meanings of enough social phenomenon to understand social reality to such an extent to recognize faces without their context: in schematic pictures (fact 1), distinguishing mother and stranger (fact 2), discriminating race (fact 3), recognizing faces through their parts (fact 6), and even selecting attractive faces (fact 7). The research of Danilov and Mihailova argued that at this stage of mental development infants cannot acquire meaning of social reality their own because of lack communication: they initiate to develop their non-verbal communication since 12-months of age [3].

– The 3- to 4-month-olds infants cannot independently understand phenomena that are not related to their social reality, which is very limited. The lack of communication noted above does not allow infants to know nature well enough to distinguish attractive cat faces from non-attractive ones (fact 8), and to know anatomy well enough to prefer the natural composition of inner facial features rather than the same features, but in an unnatural position, recognizing faces without their context (fact 5). Regarding the fact of word categorization (Section IV), 'infants cannot themselves recognize and classify inappropriate phenomena that are absent or inaccessible to their reality; even if one forgets about the problem of assimilating of first notions and the acquiring of the first words, and supposes that infants somehow themselves have already learned some basic set of meanings, there is another problem of comprehension of abstract phenomena – the above-noted fishes and dinosaurs are not suitable objects for the categorization experiment with 3- to 4-months-old infants; it is very hard to believe that without the help of adults they can categorize such abstract phenomena [3, p. 155].'

VI. Conclusion

These achievements of infants are possible only through their collaboration with adults. Adults somehow guide infants without any perceptual instruction and/or hints to them. This supposition is also supported by the facts that: the preference of 3- to 4-month-olds infants depends on their caregivers (fact 4); infants from cross-race environment did not show ORE (fact 10); and infants independently can solve tasks even difficult for adults: the 6- to 9-month-olds infants recognize race even through observing grayscale faces in black-and-white photographs (fact 9). Hence, taking all arguments together it is possible to conclude that the initial social learning occurs through non-perceptual social interaction at least partly. One possible explanation for this phenomenon was introduced by Danilov in the theory of Coherent intelligence: 'Coherent Intelligence is an effect of unconscious collaboration provided by interconnection of many brains united by entanglement state of their neurons – the phenomenon of quantum entanglement of particles – which is stimulated by common emotional arousal. This connection of entangled neurons may unite neural chains of different cerebrums and maintain their coherent mental process [33, p. 109].' This theory supposes that the phenomenon emerges from collaboration of many individuals if they solve an important problem for them at the same time within the framework of single emotional stimulation [33]. Recent research by Danilov and Mihailova [3] on language acquisition in adults supported this conclusion showing the increase of group performance provided by such unconscious mental collaboration. The theory corresponds to the laws of quantum physics and future research may supplement it with a mathematical model. The long-term study of this rudimental non-perceptual social interaction, which was developed before the emergence of the 5 perceptual senses could complement the understanding of human development within the framework of the modern paradigm of evolutionary theory. The growing field of knowledge and the multicultural environment of its development require improving teaching methods that include higher-order thinking with deeper levels of information processing to create richer memory structures for students. The author believes that long-term studies can help to develop an advanced curriculum based on the non-perceptual social interaction. This method can facilitate learning in various academic disciplines by introducing knowledge even unconsciously while studying the program.

VII. Future Work

Recent studies show that group collaboration in problem-solving can significantly increase memorization by 28%, the effect of which increases to 30% in a month. 'Taking part in a relevant group discussion had a direct positive impact on recall, whilst this positive effect persisted over a longer period only for those who had given explanations during the discussion [34]'. This probably means that a learning method based on problem-solving – such as the Problem Based Learning (PBL) method – may suit such a procedure which helps learners to increase implicit memory during solving problems. The crucial point of the PBL is a discovery or insight, which is still inexplicable, unpredictable and uncontrollable process [35]. Some recent researches [36] questioned the efficiency of knowledge acquisition in the PBL. Colliver [36] argued: 'this review of the research on the effectiveness of PBL curricula provides no convincing evidence that PBL improves knowledge base and clinical performance, at least not of the magnitude that would be expected given the extensive resources required for the operation of a PBL curriculum'. He also summarized that the results of the PBL method to accelerate learning are not significant enough in respect of efforts required. This is considering how many resources the PBL needs to be applied in opposition to the classical learning and also the fact that the speed of this type of learning is less than in the one-to-one tutoring [36].

Contemporary studies on the PBL method concentrate more its development towards efficiency in criticism training of students rather than to accelerate their knowledge acquisition. Numerous studies, such as one by Rotgans and Schmidt [37], and another one by Masek and Yamin [38], have shown that the PBL method can effectively help students to develop various abilities such as critical thinking and practical skills (as well as enhance their learning motivation and volition): 'Based on the review, it is concluded that 1) the specific processes in PBL theoretically support students' critical thinking development according to the design applied, 2) empirical evidence in general is inconclusive in explaining the effect of PBL on students' critical thinking ability, especially the studies outside of medical field, 3) some evidence indicates that PBL requires a long term exposure to foster students' critical thinking ability, 4) several predictors might also influence the relationships of PBL and critical thinking such as age, gender, academic achievement, and educational background, which calls for further research work. The implication is that, PBL curriculum must carefully be designed and concerned on the critical elements contributing to PBL effectiveness [38]'.

It seems that the modern PBL method is focused on stimulating students to interactive collaboration, by pushing their motivation and interest, which of course is necessary, but does not distinguish clearly the PBL from other methods of training and does not achieve its contemporary goal to accelerate knowledge acquisition. It should be noted that the problem-based essence of the PBL method requires to include in the learning process the actual problem solving activity. This by make students overcoming staged difficulties through their own insight. So not only reaching the solution of simple tasks that doesn't involve cognitive processes of higher-order thinking like the more classic learning methods. The PBL method was established to involve problem solving in the learning process at every stage. 'In PBL, the problem comes first [39]'. The teacher needs to create quite difficult problems to 'switch on' the phenomenon of insight in students. It shouldn't be just a set of tasks as a formal pretext to invite students into an entertaining lesson.

Taking into account all the mentioned above challenges in the contemporary society, the PBL requires confident involvement in its process of high-order thinking with deep levels of information processing and critical thinking skills to achieve success. The author believes that future researches on non-perceptual interaction could be able to develop a PBL method in which teachers can predictably improve the implicit memory of students, incorporating higher-order thinking with deeper levels of information processing in learning. More research is needed to expand our knowledge on non-perceptual social interaction in order to support the development of advanced curriculum based on the PBL method.

Acknowledgment

The author thanks Dr. Sandra Mihailova for her collaboration in research and also expresses his gratitude to Dr. David Vernon and Dr. Tullio Rizzini for their help in preparing this review.

References

1. I. Val. Danilov, "Ontogenesis of Social Interaction: Review of Studies Relevant to the Fetal Social Behavior," J Med - Clin Res & Rev. 2020; 4(2): 1-7. Available from: http://scivisionpub.com/pdfs/ontogenesis-of-social-interaction-review-of-studies-relevant-to-the-fetal-social-behavior-1081.pdf.
2. M. Tomasello, "Constructing a Language: A Usage-Based Theory of Language Acquisition," Cambridge: Harvard University Press. 2003
3. I. Val. Danilov and S. Mihailova, "Social interaction shapes infants' earliest links between language and cognition," Social Sciences Bulletin, 2019 2 (29), ISSN 1691-1881, eISSN 2592-8562.
4. S. R. Waxman and E. M. Leddon, "Early Word-Learning and Conceptual Development," The Wiley-Blackwell Handbook of Childhood Cognitive Development. 2010. [retrieved: 02, 2020]: https://www.academia.edu/12821552/Early_Word-Learning_and_Conceptual_Development.
5. G. Csibra and G. Gergely, "Natural pedagogy," Trends Cogn. Sci. 13, pp. 148–153, 2009.

6. P. Silverstein, T. Gligab, G. Westermanna, and E. Parise, "Probing communication-induced memory biases in preverbal T infants: Two replication attempts of Yoon, Johnson and Csibra (2008)," Infant Behavior and Development, 55, pp. 77–87, 2019. https://doi.org/10.1016/j.infbeh.2019.03.005.
7. S. S. Jones, "The development of imitation in infancy," Phil. Trans. R. Soc. B, 364, pp. 2325–2335, 2009. doi:10.1098/rstb.2009.0045.
8. T. Rizzini, "The Cultural Linguistic Code," Journal of Life Sciences, 12, pp. 59-63, 2018. doi: 10.17265/1934-7391/2018.01.006.
9. L. L. Namy and L. C. Nygaard, "Perceptual-motor constraints on sound-to-meaning correspondence in language," Behavioral and brain sciences, 31, 5, 2008. doi:10.1017/S0140525X08005190.
10. R. Plomin, J. C. DeFries, V. S. Knopik, and J. M. Neiderhiser, "Top 10 replicated findings from Behavioral genetics," Perspect Psychol Sci. 11(1): pp. 3–23. 2016. doi:10.1177/1745691615617439.
11. U. Eco, "On Ugliness," Maclehose, 2011. ISBN 0857051628, 9780857051622.
12. D. A. Puzzo. "Racism and the Western Tradition," Journal of the History of Ideas, 25 (4), pp. 579–86, 1964. doi:10.2307/2708188.
13. D. J. Witherspoon, S. Wooding, A. R. Rogers, E. E. Marchani, W. S. Watkins, M. A. Batzer, and L. B. Jorde, "Genetic Similarities Within and Between Human Populations. Genetics," 176(1), pp. 351–359, 2007. doi: 10.1534/genetics.106.067355.
14. J. Burger, M. Kirchner, B. Bramanti, W. Haak, and M. G.Thomas, "Absence of the lactase-persistence-associated allele in early Neolithic Europeans," Proceedings of the National Academy of Sciences USA, 104, pp. 3736 – 41, 2007.
15. C. C. Goren, M. Sarty and P. Y. K. Wu, "Visual following and pattern discrimination of face-like stimuli by newborn infants," Pediatrics, 56. pp. 544-1-549, 1975.
16. M. H. Johnson, S. Dziurawiec, H. Ellis and J. Morton, "Newborns' preferential tracking of face-like stimuli and its subsequent decline," Cognition, 40, pp. 1-19, 1991. DOI: 10.1016/0010-0277(91)90045-6.
17. I. W. Bushnell, F. Sai, and J. T. Mullin, "Neonatal recognition of the mother's face," British Journal of Developmental Psychology, 7, pp. 3–15, 1989.
18. T. M. Field, D. Cohen, R. Garcia, and R. Greenburg, "Mother–stranger face discrimination by the newborn," Infant Behavior and Development, 7, pp. 19–25, 1984.
19. O. Pascalis, S. de Schonen, J. Morton, C. Deruelle, and M. Fabre-Grenet, "Mother's face recognition in neonates: a replication and an extension," Infant Behavior and Development, 17, pp. 79–85, 1995.
20. I. W. R. Bushnell, "Mother's face recognition in newborn infants: learning and memory," Infant Child Dev., 10, pp. 67–74. 2001.
21. O. Pascalis and S. de Schonen, "Recognition memory on 3- to 4-day-old human neonates," Neuro Report, 5, pp. 1721–1724, 1994.
22. D. J. Kelly, S. Liu, L. Ge, P. C. Quinn, A. M. Slater, K. Lee, O. Liu and O. Pascalis, "Cross-Race Preferences for Same-Race Faces Extend Beyond the African Versus Caucasian Contrast in 3-Month-Old Infants," Infancy, 11(1), pp. 87–95, 2007. doi:10.1080/15250000709336871.
23. P. C. Quinn, J. Yahr, A. Kuhn, "Representation of the gender of human faces by infants: A preference for female," Perception, Vol 31, pages 1109 – 1121, 2002. DOI:10.1068/p3331, p. 1109.
24. C. Turati, E. Valenza, I. Leo, F. Simion, "Three-month-olds' visual preference for faces and its underlying visual processing mechanisms," Journal of Experimental Child Psychology 90 255–273, p. 268. 2005. doi:10.1016/j.jecp.2004.11.001 .
25. F. Simion, I. Leo, C. Turati, E. Valenza, and B. D. Barba, "How face specialization emerges in the first months of life," Progress in Brain Research, Vol. 164. Elsevier B.V., p. 182, 2007. DOI: 10.1016/S0079-6123(07)64009-6 .
26. P. C. Quinn, D. J. Kelly, K. Lee, O. Pascalis, and A. M. Slater, "Preference for attractive faces in human infants extends beyond conspecifics," Developmental Science, 11, 1, pp. 76–83. p.76, 2008. DOI: 10.1111/j.1467-7687.2007.00647.x.
27. G. Anzures, O. Pascalis, P. C. Quinn, A. M. Slater, K. Lee, "Minimizing Skin Color Differences Does Not Eliminate the Own-Race Recognition Advantage in Infants," Infancy, 16(6), pp. 640–654, International Society on Infant Studies (ISIS), 2011. DOI: 10.1111/j.1532-7078.2010.00066.x.
28. Y. Bar-Haim, T. Ziv, D. Lamy and R. M. Hodes, "Nature and nurture in own-race face processing," Psychological Science, 17, pp. 159–163, 2006.
29. S. E. Gaither, K. Pauker and S. P. Johnson, "Biracial and monoracial infant own-race face perception: an eye tracking study," Developmental Science, pp. 1–9, 2012. DOI: 10.1111/j.1467-7687.2012.01170.x .
30. A. M. Borghi, "Object concepts and action. In Grounding Cognition: The Role of Perception and Action in Memory, Language, and Thinking," Edited by Diane Pecher and Rolf A. Zwaan. New York: Cambridge University Press, pp. 8–34. 2005.
31. A. L. Ferry, S. J. Hespos, S. R. Waxman, "Categorization in 3- and 4-Month-Old Infants: An Advantage of Words Over Tones," Society for Research in Child Development, Inc., 2010. https://doi.org/10.1111/j.1467-8624.2009.01408.x.
32. D. R. Perszyk and S. R. Waxman, "Infants' advances in speech perception shape their earliest links between language and cognition," Scientific reports, 9, p. 3293, 2019. https://doi.org/10.1038/s41598-019-39511-9.
33. I. Val. Danilov. Unconscious Social Interaction: Coherent Intelligence. Second edition complemented. [e-book]. 2019. [retrieved: 02, 2020] https://www.amazon.com.
34. F. M. Van Blankenstein, D. H. J. M. Dolmans, C. P. M. Van der Vleuten, and H. G. Schmidt, "Which cognitive process support learning during small-group discussion? The role of providing explanations and listening to others," Instructional Science, 39(2), pp. 189-204, 2011. Online [retrieved: 02, 2020]: https://link.springer.com/article/10.1007/s11251-009-9124-7.
35. D. Boud and G. I. Feletti, "The Challenge of Problem-based Learning," London: Kogan Page, pp. 40-41. 1997.
36. J. A. Colliver, "Effectiveness of Problem-based Learning Curricula: Research and Theory," 2000 [retrieved: 02, 2020]: https://journals.lww.com/academicmedicine/Fulltext/2000/03000/Effectiveness_of_Problem_based_Learning_Curricula_.17.aspxResults#pdf-link.
37. J. I. Rotgans and H. G. Schmidt, "Effects of Problem-Based Learning on Motivation," Interest, and Learning. 2019. https://doi.org/10.1002/9781119173243.ch7.
38. A. B. Masek and S. Yamin, "The Effect of Problem Based Learning on Critical Thinking Ability: A Theoretical and Empirical Review," 2011. [retrieved: 02, 2020] https://www.researchgate.net/publication/266279314_The_Effect_of_Problem_Based_Learning_on_Critical_Thinking_Ability_A_Theoretical_and_Empirical_Review.
39. H. G. Schmidt, J. I. Rotgans, and E. H. J. Yew, "Cognitive Constructivist Foundations of Problem-Based Learning," The Wiley Handbook of Problem-Based Learning. Miley Blackwell. p.257, 2019.

Symbiotic Thinking … for Cognitive Modeling as Well

Marta Franova, Yves Kodratoff
LRI, UMR8623 du CNRS & INRIA Saclay
Bât. 660, Orsay, France
e-mail: mf@lri.fr , yvekod@gmail.com

Abstract— **The choice of a design paradigm influences the tools that may (or have to) be used and also the level of ambitions that may (or have to) be envisioned. This paper suggests, in Cognitive Science, exploring a particular design paradigm enabling to conceive cognitive theories that guarantee a possibility for future extensions while preserving the atemporal character of the previous achievements. One of the essential tools of this design methodology is symbiosis as a particular composition of building parts of such evolving theories. We have used these topics in a formalization of creative processes involved in the design of Symbiotic Recursive Pulsative Systems, as they are performed while designing a methodology for Automated Program Synthesis from formal specifications in incomplete domains. The paper thus concerns modeling human mental processes as well as human reasoning mechanisms.**

Keywords— Cartesian Systemic Emergence; Symbiotic Recursive Pulsative Systems; Symbiotic Thinking; cognitive models; implementation of human reasoning mechanisms.

I. INTRODUCTION

In contemporary science, a multidisciplinary systems modeling is usually performed by selecting some available logically justifiable (thus 'mathematical') tools and by adapting these tools to purposes for which these tools were not originally designed. As has been known already to Francis Bacon (see [1], p. 68), this approach may lead to artificial difficulties. More recently, Bertalanffy expressed the need for a change as follows: "It may be preferable first to have some nonmathematical model with its shortcomings but expressing some unnoticed aspect, hoping for a future development of a suitable algorithm, than to start with premature mathematical models following known algorithms and, therefore, restricting the field of vision" [3], p. 24.

We have relied on Bertalanffy's suggestion in our work with a design of a particular problem-solving system, namely a system that constructs recursive programs from formal specifications in incomplete domains (called here Program Synthesis in Incomplete Domains, PSID, for short). We realized that a necessary condition for the success of our task is including 'symbiosis' into the design of the system (thus conceiving a symbiotic system) and to our scientific reflection as well (thus performing 'symbiotic thinking'). Roughly speaking, symbiosis concerns a particular composition of the parts of a system. Namely, the essential feature of a symbiotic composition is that, when eliminating an arbitrary part of a symbiotic system, not only the whole system but also all the remaining parts collapse, i.e., the system and its parts cease to exist or are mutilated. A typical example of a symbiotic system is provided by Peano's definition of Natural Numbers (NAT). If we use the symbol ♦ for symbiotic compositions, a formal representation of the systemic definition of NAT reads as: NAT = 0 ♦ Suc ♦ NAT, where Suc is the successor function. If we eliminate one part from this system, for instance 0, we may no more speak of Suc nor of NAT as such. This example illustrates that, while it might not be obviously noticeable, symbiosis is present in formulating primitive notions (such as 0, Suc, Nat) of deductive theories.

The exactness required by mathematical sciences (see [12]) is not suitable for handling symbiosis. This maybe explains why Cognitive Science (CS) relies on modular tools and formulates modular models [2]. In this paper, we want to point out the advantage of designing evolving symbiotic systems/models not only in Computer Science (as illustrated by our work in PSID) but in CS as well. Indeed, such an evolving teleological orientation (*teleos*, lat. "end") of CS research allows handling, in a creative way, problems that are out of the scope of modular systems. For instance, consider the goal specified informally by the following sentence:

(g1) "Construct a scientific model of the human brain that solves all the questions and problems related to a formalization of the brain mental processes".

Researchers in CS will certainly argue that this goal is impossible. We would like to point out that this notion of 'impossible' is related to the present scientific knowledge, scientific tools and models. In this paper, we will present some notions and tools that diminish the strength of this contemporary verdict 'impossible' to a somewhat weaker notion of 'reasonable and achievable, provided that we change our paradigms, tools and that we put in an adequate effort'. Of course, a trade-off of this new approach is replacing the requirement of exactness by the requirements of rigor, control and prevention. By control is meant here the requirement to consider all secondary effects of the evolution in the process of construction of a particular system so that the constructed system needs *no future maintenance*, as it is, for instance, the case for Peano's axioms. By prevention is meant here some careful anticipation of possible future practical needs, opening thus a way to a smooth extension of a previously, practically sufficient system. This can be illustrated by a smooth extension of NAT up to complex numbers. In other words, the acceptance of new essential values leads to interesting by-products, namely, to a creative freedom enabling to consider evolving systems and to non-obsolesce of these systems at each stage of its evolution.

Concerning these essential competitive returns of considering symbiosis in the systems design and modeling, our aim in this paper is to share the essential knowledge we have used in PSID and that we deem useful also for CS.

The paper is structured as follows. Section II specifies the context of this paper. Section III introduces some fundamental notions that are necessary for understanding the topic of this paper. Section IV presents the main problems related to the use of Symbiotic Thinking in creation and modeling symbiotic systems. Finally, Section V presents related and future work.

II. THE CONTEXT

PSID as well as the brain are complex problem-solving systems. Therefore, it is necessary to point out how symbiosis is related to basic problem-solving paradigms. In this section we are going to recall two of these paradigms. We will explain also how symbiosis and modularity are related to these paradigms. Then, we present Cartesian Systemic Emergence as an effort to formalize a particular kind of scientific creativity.

A. Paradigms

Let us briefly draw the difference between modular and symbiotic Paradigms.

In a *modular* system, the parts (called *modules*) of the system are units, entities or operations that can exist all by themselves, though in the modular system they are intended to be used together. Modular systems are designed usually via the paradigm that can be represented by the following formula:

$\forall$ Problem $\exists$ System solves(System,Problem). (P1)

(P1) states that for any problem Pb_i one can build at least one system (or a module) S_i able to solve Pb_i. Usually, S_i is not able to solve a problem Pb_j, for $j \neq i$. This is why we call here heuristics such solutions. Relying on (P1) while constructing a system leads to a library of particular heuristics. One can therefore design a modular system S that is a modular composition of S_i that were previously built. Of course, this does not imply that S necessarily represents a global solution for all possible problems Pb_j, since a global solution is a unique universal method for all problems. Paradigm (P1) is useful when one of the main goals is to guarantee a simple maintenance of resulting systems [18] [13]. Most system designing approaches are thus based on this paradigm [6] [13] - [15] [18].

In contrast to modular systems, the creation of symbiotic systems usually relies on the paradigm expressed by the following formula:

$\exists$ System $\forall$ Problem solves(System,Problem). (P2)

(P2) states that one may build at least one system that will solve all problems. The construction of a system via (P2) largely differs from the one of via (P1). (P2) has to result in a single universal system S. For instance, Peano's arithmetic for NAT is an illustration in which (P2) has been used. Note that this illustrates that it is meaningful to rely on (P2) while creating a global system, even though the resulting system may not verify the completeness requirements. In other words, Gödel's results [12] are not an obstacle for the use of (P2) while designing real-world problem-solving systems.

In this paper, the systems conceived via paradigm (P2) are called P2-systems and the solutions to a problem conceived via (P2) are called P2-solutions. Recall once again that the main difference between a P2-system and a P1-system lies in the fact that a P2-solution is a single unified universal method while a P1-solution is a modular library of heuristics.

B. Cartesian Systemic Emergence

In [5], the author gives an example of a highly smart people group failure to solve a multidisciplinary problem. The main reason for this failure is a lack of effort to build a common vocabulary allowing to integrate skills and knowledge of this group. This illustrates that collaboration on a multidisciplinary topic, as are PSID and (g1), being itself a complex dynamic system (see [21]) requires a preliminary elaboration of a 'meta' action-oriented theory to avoid failures due to missing directed integration of multidisciplinary knowledge and skills. Being aware of the importance of developing and studying symbiotic P2-systems as well as a rather unusual character of *symbiotic* collaborations, we felt necessary to create solid foundations for this new type of research. We call Cartesian Systemic Emergence (CSE) the theory intended to represent these foundations [9]. In [22], we present a preliminary toy example to illustrate CSE in action.

In this paper, we work exclusively in the context of symbiotic P2-systems. The next section presents the most important notions necessary for understanding the complexity and the essential advantages (and drawbacks) of considering symbiotic systems.

III. SOME FUNDAMENTAL NOTIONS

As said above, CSE is intended to become a theory to represent the foundations enabling to understand, perform and evaluate research on symbiotic P2-systems, be it in the form of a design or of a modeling of symbiotic P2-systems. More accurately, the goal of CSE is to formalize strategic aspects of human creation of *informally* specified *symbiotic deductive-like problem-solving systems* in incomplete domains following our *pulsation* model. This formalization is performed to prepare fundamentals for *designing automated tools* that help humans or that may even be able to perform alone this complex task. The goal of CSE is expressed in terms of five fundamental notions.

Since the goal of CSE is to be considered in a P2-framework, i.e., CSE aims at a formalization that is a symbiotic P2-system. Therefore, all the fundamental notions that we need to define are symbiotically interrelated. As a consequence, each of these fundamental notions cannot be clearly described without referring to the other fundamental notions. This is why, in order to introduce such complex descriptions, we will present, at first, a rough description of their meaning independently of their aim to represent a basis of a P2-system. Such a rough description can also be used in the context of modular P1-systems.

As roughly described above, the symbiosis of parts of a system means that, if even only one of these parts is eliminated, not only the system collapses but also all the other symbiotic parts collapse as well. An informal specification of a system is a description of this system that is somewhat vague, i.e., what the words in this description exactly mean may be unclear. Standard deductive-like problem-solving systems are systems that have to be defined exactly by their corresponding axiomatic system. Incomplete domains are domains that are insufficiently formalized in the sense that there might exist several different interpretations corresponding to the considered formalization of the domain. Pulsation is a model for a particular kind of systems evolutive improvement.

We will now provide more details about these notions.

A. *Symbiosis*

In the design of a deductive-like problem-solving system, we need to be aware of a particular interdependence, called here symbiosis, of the parts of the resulting system. By ***symbiosis***, we understand a composition of several parts that is vitally separation-sensitive. By *vital separation-sensitivity* of a composition, we mean that eliminating one of its parts has three possible consequences. It may be a complete destruction or a non-recoverable mutilation or uselessness of the remaining parts. This implies that the divide and conquer strategy, as well as analysis and synthesis are inappropriate tools when creating and observing symbiotic systems. Symbiosis is therefore different from synergy that is a mutually profitable composition of elements that are not destroyed nor mutilated by separation.

A well-known picture that may be used for an intuitive understanding of symbiosis is the well-known so-called 'duck-rabbit' illusion. This picture may be seen as a symbiosis of two parts, namely the 'rabbit' and the 'duck'. In this picture, the result of removing one of its parts (the 'duck', for instance) gives 'nothing'. In other words, the 'rabbit' disappears as well. This is an example of what we mean by 'destruction' in our definition of symbiosis.

The symbiotic parts, however, do not necessarily need to coincide in the final symbiotic object as it is in the case of the just mentioned picture. They may have a symbiotic, possibly a hidden one, intersection that makes their whole symbiotic. From a systemic point of view, symbiosis of a system is embodied by the *vitally separation-sensitive interdependence* of all the notions and the parts of this system.

B. *Informal specification*

In the framework of CSE, an ***informal specification*** of a system is a description of this system by a *sentence* in which occur terms that are not yet exactly defined; they are underspecified. When considered out of a particular context, such a description, i.e., informal specification, may even seem absurd or the goal specified by it may seem impossible to reach. These terms in which a given concrete informal specification is expressed will evolve during the system construction. In other words, depending on some constraints and opportunities that will arise during the construction of the system, the meaning of the terms used in the starting specification will evolve and will make a part of the solution. The initial ambiguity of terms occurring in a given informal specification is eliminated by the provided solution. Their evolution will also bring an exact specification of the context to be considered.

For instance, let us consider the above goal (g1). The notion of 'brain' is specified here informally, since no definite agreement has been provided as to what aspects, functions, *etc.* have to be considered. The same holds about the notion of 'model', 'solve'. In order to point out that these notions will evolve during the research on this imprecisely formulated goal, in the framework of CSE, the notion of informal specification needs to be completed by stressing the difference between the notions of formalized (rigorous) and the one of formal (exact) specification. In CSE, a ***formalized specification*** is an intermediary state in the progress from informal to formal specification. It consists in a collection of not yet uniquely defined definitions and not yet exactly defined tools that plausibly point at a successful completion process. In such a completion process, some inventive steps may still be needed to complete these inexact but rigorous working definitions and tools so that their use and their evolution, through suitable experiences, lead to their final form (i.e., their exact form). A formalized specification allows thus to perform rigorous thinking. In CSE, a ***formal specification*** then consists in a complete solution represented by the working system and the complete knowledge necessary to the system construction, i.e., a particular kind of meta-knowledge. These all are needed in order to be used in further evolutive improvement. The notion of evolutive improvement will be introduced in Section D.

The notion of informal specification plays an important strategic role in the Multidisciplinary Systems Design and Modeling (MSD) since it fulfills the role of balance between rigor and freedom known to be necessary in complex systems for them to evolve, transform and adapt [21].

To give illustrations of a formalized and of a formal specification, we need to introduce the notions of deductive-like problem-solving system (in Section C) and of Pulsation (in Section D). These notions will help us also better illustrate what we mean by symbiosis.

C. *Deductive-like Problem-Solving Systems*

In P2-oriented MSD, explaining what we mean by a deductive system is important, since the goal of CSE is to build a deductive-like P2-system formalizing human creation of P2-symbiotic systems. By ***deductive systems*** we understand a particular kind of axiomatic systems in the sense that these systems formalize, in a compact finite way, the knowledge about a Real World Situation (RWS) with the aim to handle this knowledge in an efficient uniform way.

Peano's Axiomatic Definition (PAD) of NAT and Euclid's Geometry (EG) are the best-known examples of deductive systems. They make a part of what has been called, in the above section, a formal specification.

As can be illustrated by the evolution of PAD and EG, a formalization of an RWS leading to a deductive system consists of a 'selection' of essential primitive notions and axioms representing the essential relationships among these notions.

Primitive notions are the notions that are *not* defined with the help of previously defined notions. Before a full formalization of an RWS, the meaning of these notions is specified, informally, by a *large experience* in RWS which shows that they are useful and essential for considering RWS. For instance, if we consider NAT, a large experience in natural numbers shows that the primitive notions in a formalization of NAT are not only 0 and Suc, but also NAT themselves. Indeed, we cannot (or do not know how to) provide a clear understanding of what we mean by natural numbers by referring to other already defined notions. The primitive notions of a deductive system are, in principle, symbiotic. For instance, as said above for NAT, we cannot specify informally what 0 signifies in another way than by referring, in this informal description, also to Suc and NAT.

As said above, ***axioms*** of a deductive system express the statements about the relationships among the primitive notions. The essential particularity of these relationships is that, together, they provide a formal definition of all the primitive notions. In other words, it is not a particular axiom that defines a particular notion, all axioms are symbiotically necessary to provide a clear understanding (and thus a definition) of the meaning of a particular primitive notion.

Since the primitive notions of PAD and EG are symbiotic, their axioms could not be determined via (P1). The axiomatic constructions of both these systems were determined via (P2) since in both cases the aim was to obtain one global system describing respective RWS.

We shall now informally define what we mean by a deductive-like P2-symbiotic system.

By a ***Deductive-like P2-Symbiotic System*** (P2-DSS) we mean a system such that its primitive notions are specified informally and the essential relationships among them, expressed by a finite number of axioms, provide their exact definition.

Note that, to the best of our knowledge, the symbiotic character of the primitive notions and the axioms of a deductive system has never been mentioned in the literature before.

D. Pulsation

Pulsation is a model for evolutive improvement, including creation, of practically complete systems that are concerned with the factors of control and prevention. In other words, pulsation provides a rigorous framework for the completion process of incomplete systems. In similarity to the infinite sequence which is used in [10] to *construct* Ackermann's function (see its standard definition in [20]), Pulsation relies on a *construction* of a potentially infinite sequence of systems that might be used to construct a global *'Ackermann's system'* that contains all of these systems. In our work, by Pulsation we thus understand a progressive construction of a potentially infinite sequence $S_0, S_1, \ldots, S_n, S_{n+1}, \ldots$ such that

1. S_0 is the initial informal specification,
2. S_i, for $i > 0$, is an incomplete, but a practically complete deductive system,
3. $S_i \subset S_{i+1}, S_i \neq S_{i+1}$ (for $i = 0, 1, 2, \ldots$), and
4. an infinite limit of this sequence represents an ideal, complete deductive system S.

We say here that S_{i+1} is a *practical completion* of S_i (for $i = 0, 1, 2, \ldots$). The fourth requirement can formally be written in the form

$$\lim_{n \to \infty} S_n = S. \tag{1}$$

Note that, in a potentially infinite sequence $S_0, S_1, \ldots, S_n, S_{n+1}, \ldots$, S_0 is an informal specification, while S_1 is a practically complete system. Therefore, the transition from S_0 to S_1 is the most difficult process, since it requires to go from informal specifications to designing all the formal specifications of the notions, the rules and the on-purpose tools that are to be used to describe S_1. The transition from S_i to S_{i+1} is an easier task not only because experience with handling symbiotic parts has been further developed but also because in this transition the notions and the tools of S_i are considered in their formalized version. CSE is being developed to provide a reasonable solution to these two kinds of problems as well.

E. Complementary Notions and Remarks

In the MSD-framework, to consider the above-introduced notions as symbiotically interrelated, i.e., defined in terms of each other, is important for understanding the process of construction of a P2-DSS. For an RWS of a Problem-Solving System (PbSS) expressed by a P2-DSS, the *primitive notions* are specified by informal specifications of the goal of each primitive notion in the context of PbSS. In other words, the informal specifications of primitive notions express the '*what*' behind these notions. The axioms of P2-DSS, conceived for PbSS, express then the '*how*' corresponding to each informally specified '*what*'. In other words, the *axioms are procedures* of PbSS. These procedures are defined symbiotically in a similar way as it can be perceived from the symbiosis of the axioms in PAD.

This has a large implication for understanding the process of construction of a P2-DSS. Namely, it is necessary to understand that the process of specifying the primitive notions is symbiotic with the process of 'introducing' the axioms. In other words, the primitive notions and the axioms 'emerge' together in the process of construction of P2-DSS for a considered RWS.

Above, we have introduced the fundamental notions that contribute to understanding CSE and ST. These notions allow us to introduce, in multidisciplinary systems design, the notion of *Symbiotic Recursive Pulsative Systems* (SRPS) that are, by definition, systems that are implicitly or explicitly symbiotic, that are recursive either by systemic recursion or by the process of evolutive improvement via Pulsation, and that are pulsative, whenever the model of Pulsation (together with the notion of practical completeness) is used in their design. To point out that SRPS are developed via paradigm (P2), we may call them P2-SRPS.

Let us consider an example of a symbiotic system for which we put symbiosis together with recursion, Pulsation and P2-paradigm. Thus, let us consider the above informal specification (g1) from CS. Now, we may ask whether a solution might not be something like

$$\lim_{n\to\infty} \text{Brain}_n = \text{Brain}, \qquad (2)$$

where

$\text{Brain}_n = \text{Left\_Brain}_n \blacklozenge \text{Right\_Brain}_n \blacklozenge \text{RNK}_n$ &

$\text{Left\_Brain}_n = \text{Brain}_{n-1} \blacklozenge \text{RNK1}_n$ &

$\text{Right\_Brain}_n = \text{Brain}_{n-1} \blacklozenge \text{RNK2}_n$

Here, RNK_n is a new knowledge related to symbiotic composition of left and right brains in the n-th pulsation step, RNK1_n and RNK2_n are relevant new knowledge extending, by the process of practical completion, the previous knowledge respectively about Left_Brain_{n-1} and Right_Brain_{n-1}. This means that, with respect to mental processes instead of studying the brain as a synergy of two elements (left and right brain) [2], it might be interesting to explore the potential of this new symbiotic paradigm. Note also that (2) represents a recursive model of the brain, which explicitly indicates its evolutive character.

The next section presents more information about ST.

IV. SYMBIOTIC THINKING

The goal of ST is, in the process of CSE, to create symbiotic compositions as well as to contribute to a relevant suggestion of missing parts relative to a designed P2-SRPS system. Thus, as a by-product of this goal, CSE also aims at a formalization of a particular kind of scientific invention of new scientific concepts (different from scientific discovery [4]) in the design process of a P2-SRPS system. ST is therefore the most complex facet of CSE.

In order to describe ST, let us consider the goal of constructing a Problem-Solving System (PbSS) specified by an Informal Specification (InfS). Note that, as far as mental processes are concerned, the human brain can be considered as a real-world instance of a PbSS. As said above, ST is a conscious construction process aiming at two goals. One goal deals with a relevant evolving symbiotic composition of PbSS's parts. The second deals with a relevant suggestion of missing parts. Achieving these two goals indirectly leads to a progressive refinement and completion of the notions in InfS.

ST is indeed very complex since, in the PbSS's design process, it simultaneously handles three tasks. The first deals with the symbiotic character of all parts of CSE. The second does with the symbiotic character of all parts of a PbSS (even those that are not yet specified in the construction process). The third deals with the symbiotic character of the environment for which PbSS is being developed.

In the process of constructing a PbSS, some elementary parts of the system are specified by the needs that have been recognized in a relevant preliminary theoretical and experimental study of the given informal specification InfS. The consideration of the suggested parts as being informally specified and symbiotic allows

(a) a freedom to design them in an original manner,
(b) letting these parts evolve relying on the requirements that will appear in the design process,
(c) their imperfections (from a theoretical or practical point of view) to be compensated by the other parts of the system or by the system itself,
(d) a natural emergence of minimal forms of complementary constraints on the system, on its parts or on the environment.

These particular competitive advantages of ST and CSE, provided an adequate effort, *enlarge* the possibilities of MSD in that they hand over realistic goals that have before been considered unreachable.

For instance, for brain modeling, (a) and (d) together reflect considering complex experiences from the start so as avoiding simplicity factors to become, in future, obstacles to an effective ideas-activating process. The advantages (b) and (c) together reflect accepting the fact that research on symbiotic systems itself is a complex system [21] and thus it cannot be evaluated from a short-sided perspective of short or mid-term projects, as it is unfortunately usual in contemporary science.

Note that, in this section, our aim is solely to present the role of ST and its advantages for designing a P2-SRPS. We will not describe here its execution. The reason for this restriction lies in the fact that it would also require a detailed description of the strategic aspects of Program Synthesis from underspecified informal specifications in incomplete domains. We shall, therefore, address this topic in our future work.

V. RELATED WORK

In [9], we have pointed out that CSE might well be part of a challenge for CS, namely by developing CS models that capture all the essential characteristics of CSE, by finding methods and tools to study the emergence process in an active performance and developing on-purpose computational models for this particular way of thinking. Here we can enlarge our observation of CS problems that are similar to ST to conceptual blending as studied in [8]. As expressed by Fauconnier and Turner, conceptual blending is a non-deterministic intuitive process performed on small conceptual pockets constructed for purposes of local understanding and action ([8], p. 40), In contrast to this, ST performs consciously a goal-oriented symbiosis taking into account all the aspects (local as well as global, methodological as well as teleological, *etc.* as described in the above section).

Furthermore, if Wittgenstein points out, in [19], the interest for duck-rabbit illusion from the philosophical and psychological points of view, thus formulating a challenge for CS from perception modeling perspective of unusual 'objects', we point out here the challenge of modeling technological aspects of *creating/modeling* symbiotic systems.

Even though the topic of considering ST (and CSE) in CS is challenging, we are convinced that a strong desire or need to solve problems that CSE and ST suggest to CS will lead soon or later to fruitful empowerment of CS.

VI. CONCLUSION AND FUTURE WORK

The novelty of Cartesian Systemic Emergence lies in the fact that CSE is concerned with a formalization of the creation process of P2-SRPS *axioms*. So far, this problem has not been dealt with in modern exact sciences. However, the philosophical works of Francis Bacon [1], René Descartes [7], Peirce [16] and others express that experiences/experiments play an important role in creating the axioms. The symbiosis of axioms points out that these experiments/experiences have to be performed taking into account this particular feature of axioms. For Cognitive Science it would mean to revise all the knowledge on mental processes of the human brain in the light of a possible presence of symbiotic processes that necessarily would mean the presence of symbiotic parts in the brain. Our creative process and its creative formalization process lead us to be firmly persuaded about the presence of symbiotic processes in our brain. Researchers usually do not examine carefully their creative efforts (except for mentioning intuitive unconscious character of their productions, such as [17]). However, once we work in the framework that requires control and prevention, we no more have 'unconscious intuitions' since all the mental processes are conscious. Of course, with respect to an enormous amount of experiences gained in the teleological experimentation process, the included knowledge is not expressed verbally in its formal form but in the form of their 'rigorous' informal specifications. This may be explained by an analogy of representing local computations of Ackermann's function in the form of an on-purpose generated finite sequence of primitive recursive functions replacing the computationally intractable process (i.e., considering all the details of the considered knowledge) by a sequence of primitive recursive functions (i.e., the relevant details pointed out in the form of rigorous informal specifications).

In this paper, we aimed at pointing out the advantages of considering symbiotic pulsative recursive systems also in Cognitive Science. Even though Symbiotic Thinking and CSE are not easy to grasp for formalistic minds (as implicitly shown in [11]), it seems to us that Cognitive Science can, hopefully with our help, benefit from an intensive exploration of recognition and of construction potentials present in Symbiotic Thinking and CSE.

As for our future work on ST, describing ST in action shall need a description of the particularities of strategic aspects of PS from informal specifications in incomplete domains.

REFERENCES

[1] F. Bacon, Novum Organum, P.U.F, 1986.

[2] J. L. Bermúdez, Cognitive Science: An Introduction to the Science of the Mind, Cambridge University Press, 2014.

[3] L. von Bertalanffy, General Systems Theory, George Braziller, 1969.

[4] M. Boden, "Computational models of creativity", in R. J. Sternberg, (ed.): Handbook of Creativity, Cambridge University Press, 1999, pp. 351–373.

[5] R. Chauvin, Les Surdoués, Stock, 1975.

[6] J. A. Crowder, Multidisciplinary Systems Engineering: Architecting the Design Process, Springer, 2018.

[7] R. Descartes, "Principles of Philosophy" (« Les principes de la philosophie »), in R. Descartes, Œuvres philosophiques (3 vol.), Edition de F. Alquié. T. 3, Classiques Garnier, Bordas, 1989, pp. 87-525.

[8] G. Fauconnier and M. Turner: The Way We Think: Conceptual Blending And The Mind's Hidden Complexities, Basic Books, 2003.

[9] M. Franova and Y. Kodratoff, "Cartesian Systemic Emergence - Tackling Underspecified Notions in Incomplete Domains", in O. Chernavskaya and K. Miwa (eds.), Proc. of COGNITIVE 2018: The Tenth International Conference on Advanced Cognitive Technologies and Applications, ISBN: 978-1-61208-609-5, 2018, pp. 1-6.

[10] M. Franova and Y. Kodratoff, Cartesian Systemic Pulsation – A Model for Evolutive Improvement of Incomplete Symbiotic Recursive Systems, International Journal On Advances in Intelligent Systems, vol 11, no 1&2, 2018, pp. 35-45.

[11] J. Y. Girard, "The sign field or the bankruptcy of reductionism" (« Le champ du signe ou la faillite du réductionnisme »), in T. Marchaisse, (dir.), Le théorème de Gödel, Seuil, 1989, pp. 145-171.

[12] K. Gödel, Some metamathematical results on completeness and consistency, On formally undecidable propositions of Principia Mathematica and related systems I, and On completeness and consistency, in J. van Heijenoort, From Frege to Godel, A source book in mathematical logic, Harvard Univ. Press, 1967, pp. 592-618.

[13] H. Kopetz, Simplicity Is Complex: Foundations of Cyber-physical System Design, Springer, 2019.

[14] J. L. Le Moigne, General system theory, modeling theory (« La théorie du système général, théorie de la modélisation »), P.U.F, 1984.

[15] M. S. Levin, Modular system design and evaluation, Springer, 2015.

[16] C. Peirce, In search of a method (A la recherche d'une méthode), Théétète - éditions, 1993.

[17] H. Poincaré, L'invention mathématique, in J. Hadamard, Essai sur la psychologie de l'invention dans le domaine mathématique, Editions Jacques Gabay, 1993, pp. 139-151.

[18] C. S. Wasson, System Engineering Analysis, Design, and Development: Concepts, Principles, and Practices, Wiley-Blackwell, 2015.

[19] L. Wittgenstein, Remarks on the Philosophy of Psychology, Vol. 1, Wiley-Blackwell, 1991.

[20] A. Yasuhara, Recursive Function Theory and Logic, Academic Press, New York, 1971.

[21] H.P. Zwirn, Complex Systems: Mathematics and Biology (Les systèmes complexes: Mathématiques et biologie), Odile Jacob, 2006.

[22] Y. Kodratoff and M. Franova, "Resonance Thinking and Inductive Machine Learning", in. S. Sendra Compte (eds.), Proc. of The Fourteenth International Conference on Systems, ICONS 2019, ISBN: 978-1-61208-696-5, 2019, pp. 7-13.

SensAI+Expanse
Emotional Valence Prediction Studies with Cognition and Memory Integration

Nuno A. C. Henriques
BioISI
Faculdade de Ciências
Universidade de Lisboa
Portugal
nach@edu.ulisboa.pt

Helder Coelho
BioISI
Faculdade de Ciências
Universidade de Lisboa
Portugal
hcoelho@di.fc.ul.pt

Leonel Garcia-Marques
CICPSI
Faculdade de Psicologia
Universidade de Lisboa
Portugal
garcia_marques@sapo.pt

Abstract—**The humans are affective and cognitive beings relying on memories for their individual and social identities. Also, human dyadic bonds require some common beliefs, such as empathetic behaviour for better interaction. In this sense, research studies involving human-agent interaction should resource on affect, cognition, and memory integration. The developed artificial agent system (SensAI+Expanse) includes machine learning algorithms, heuristics, and memory as cognition aids towards emotional valence prediction on the interacting human. Further, an adaptive empathy score is always present in order to engage the human in a recognisable interaction outcome. The developed system encompass a mobile device embodied interacting agent (SensAI) plus its Cloud-expanded (Expanse) cognition and memory resources. The agent is resilient on collecting data, adapts its cognitive processes to each human individual in a learning best effort for proper contextualised prediction. The current study make use of an achieved adaptive process. Also, the use of individual prediction models with specific options of the learning algorithm and evaluation metric from a previous research study. The accomplished solution includes a highly performant prediction ability, an efficient energy use, and feature importance explanation for predicted probabilities. Results of the present study show evidence of significant emotional valence behaviour differences between some age ranges and gender combinations. Therefore, this work contributes with an artificial intelligent agent able to assist on cognitive science studies, as presented. This ability is about affective disturbances by means of predicting human emotional valence contextualised in space and time. Moreover, contributes with learning processes and heuristics fit to the task including economy of cognition and memory to cope with the environment. Finally, these contributions include an achieved age and gender neutrality on predicting emotional valence states in context and with very good performance for each individual.**

Keywords—emotional valence prediction; context; cognition; memory; human-agent interaction.

I. INTRODUCTION

The human agents may be seen like self-consciousness, emotion-driven, cognitive beings with a bond between the evolutionary way of emotions and their supporting physical structure, as proposed in [1]. In a sense, an agent's behaviour depends on its affective states besides cognition to cope with the environment. Thus, the ability to predict some dimension of those affects would undoubtedly be of great value towards better adaptation and interaction with others. Furthermore, an artificial agent, like in humans, may be conceived with a decision process influenced by facts, reason, memories [2] and emotional pressure for the basic needs to the entity's homeostasis [3]. Additionally, using the concept of empathy [4][5] as a starting point for two-agent bonding may bring better dyadic interaction and communication. Therefore, an artificial agent adjusting empathetically towards the interacting human current behaviour and affective state may be conceived [6][7]. Further, Human-Agent Interaction (HAI) should be open to each entity own perception, such as the perceived human affective states in a multimodal approach [8][9]. Accordingly, the use of a wearable or mobile device, such as a smartphone seems suitable for the task of collecting data towards affect sensing and reasoning. Twenty years ago, the American College of Medical Informatics (ACMI) has already approached the subject during the 1998 Scientific Symposium: "Monitor the developments in emerging wearable computers and sensors — possibly even implantable ones — for their potential contribution to a personal health record and status monitoring" [10]. Currently, the mobile device as a sensing tool for behavioural research is thriving with active discussions [11][12] including exploration on correlates between sensors' data and depressive symptom severity [13].

This paper describes the SensAI+Expanse system ability to predict human emotional valence states in geospatial and temporal context without evidence of any bias regarding demographics, such as age and gender. This prediction ability is supported by cognition and memory integration in learning mechanisms within an adaptive process. Further, human population in current study comprise distinct behaviour, age, gender, and place of origin. Meaning, the need for proper adaptation on reasoning about each individual and respective collected data in order to assure demographics neutrality. Accordingly, the system developed for the affective studies encompasses an integration of cognition and memory resources distributed between a smartphone embodied agent (SensAI) and its Cloud-expanded (Expanse) continuity. SensAI collects data from multimode sources, such as (a) device sensors (e.g., Global Positioning System (GPS)); (b) current timestamp in user calendar time zone; and (c) human text writings from in-application diary and social network posts (e.g., Twitter). These written texts in (c) will be subjected to a rule-based lexical processing [14] in order to obtain a valence value, i.e., instantaneous sentiment analysis on demand with efficient energy use. The human reports emotional valence ground truth by means of three available buttons regarding positive, neutral, and negative sentiment classes. Simultaneously, an empathy score progress bar is visible during this interaction (Figure 1) and may change on events, such as the human reporting frequency. The score decays over time and it is designed to be the human-agent current value of empathy. Complementary, the available algorithms and heuristics included in Expanse are used by a pipeline process in order to reason about the data set of each human individual. These machine learning services comprise (a) unsupervised algorithms, such as location clustering parameters auto discovery; and (b) supervised ones, such as learning hyperparameters auto tuning. Regarding the learning model and evaluation metric, the choice is based on a previous study [15] where Extreme Gradient Boosting and F1 score achieved good results for several data sets. As depicted in Figure 2, the prediction performance of the agent achieved a score greater than 0.9 for almost two thirds of the population (31 eligible out of 49 from a total of 57), one third distributed between 0.7 (exclusive) and 0.9, with only one subject scoring slightly less than 0.7 (0.68).

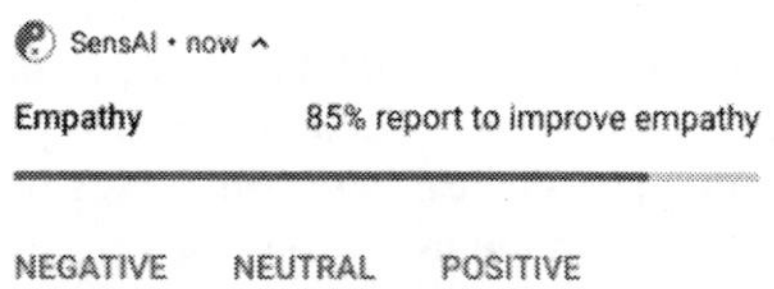

Figure 1. Empathy score notification and emotional valence report buttons.

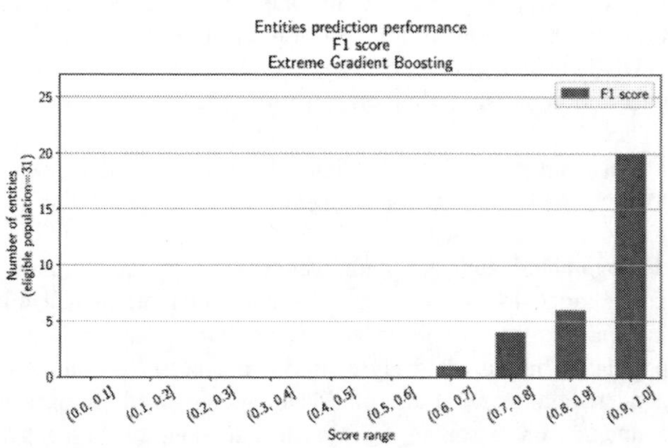

Figure 2. Prediction performance on all individuals by F1 score range.

This first section introduced the current investigation purpose and the work done so far. Next, Section II briefly describes the cognitive and memory mechanisms in place for the developed system reasoning capabilities on emotional valence prediction. Section III describes the research study followed method and the achieved results, including the scope restrictions of this and similar studies using smartphone sensing. Finally, Section IV summarises the outcomes and presents a future perspective.

II. Cognition and Memory in SensAI+Expanse

In order to enable SensAI+Expanse as a trustable research tool for affective studies, this section briefly describes the achieved cognition and memory integration in the developed system. In a sense, this agent is more than an instrument by means of some bio-inspired concepts on its design and implementation. Regarding natural brains, to some extent may be seen as mainly about cognitive processing and memory use towards learning in order to adapt and survive. All this, of course, besides identity, social and cultural aspects. Moreover, emotions in humans are of great importance by helping on decision-making and also with the persistence of episodic memories, amongst other useful regulations [16][17]. Simultaneously, "Forgetting to remember" [18] is required to sustain adequate processing and storage when coping with the information stream that flows through perception sensors. Thus, the concept of cognitive economy is introduced comprising some exclusions from memory to foster savings by means of (a) sustaining last collected data value without change from a sensor during a well-defined time interval (e.g., 15 minutes); and (b) discarding data below relevant thresholds (e.g., location changed less than 10 meters). The resulting information gaps in (a) are filled *a posteriori* in Expanse cognition. This reconstruction is done strictly with the same time interval values used by SensAI thus avoiding any data bias.

As already referred, adaptive mechanisms including cognitive and memory ones are described in a previous paper [15]. Although, there are some of this Automated Machine Learning (AutoML) process aspects relevant to emphasise once more. Regarding system communication, SensAI and its Expanse are connected through an end-to-end secure Web service. The data flows mainly from the mobile device sensors collected by SensAI to the Expanse storage for posterior processing in a pipeline. SensAI has in-device reasoning and memory abilities yet the Expanse does the heavy work by means of several adaptive mechanisms regarding collected data from human behaviour. In the end, the system functions as a distributed, fault-tolerant, mobile and Cloud-based artificial intelligent agent. It may be used as a robust, continuously, online research tool for gathering and processing human emotional valence data towards contextualised predictions, and also affective studies.

A. *SensAI*

The mobile device agent is embodied, encompassing several functions as a whole, towards proper interaction, data collecting, reasoning, and storage. The ground truth values for emotional valence prediction are reported by humans. The main interface includes three emoticon in buttons representing the available discrete valence classes of negative, neutral, and positive, as in the persistent notification (Figure 1). Further, this mechanism is robust to interaction bias, such as high-frequency repeated button (emoticon) clicks. Also, to cases of mistaken valence reported and promptly corrected by an additional hit on a different class. Moreover, a simple yet effective heuristic of accounting only for the last hit during a defined short time interval is in place. All these happenings are properly contextualised by collecting the location and moment of the event. SensAI is focused mainly on:

Smooth HAI towards engaged empathetic relationship, reasoning about current emotional valence state of the human, and keeping all interaction very much passive only with seldom actions. The empathetic engagement relies on a score to be perceived by the human as the HAI empathy level. This metric is sensible to the frequency of human reporting. It decays over time (e.g., 24-hour cycle) and the decay rate may change with other actions, such as pausing the data collection. The agent writes some periodic messages using the in-application diary with useful information, such as the detected activity (e.g., running) and the current computed emotional valence value. All these actions, specifically empathy level notifications, are kept silent, only notifying when the human is interacting. Additionally, displays summary data such as physical activity by means of six recognised classes (e.g., walking) in a main dashboard. Also, a sentiment chart is available with interactive zoom and pan along the local memory chronological limit (e.g., 28 days) of sentiments reported and detected (e.g., Twitter status).

Efficient data collection as much as possible and allowed in a relatively low energy consumption. Accordingly, a practical data acquisition rhythm, such as $active = 2s$, $inactive = 8s$, $f = 1/5Hz$, and $D = 20\%$ is devised and implemented in order to acquire relevant data without too much power drain (below two-digit percentage points on average for several assessments). This rhythm and other thresholds (e.g., $100ms$ minimum interval between sensor fetches) may be subjected to automatic adaptation within environment changes. Regarding the sentiment analysis [14] of written texts, a custom heuristic is implemented [15] integrating language detection, translation, and emoticon processing. All in a best effort to get the sentiment value along with the language (English and Portuguese supported). This process adapts to the cases of mixed languages, emoticon-only text, and no language detected but emoticon available to extraction on analysing these short messages. Additionally, a display with the statistics about all sensors collected events is available. It includes sensor event count in local memory and already Cloud synced, last data sync, and percentage of collecting activity relative to application existence.

Environment adaptation in order to keep local resources healthy and survive to sudden contingencies, such as application crashes. An homeostasis-based implementation runs periodic checks, such as database health and data feed. It will take proper actions, such as recovering the data collection from sensors, and even a local database maintenance. The agent does a system registration at first start to deal with device boot and application upgrade special states. Also, guarantees the reviving by the Android operating system in cases of unexpected crash and removal from the running state. Regarding Cloud data syncing, it is robust to failures using a mechanism inspired in the relational database management system transaction. Only synced data will be marked for removal after local cache persistence threshold. Moreover, if no suitable data connection is available then it will adapt by increasing verification frequency for further try to sync. All these mechanisms of local cache and Cloud sync are paramount to keep healthy memory consumption and guarantee proper data collection.

B. *SensAI Expanse*

The Expanse comprises Cloud-expanded resources for the SensAI agent. These are able to supplement the smartphone restricted local memory, processing, and power. In a sense, it augments the agent cognition and memory. Regarding persistence, there is storage available for data since first value collected until the present. All data is secured and stored anonymously. Because of an efficient data collection, fewer data stored represents more after proper processing. There is a step during the machine learning pipeline where a transformation acts on cleaning and reconstructing collected data. This includes upsampling data within the actual thresholds previously used to save resources in the mobile device. Moreover, processing all eligible data through the available myriad of heuristics and other algorithms towards AutoML requires (a) an adaptation to the multiple human behaviours revealed in the data set; and (b) Bayesian efficient auto discovery on parameters.

The developed custom pipeline for SensAI learning uses various heuristics and other algorithms towards AutoML. These include data classes (negative, neutral, positive) imbalance (reports count) degree check from [19]. And also, a custom heuristic for class verification and learning process adaptation in cases, such as no reports for one (or even two) classes. After all these reasoning, the achieved entities are the ones eligible for the machine learning final step towards emotional valence prediction in context. Regarding location, the learn process make use of the unsupervised HDBSCAN algorithm clustering coordinates which accurately drops outliers. For each individual case, the relevant steps may be summarised as (a) calling HDBSCAN on provided `min_samples` (using $[1, 10, 100]$) in order to find the best `min_cluster_size` parameter; and before each call to the elected supervised multi-class classification algorithm Extreme Gradient Boosting (b) an auto search is run for the best cross validation K splits (K-fold) regarding the algorithm minimum count of accepted classes. Next, Bayesian optimisation is used for hyperparameter auto tuning with cross validation for each specific model. Finally, the model fit for each human current data is achieved and performance metrics are computed. The actual knowledge from the learning process is stored efficiently with a very small memory footprint. The system prediction ability is ready to serve answers about contextualised emotional valence for each individual.

III. STUDY

This section encompasses the outcomes and method used in a research study running on a long-term interaction between SensAI and a population of human individuals in the field (anonymous participants outside the laboratory).

A. Method

The participants in this study are neither targeted nor recruited from anywhere. Instead, the goal to avoid a laboratory known [20] frequent bias of sampling only from Western, Educated, Industrialized, Rich, and Democratic (WEIRD) societies is accomplished by collecting data in the wild and worldwide. Smartphone sensing [21] is in place by means of an Android application. Moreover, privacy is enforced by removing all identifiable data before storing in Expanse. Furthermore, text in the Diary activity is kept local and will be destroyed by SensAI uninstallation. The user is informed on first install and by using the help option. A total of 57 participants (ten countries and four continents) installed SensAI, eight were discarded for not sharing age and gender thus 49 remained eligible for analysis before machine learning pipeline further restrictions. Moreover, some ten-year age range classes revealed to be under-represented hence a dichotomy approach is in place using age median ($M = 34$). Therefore, a reasonable distribution of all genders by the two age ranges, $[10, 34)$ vs. $[34, 70)$, is attained despite some gender disproportion in each range. The age range count relative difference from $[10, 34)$ to $[34, 70)$ is only 4.2% (one individual) as presented in Table I.

TABLE I. ELIGIBLE POPULATION FOR ANALYSIS

	Age range	
	$[10, 34)$	$[34, 70)$
Female	9	9
Male	15	16
Total	24	25

B. Results

Regarding the emotional valence states reported by the humans, there is evidence of valence proportion differences between some groups. In order to assess the statistical significance of this evidence depicted in Figure 3, the Mann-Whitney U test is used. The results presented in Table II show that the null hypothesis (H_0: two sets of measurements are drawn from the same distribution) can be rejected for all but two tests, i.e., evidence of significant differences on three comparisons of two groups each as described next:

$[10, 34)$ **vs.** $[34, 70)$ show differences between two age ranges mainly driven by the female gender.

$[10, 34)$ female **vs.** $[34, 70)$ female evidence a difference in behaviour where the older age group reported significantly less negative and neutral emotional valence and an order of magnitude more positive reports.

$[34, 70)$ female **vs.** $[34, 70)$ male evidence the overwhelming positive reports by female versus male in this age range group.

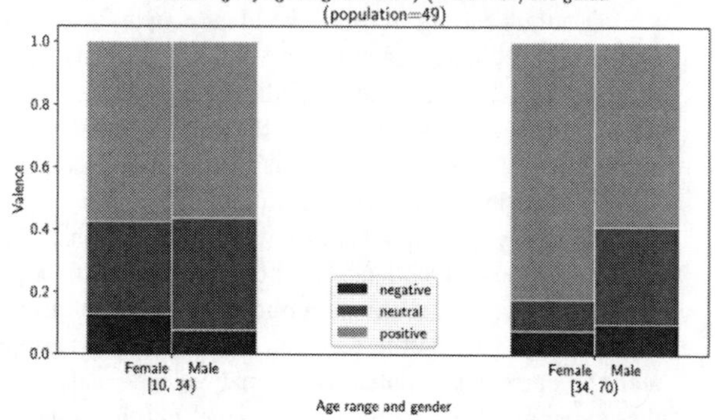

Figure 3. Emotional valence reports percentage by age range and gender.

TABLE II. AGE AND GENDER GROUPS COMPARISON (FIGURE 3): MANN-WHITNEY U TEST RESULTS

Age range and gender	p value	H_0 ($\alpha = 0.05$)
$[10, 34)$ vs. $[34, 70)$	1.161×10^{-30}	rejected
$[10, 34)$ female vs. $[34, 70)$ female	5.539×10^{-14}	rejected
$[10, 34)$ male vs. $[34, 70)$ male	1.561×10^{-1}	not rejected
$[10, 34)$ female vs. $[10, 34)$ male	3.938×10^{-1}	not rejected
$[34, 70)$ female vs. $[34, 70)$ male	7.027×10^{-67}	rejected

Regarding the system prediction performance, a previous study [15] revealed Extreme Gradient Boosting with F1 score as the best option on average for the population individuals, as already depicted in Figure 2. The sample is reduced to 31 eligible individuals due to valence classes imbalance restrictions further applied in the machine learning pipeline process. Regarding these entities, the high scores achieved were independent of age and gender, no pattern whatsoever was revealed. Further, inspection of the feature importance contribution to the prediction revealed that most of the population is more sensible to the time dimension than the location. Specifically, weekday (`moment_dow`) is the most, 64.5% of the cases, influential for emotional valence predictions followed by hour (`moment_hour`) with 25.8%, and location (`mgrs_...`) with 9.7%. This ranking is obtained using SHapley Additive exPlanations (SHAP) on all entities prediction model for the feature ranked first on each entity. Meaning that for almost all entities the moment, weekday and hour, is decisive to obtain a prediction whereas for a few (e.g., entity 5 as depicted in Figure 4) some locations strongly compete for emotional valence prediction.

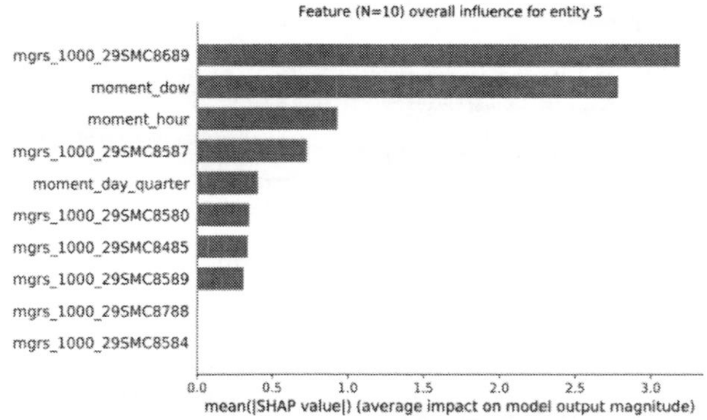

Figure 4. Feature overall influence for entity 5.

Regarding the common behaviour, entity 24 is a typical individual where the time dimension prevails on emotional valence prediction. In this case, Sunday is a weekday where all locations are expected to have positive value predictions. Accordingly, Figure 5 shows the expected positive emotional valence on a Sunday in the future at 8:00 a.m. for the top seven locations (most influential).

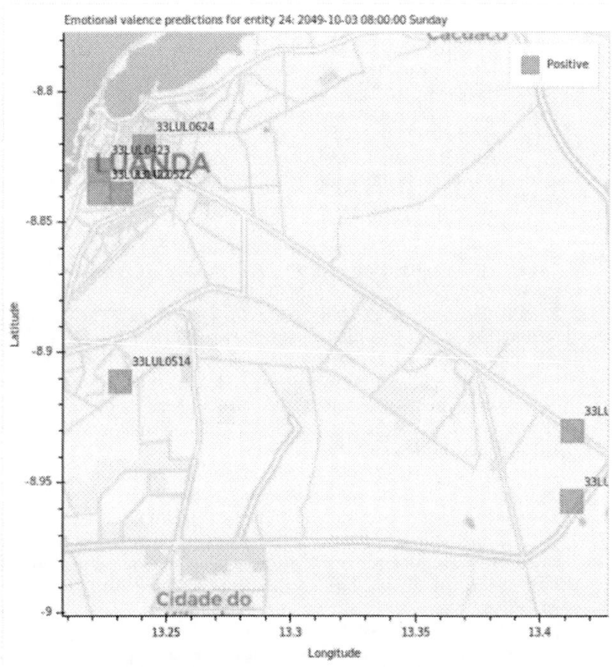

Figure 5. Entity 24: Sunday valence probability for the top 7 locations.

Regarding the same top seven locations and hour of the day, Figure 6 depicts a quite different day from the previous Sunday. The computed probabilities are in order with the expected for a business day for this entity at 8:00 a.m.

The map areas of emotional valence prediction measure 1000 m square side due to reasonable cell size for same place sentiment and a feasible number of cells able to use as features in the learning process. Moreover, world map is divided into

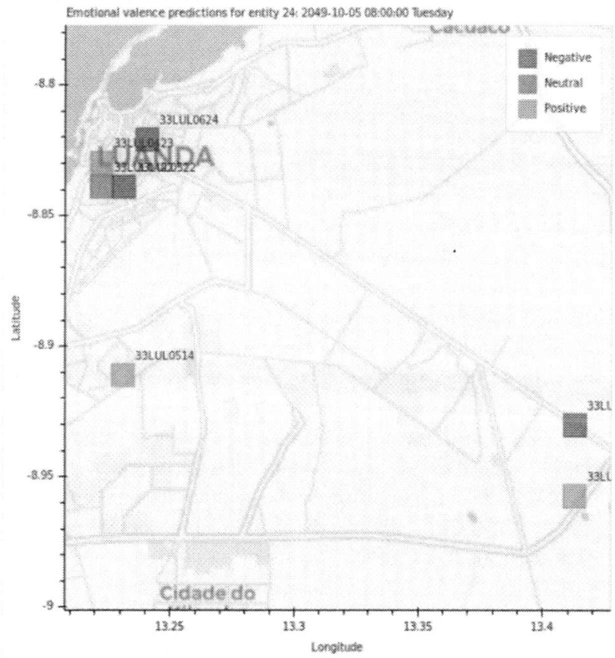

Figure 6. Entity 24: Tuesday valence probability for the top 7 locations.

cells following the Military Grid Reference System (MGRS). These maps are obtained with a developed prototype (Jupyter notebook and Python) for prediction analysis online using the last AutoML results for each entity. The tool is interactive including zoom and more information on hover each location.

Every scientific study has limitations. In order to clarify under which conditions the results should be interpreted, the identified limitations of the present work are (a) no prior health information about the users that may impact the engagement effect including prediction result bias; (b) interacting with a non-anthropomorphic versus human-like agent [22] may impact the emotional valence state reported; and (c) affective reactivity and regulation gender differences on emotional response to context are not considered as proposed in [23]. Although, gender and age neutrality is achieved by SensAI+Expanse results on predicting emotional valence states. Moreover, there is no evidence of any bias in the prediction scores achieved regarding the individual gender.

IV. CONCLUSION AND FUTURE WORK

This paper described the SensAI+Expanse system ability to predict emotional valence states (a) in spatial and temporal context; (b) with very good performance; and (c) age and gender neutral on revealing some individuals' idiosyncrasies. Moreover, this smartphone sensing-based system is robust to unexpected behaviours from humans, Cloud, and mobile demanding environments. The SensAI agent first adapts to the operating system restrictions on mobile resources use, such as keeping battery consumption below two-digit percentage points on average. Then, it uses a myriad of heuristics and other algorithms in order to achieve the best possible prediction whichever human behaviour encounters within the collected data. The outcomes presented show evidence, restricted to population and data samples in this study, of differences in behaviour amongst some combinations of age ranges versus gender. Regardless, SensAI+Expanse was able to adapt and learn to predict emotional valence states with very good scores for every individual on average (Figure 2). Thus, SensAI is able to reveal idiosyncratic factors on human's emotional valence changes without any bias regarding age and gender. Moreover, adding features to the learning process may reveal distinct factors not yet discovered, such as influence of physical activity (e.g., riding a bike). The accelerometer data may be used to correlate physical activity with valence (positive) state [24]. This course of action may be taken as future work. Therefore, SensAI+Expanse contributes as a novel platform for affective and cognitive studies about human emotional valence changes in context. Further, it may complement and eventually supersede laboratory usually long-list self-appraisal questionnaires. Moreover, it reinforces smartphone sensing contribution as a tool for personalised health studies, such as emotional disturbances accompanied by healthcare professionals. Furthermore, all the source code is published as free software under the Apache License 2.0. Future work may include prior health information from each human. Thus, adapting interaction and learning process towards better predictions. Furthermore, SensAI may enable classifying options (e.g., Likert scale) at some specific events for the human to grade the agent behaviour hence tailoring future actions. This course of action may diminish the identified limitations described in the previous section and contribute to better studies.

ACKNOWLEDGEMENT

N.A.C.H. thanks Jorge M. C. Gomes for the precious contributions. This work is partially supported by *Universidade de Lisboa* [PhD support grant May 2016–April 2019]. Partially supported by *Fundação para a Ciência e Tecnologia* [UID/MULTI/04046/2019 Research Unit grant from FCT, Portugal (to BioISI)]. This work used the European Grid Infrastructure (EGI) with the support of NCG-INGRID-PT.

REFERENCES

[1] A. Damásio, *Self Comes to Mind: Constructing the Conscious Brain*, 1st ed. ["O Livro da Consciência: A Construção do Cérebro Consciente", Círculo de Leitores, ISBN:9789896441203], 2010.

[2] R. Wood, P. Baxter, and T. Belpaeme, "A review of long-term memory in natural and synthetic systems," *Adaptive Behavior*, vol. 20, no. 2, pp. 81–103, 2012. DOI:https://doi.org/10.1177/1059712311421219

[3] S. C. Gadanho and J. Hallam, "Robot learning driven by emotions," *Adaptive Behavior*, vol. 9, no. 1, pp. 42–64, 2001. DOI:https://doi.org/10.1177/105971230200900102

[4] K. Stueber, *Empathy*, winter2014 ed., E. N. Zalta, Ed. Metaphysics Research Lab, Stanford University, 2014. URL:http://plato.stanford.edu/archives/win2014/entries/empathy

[5] F. B. M. de Waal, "Putting the altruism back into altruism: The evolution of empathy," *Annual Review of Psychology*, vol. 59, pp. 279–300, 2008. DOI:https://doi.org/10.1146/annurev.psych.59.103006.093625

[6] R. W. Picard, *Affective Computing*. Cambridge, MA, USA: MIT Press, 1997. ISBN:0-262-16170-2

[7] M. Perusquía-Hernández, D. A. G. Jáuregui, M. Cuberos-Balda, and D. Paez-Granados, "Robot mirroring: A framework for self-tracking feedback through empathy with an artificial agent representing the self," 2019. arXiv:http://arxiv.org/abs/1903.08524v1

[8] L. Tavabi, "Multimodal Machine Learning for Interactive Mental Health Therapy," in *2019 International Conference on Multimodal Interaction on - ICMI '19*. New York, New York, USA: ACM Press, 2019. DOI:https://doi.org/10.1145/3340555.3356095 pp. 453–456.

[9] C. Tsiourti, "Artificial agents as social companions: design guidelines for emotional interactions," phdthesis, Université de Genève, 2018.

[10] R. A. Greenes and N. M. Lorenzi, "Audacious Goals for Health and Biomedical Informatics in the New Millennium," *Journal of the American Medical Informatics Association*, vol. 5, no. 5, pp. 395–400, 1998. DOI:https://doi.org/10.1136/jamia.1998.0050395

[11] K. Denecke, E. Gabarron, R. Grainger, S. T. Konstantinidis, A. Lau, O. Rivera-Romero, T. Miron-Shatz, and M. Merolli, "Artificial Intelligence for Participatory Health: Applications, Impact, and Future Implications," *Yearbook of Medical Informatics*, 2019. DOI:https://doi.org/10.1055/s-0039-1677902

[12] I. R. Felix, L. A. Castro, L.-f. Rodriguez, and O. Banos, "Mobile sensing for behavioral research: A component-based approach for rapid deployment of sensing campaigns," *International Journal of Distributed Sensor Networks*, vol. 15, no. 9, pp. 1–17, 2019. DOI:https://doi.org/10.1177/1550147719874186

[13] S. Saeb, M. Zhang, C. J. Karr, S. M. Schueller, M. E. Corden, K. P. Kording, and D. C. Mohr, "Mobile Phone Sensor Correlates of Depressive Symptom Severity in Daily-Life Behavior: An Exploratory Study." *Journal of medical Internet research*, vol. 17, no. 7, p. e175, 2015. DOI:https://doi.org/10.2196/jmir.4273

[14] C. J. Hutto and E. Gilbert, "VADER: A Parsimonious Rule-based Model for Sentiment Analysis of Social Media Text," in *Proceedings of the Eighth International AAAI Conference on Weblogs and Social Media*, Ann Arbor, Michigan, USA, 2014, pp. 216–225.

[15] N. A. C. Henriques, H. Coelho, and L. Garcia-Marques, "SensAI+Expanse Adaptation on Human Behaviour Towards Emotional Valence Prediction," pp. 1–6, 2019. arXiv:http://arxiv.org/abs/1912.10084v4

[16] B. Goertzel, R. Lian, I. Arel, H. de Garis, and S. Chen, "A world survey of artificial brain projects, Part II: Biologically inspired cognitive architectures," *Neurocomputing*, vol. 74, no. 1-3, pp. 30–49, 2010. DOI:https://doi.org/10.1016/j.neucom.2010.08.012

[17] A. Damásio, *Descartes' Error: Emotion, Reason, and the Human Brain*, 2nd ed. ["O Erro de Descartes: Emoção, Razão e o Cérebro Humano", Círculo de Leitores, ISBN:9724211290], 1994.

[18] E. M. Altmann and W. D. Gray, "Forgetting to remember: The functional relationship of decay and interference," *Psychological Science*, vol. 13, no. 1, pp. 27–33, 2002. DOI:https://doi.org/10.1111/1467-9280.00405

[19] R. Zhu, Z. Wang, Z. Ma, G. Wang, and J. H. Xue, "LRID: A new metric of multi-class imbalance degree based on likelihood-ratio test," *Pattern Recognition Letters*, vol. 116, pp. 36–42, 2018. DOI:https://doi.org/10.1016/j.patrec.2018.09.012

[20] J. Henrich, S. J. Heine, and A. Norenzayan, "The weirdest people in the world?" *Behavioral and Brain Sciences*, vol. 33, no. 2-3, pp. 61–83, 2010. DOI:https://doi.org/10.1017/S0140525X0999152X

[21] V. P. Cornet and R. J. Holden, "Systematic review of smartphone-based passive sensing for health and wellbeing," *Journal of Biomedical Informatics*, vol. 77, pp. 120–132, 2018. DOI:https://doi.org/10.1016/j.jbi.2017.12.008

[22] S. Schindler and J. Kissler, "People matter: Perceived sender identity modulates cerebral processing of socio-emotional language feedback," *NeuroImage*, 2016. DOI:https://doi.org/10.1016/j.neuroimage.2016.03.052

[23] K. McRae, K. N. Ochsner, I. B. Mauss, J. J. D. Gabrieli, and J. J. Gross, "Gender Differences in Emotion Regulation: An fMRI Study of Cognitive Reappraisal," *Group Processes & Intergroup Relations*, vol. 11, no. 2, pp. 143–162, 2008. DOI:https://doi.org/10.1177/1368430207088035

[24] N. Lathia, G. M. Sandstrom, C. Mascolo, and P. J. Rentfrow, "Happier People Live More Active Lives: Using Smartphones to Link Happiness and Physical Activity," *PLOS ONE*, vol. 12, no. 1, p. e0160589, 2017. DOI:https://doi.org/10.1371/journal.pone.0160589

Introduction of a Model-Based Approach to Psychology Class: Class Practice for Serial Position Effect Experiments

Kazuhisa Miwa*, Kazuaki Kojima†, Yuki Ninomiya* and Asaya Shimojo*
*Graduate School of Informatics, Nagoya University
Nagoya, Japan 464-8601
Email: miwa@is.nagoya-u.ac.jp, {shimojo,ninomiya}@cog.human.nagoya-u.ac.jp
†Learning Technology Lab. Teikyo University
Utsunomiya, Japan 320-8551
Email: kojima@lt-lab.teikyo-u.ac.jp

***Abstract*—We report an example class practice that introduces the model-based exercises into a psychology class in which participants investigate the serial position effect of the human memory. To the class, a rule-based cognitive model that simulates human memory processes was introduced. The participants themselves manipulated the parameters of the model and performed simulations that examined psychological experiments with a variety of experimental settings and experiments by participants of various working memory capabilities. Analysis confirmed that about two-thirds of the participants experienced good exploration processes and successfully compiled the research reports.**

Keywords - science education; model-based approach; serial position effect

I. INTRODUCTION

In science education, simulations using computer-executable models are widely used. For example, phET at the University of Colorado has released simulations developed based on science education research. Rutten et al. also reviewed studies on simulation-based learning and reported that is widely adopted in biology, physics, science, engineering, general science, earth sciences, and information science [1].

In this study, we report a simulation-based university class design and the results of its practice in psychology education. Compared to the vast practice in natural sciences, simulation-based class practices in psychology have been reported only in very limited cases. The current study focuses on cognitive psychology and cognitive science, which seek to understand the human internal processing mechanisms. In this field, as in other empirical sciences, computer models also play an important role as research tools.

In natural science, models are used not only in research but also in education for learning about various scientific phenomena. However, in psychology education, models are rarely used in class contexts; rather experience-based learning with experiments and observations is more popular. The model-based approach realizes the human internal processing mechanisms on a computer; and it is thought that by such models, unobservable internal processes can be objectively understood with the use of these models. This nature of computer modeling may enable students to learn about psychological phenomena more deeply and precisely.

Jong distinguishes between simulations that are based on conceptual versus operational models [2]. Conceptual models include principles and concepts in the system, and operational models include procedures and perform information processing. Jong points out that science education has focused on various conceptual models. In contrast, this study focuses on operational models that deal with how information is processed based on the internal mechanism. Both types of models exist in cognitive psychology and cognitive science, but in the information processing approach, models that reveal how information is processed in the internal mechanism take the leading role.

Example learning environments reported in preceding studies that support the construction of operational models in science education include DynaLearn [3] and Model-It [4] for understanding the dynamic behavior of environmental systems. For example, Model-It is intended for building ecosystem models, where learners can define specific objects such as animals, plants, and water, as well as define static and dynamic relationships between those objects. In the operational models in these previous studies, static, and dynamic relationships between multiple components are defined by mathematical formulas and graphs.

On the other hand, operational models related to the human cognitive processing describe not the definition of the relationship between components but rather the operations that transit the internal or external states. In the studies of human cognition, descriptions and understandings related to such operations are extremely important. For example, research on traditional human problem-solving analyzes cognitive processes by describing internal or external actions and state transitions that occur through the operations [5].

The subject of the lesson practice in this paper is the serial position effect in the human memory [6]. In Section 2, we explain the serial position effect, the computational model used for practice, and summary of our class practice. Followed by the section, we report two class practices in Sections 3 and 4, respectively. Section 5 is the discussion and conclusions section.

II. SERIAL POSITION EFFECT

The research topic, the serial position effect, observed in human memory experimentation will be briefly explained.

A. Primacy and recency effects

The serial position effect is a phenomenon in which, when a list of words is sequentially stored and free reproduction is performed, the memory performance of the first and last several items in the list is higher than the performance of the items presented in the middle of the list. The effect of the head of the list is called the primacy effect, and the effect of the ending is called the recency effect. These effects are recognized as robust experimental evidence that distinguishes between the short-term and long-term memory.

An established theory of the human memory system is summarized as follows. Information from the outside world is temporarily stored in the iconic memory. Information selectively focused on the iconic memory is sent to the short-term memory; however, it is maintained only for about 15 to 30 seconds. Without rehearsals of the items, they are soon erased from short-term memory. Through rehearsal processes, information in the short-term memory is encoded into the long-term memory. Once information is encoded in the long-term memory, it is never forgotten.

The primacy effect emerges because only words presented earlier are encoded into long-term memory through rehearsals. The recency effect appears because words from the end remain in the short-term memory and are directly retrieved from it when asked to be reported. In contrast, words in the middle of the list have been present too long to be held in short-term memory, but not long enough to be encoded into long-term memory.

B. *Two storage model*

The mechanisms of the short- and long-term memory, and the interaction of the two have been explained as the dual-storage model theory. In this study, based on the theory, a rule-based model that reproduces the serial position effect experiment was constructed. A computational architecture for cognitive modeling used in this practice was DoCoPro, an educational production system architecture developed by the authors [7].

Table I shows the main rules that construct the model. Figure 1 shows flows of cognitive information processing performed by the model. The model has several parameters. Students, by manipulating these parameters, are able to simulate the cognitive information processing of experiment participants with various abilities in short- and long-term memory abilities. In addition, a variety of experimental situations can be examined. The list of parameters is shown in Table II.

TABLE I. RULES OF THE MODEL

Rule	Function
Presentation rule	presents an item and encodes it into the short-term memory
Two erasing rules	erase items from the short-term memory after the time limit for holding items has passed, and erase items from the short-term memory when the number of items has exceeded the working memory capacity
Rehearsal rule	performs rehearsals of items in the short-term memory
Encoding rule	encodes items into long-term memory when the number of rehearsals exceeds a threshold value
Two reporting rules	report items from the short-term and long-term memories when asked to report memorized items after all items have been presented
Two rules	for stopping the system and increasing the time counter

C. *Class practice*

This class practice was implemented as follows. The practice here was part of a cognitive science lesson directed by the first author. A total of 118 participants joined the class.

TABLE II. PARAMETERS OF THE MODEL

Parameter	Function
Presentation interval	controls an interval between two successive item presentations
Rehearsals for encoding	specifies the number of rehearsals needed for encoding items into the long-term memory
Working memory capacity	specifies the number of items that can be simultaneously stored in the short-term memory; when the number of items exceeds this limit, the oldest item that was stored earliest is erased from the short-term memory
Holding time	specifies a time limit for holding items in the short-term memory; when no rehearsals are performed beyond the time limit, the item is erased from the short-term memory

The participants first took part in the serial position effect experiment in groups. At three-second intervals, 20 words were presented, and the participants were asked to list as many words as possible immediately after memorizing them.

Figure 2 shows the results of the experiment. The pattern does not show a typical U-shape, but in the overall pattern, the primacy and recency effects can be confirmed.

Next, the participants attended a lecture on the dual-storage model theory that explains the serial position effect. The lecture also presented typical experimental results demonstrating the serial position effect in previous research.

After the lecture, the model for simulation was distributed to each participant. Each participant was able to simulate experiments with a variety of experimental situations and experiments by experiment participants of various abilities by freely setting parameters.

The participants were given the following two assignments.

III. ASSIGNMENTS

We performed two assignments. The first is a simple assignment, followed by a more advanced and complex second assignment.

A. *First assignment*

1) Tasks: In Assignment 1, the participants were divided into five groups, Groups A to E, each of which addressed the following issues:

- **Group A** Examination of the effect of the time interval of the presented words on experimental results
- **Group B** Examination of the effect of rehearsal ability (required activities for transfer to the long-term memory) on experimental results
- **Group C** Examination of the effect of capacity ability to maintain words in the short-term memory on experimental results
- **Group D** Examination of the effect of retention ability of the short-term memory on experimental results
- **Group E** Examination of the effect of the number of presented words on experimental results.

The participants were asked to submit a research report consisting of (1) hypotheses, (2) experimental designs, (3) experimental results, and (4) interpretations. The hypotheses were submitted prior to the simulation, and care was taken not to change the hypotheses after the simulation.

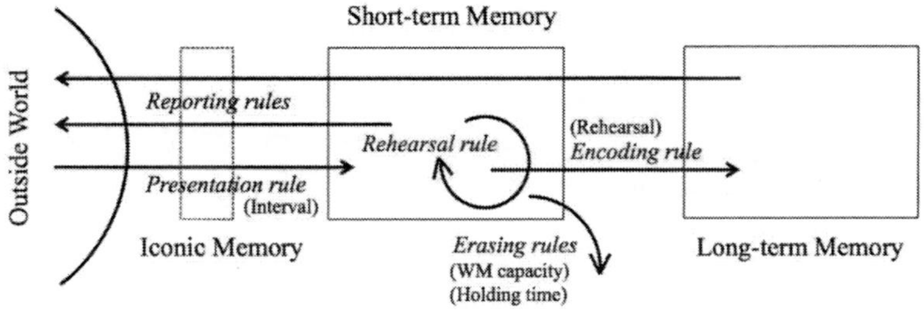

Figure 1. Summary of the production system model. Italics indicate production rules, and parentheses indicate rule parameters.

Figure 2. Experimental results by participants.

2) Results of the simulations: Figure 3 shows the results of the simulations performed while controlling the four parameters listed in Table II.

Some interesting patterns can be found.

- **Rehearsals** As the number of rehearsals required to transfer the items stored in the short-term memory to the long-term memory increases, the recall rate of words that were presented from the first to middle half of the list decreases. On the other hand, the recall ratio of words presented at the end does not decrease.
- **Presentation interval** Patterns similar to those found in the control of required rehearsals are confirmed. However, for words that were presented at one-second intervals, the recall ratio of words presented from the first to middle half of the list decreases, but, oppositely, the ratio for words presented at the end increases.

These phenomena can be understood based on explanations about why primacy and recency effects emerge in the preceding literature.

The participants manipulated the relevant parameters according to a topic set for each group, and confirmed results similar to those indicated in Figure 3. Based on these simulation results, the participants examined their initial hypotheses.

3) Scores of the participants' reports: Two expert coders analyzed the participants' reports. A perfect score was two points; and if any of the following checkpoints applied, one point was deducted.

- The hypothesis is untestable, or cannot be understood.
- The experimental design is inadequate for examining the hypothesis, i.e., incorrect factor control that cannot test the hypothesis.
- The experiment has an incorrect factorial design.
- The simulation results are obviously strange.

The data of 115 participants among 118 who submitted a report were analyzed. Table III shows the distribution of scores. It is confirmed that about two-thirds of participants planned adequate experiments based on an appropriate hypothesis, and assessed the simulation results properly.

TABLE III. DISTRIBUTION OF REPORT SCORES IN ASSIGNNMET 1

Score	0	1	2
Number (rate)	10 (0.09)	35 (0.30)	70 (0.61)

B. Second assignment

1) Tasks: In Assignment 2, based on the results of Assignment 1, the participants were asked to create a more complex hypothesis on why the primacy and recency effects would appear. To test the hypothesis more deeply, they would need to perform 2 x 2 factorial design experiments.

2) Scores of participants reports: The participants were told to submit the same style of report as in Assignment 1. The submitted reports were scored based on the same criterion as in Assignment 1. The data of 112 participants who submitted the report were analyzed. Table IV shows the distribution of scores.

TABLE IV. DISTRIBUTION OF REPORT SCORES IN ASSIGNNMET 2

Score	0	1	2
Number (rate)	6 (0.05)	43 (0.38)	63 (0.56)

IV. DISCUSSION AND CONCLUSIONS

This paper describes an example class practice that used model-based exercises in a psychology class in which participants investigated the serial position effect of the human memory. The class introduced a rule-based cognitive model built based on the dual-storage model theory as a typical theory of the human memory. This model can reproduce the primacy and recency effects in the serial position effect. The participants themselves manipulated the parameters of the model and performed simulations that examined psychological experiments with a variety of experimental settings and experiments

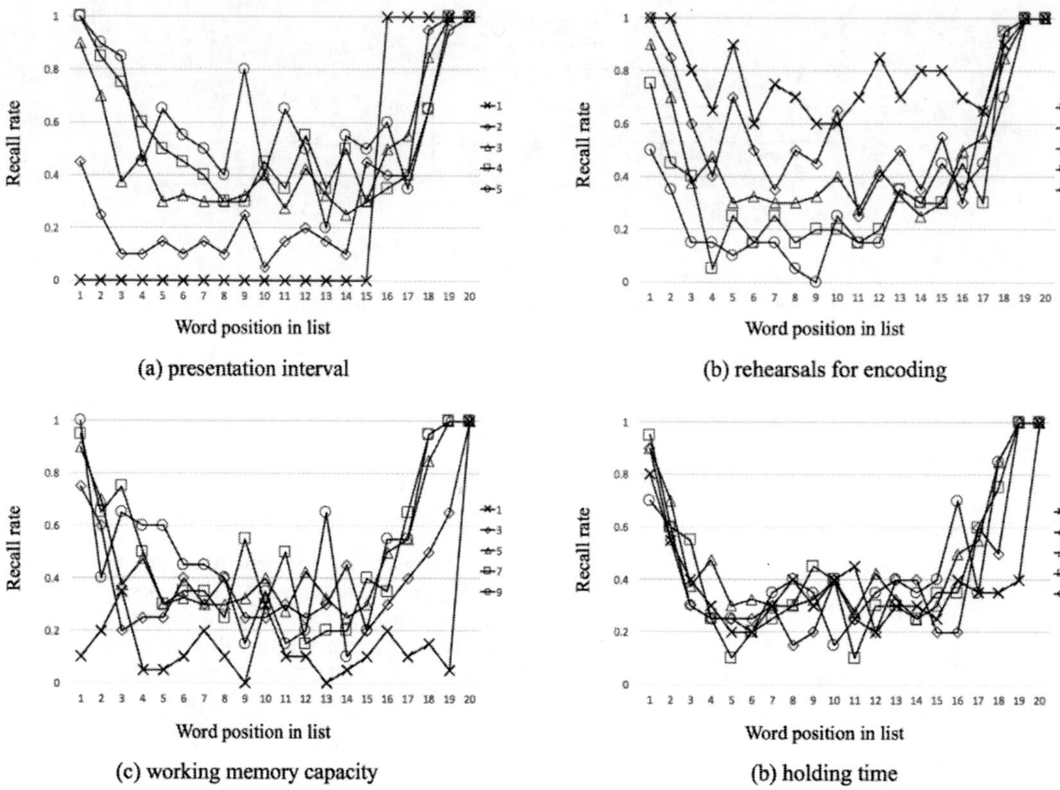

Figure 3. Results of computer simulations performed while controlling four parameters. Four parameters, (a) word presentation interval time, (b) rehearsals required for encoding items into the long term memory, (c) the number of items possible to be stored in the short term memory, and (d) holding time possible to be maintained in the short term memory, were controlled. The legend shows values of each parameter.

by participants of various working memory capabilities. After the exercise, the participants worked on research reports that followed typical psychological exploration patterns: hypotheses, experimental designs, experimental results, and discussion. Analysis of the reports confirmed that about two-thirds of the participants experienced good exploration processes and were successful in compiling the research reports.

This case practice illustrates the value of introducing the model-based approach in cognitive science, and more broadly, in cognitive psychology classes. In many psychology classes, experiments for training are widely used, but computational models are not always practiced. The lessons introduced in this paper are less costly to introduce, and it is likely that they can be applied in psychology-related lessons.

Many cognitive science researchers employ the constructive approach. On the other hand, there are not many teachers who adopt the model-based approach in education. Yet, as the analytical and constructive methods are two pillars of empirical science, it is important to give psychology students a fundamental understanding of the model-based approach as part of the general knowledge and skills they need as junior researchers investigating the human mind.

ACKNOWLEDGEMENT

This research was partially supported by JSPS KAKENHI Grant Number 18H05320.

REFERENCES

[1] N. Rutten, W. R. Van Joolingen, and J. T. Van der Veen, "The learning effects of computer simulations in science education," Computers & Education, vol. 58, no. 1, 2012, pp. 136–153.

[2] T. De Jong and W. R. Van Joolingen, "Scientific discovery learning with computer simulations of conceptual domains," Review of educational research, vol. 68, no. 2, 1998, pp. 179–201.

[3] A. Zitek, M. Poppe, M. Stelzhammer, S. Muhar, and B. Bredeweg, "Learning by conceptual modeling–changes in knowledge structure and content," IEEE Transactions on Learning Technologies, vol. 6, no. 3, 2013, pp. 217–227.

[4] S. J. Stratford, J. Krajcik, and E. Soloway, "Secondary students' dynamic modeling processes: Analyzing, reasoning about, synthesizing, and testing models of stream ecosystems," Journal of Science Education and Technology, vol. 7, no. 3, 1998, pp. 215–234.

[5] A. Newell and H. A. Simon, Human problem solving. Prentice-hall Englewood Cliffs, NJ, 1972, vol. 104, no. 9.

[6] R. C. Atkinson and R. M. Shiffrin, "Human memory: A proposed system and its control processes." In K. W. Spence and J. T. Spence (Eds.), The Psychology of learning and motivation: Advances in research and theory (vol. 2)., 1968, pp. 89 – 105.

[7] K. Miwa, J. Morita, R. Nakaike, and H. Terai, "Learning through intermediate problems in creating cognitive models," Interactive Learning Environments, vol. 22, no. 3, 2014, pp. 326–350.

On Modeling the Role of Negative Emotions and the Effect of Panic in an Artificial Cognitive System

Olga Chernavskaya
Lebedev Physical Institute (LPI)
Moscow, Russia
E-mail: olgadmitcher@gmail.com

Yaroslav Rozhylo
Ukrainian center for Social Data
Kyiv, Ukraine
E-mail: yarikas@gmail.com

***Abstract*— We continue a series of works on modeling especially the human aspects of cognitive process, such as intuition, the influence of emotions, the role of personality, etc. The Natural Constructive Cognitive Architecture proposed and analyzed in our previous works has an important design feature: the entire system consists of two connected subsystems conventionally corresponding to the cerebral hemispheres of human brain. One of them is responsible for the processing of well-known information, the other is aimed at learning new information and creative work. This paper is focused on analyzing the extreme mode of thinking process, namely, the effect of panic in creative work ("throes of creativity"). It is shown that the regime of panic in an artificial cognitive system could be imitated by chaotic fluctuations in the amplitude of self-excitation around an abnormally high level. A sharp drop in the self-excitation level below the normal value (ensuring normal system's functioning) leads to a decrease in efficiency (an analogue to the depression).**

Keywords-emotions; creativity; noise; chaotic oscillations; extreme conditions.

I. Introduction

Modeling the human cognitive process still represents a challenge in spite of considerable efforts undertaken in this field [1] – [3]. The influence of emotions to the logical thinking attracts especial attention [4] – [6], but the problem has no ultimate solution yet. In particular, this concerns the features of human thinking in difficult (extreme) situations [7], disease [8][9], stress [10], etc.

In our previous papers [11] – [15], we have proposed and elaborated the so called Natural Constructive Cognitive Architecture (NCCA). This model has an important design feature: the entire system consists of two connected subsystems (*hemi*-systems), conventionally corresponding to the cerebral hemispheres, the right (RH) and left hemi-systems (LH), respectively. One of them (LH) is responsible for the processing of well-known information (recognition, prediction, etc.), the other one (RH) is aimed at the perception of new information, learning, and creative work.

The idea that any developing system should consist of two subsystems, one for generating an information (with the obligatory participation of a random element – noise), the other one for conservation of information (noise free) had been put forward in the works of Haken [16] and Chernavskii from the theoretical physics viewpoints [17]. Independently, similar idea appeared in the works of neuro-psychologist-clinician Goldberg [3] and was supported by clinical data (tests, fMRI study, etc.). He had argued that the generating subsystem corresponds to the Right Hemisphere (RH) of human brain, while the conservation subsystem could be associated with the Left Hemisphere (LH).

Within NCCA, this specialization is ensured by the presence of random element (noise) in RH (random self-excitation of neurons). Each hemi-system represents a complex multi-level hierarchical structure of various neural processors [18] – [20], with connections between neurons are to be trained according to different rules in RH and LH. Emotions are treated as a product of interaction between cortical and subcortical structures [21][22].

In this paper, NCCA is used to analyze the extreme mode of the cognitive process – the effect of panic. We consider the panic caused not by certain external (threatening) factors, but by the need to solve urgently any complex problem (the so-called "*throes of creativity*").

The paper is organized as follows. The problems of creativity are considered in Section II. In Section III, the main peculiar features of NCCA and our hypothesis on possible panic representation are discussed. Conclusions and discussion of further perspectives are presented in Section IV.

II. Problems of Creative Work

The creativity is treated as the ability of a person to find non-standard and nontrivial new decisions, to generate and perceive fundamentally new ideas and concepts [23][24]. Up to some degree, this ability is inherent in any person who is placed in new and, especially, extreme conditions. However, very rarely a new concept invented by a person becomes socially significant and considered as a *chef-d'oeuvre,* while the person is treated as a genius. Generally speaking [24], the creativity requires:

- ability to extract key issues and ask important questions;
- striving for novelty and the ability to find new solutions even for old problems;
- ability to correlate old knowledge with new problems;
- flexibility of thinking, i.e., the ability to abandon dogmas if new information contradicts them;
- perseverance and focus on solving the problem;
- "free wandering thoughts".

But all this is not a *recipe* for creating a *chef-d'oeuvre* — such recipe does not exist at all, which is really an *enigma* [15].

From a neurophysiological viewpoint [25][26], it is believed that RH and the *prefrontal cortex* are responsible for the processing the new information and creativity. Actually, this formula is not entirely correct. Creativity is a complex process requiring participation of many brain structures in RH and LH. Thus, the flexibility of thinking and the *free wandering thoughts* are associated with *image* thinking, while *focus* requires activation of both frontal lobes. The comparison of old and new knowledge occurs in the dialogue between RH and LH, etc. [24].

Under extreme conditions, the extreme modes of the brain functioning (like *stress, hyperactivity*, etc.) could be switched on, which is accompanied by emotional instability [10]. In this case, the emotional excitation activates the latent ("sleeping") neurons (self-excitation), but there is a huge expenditure of energy. Naturally, such regime cannot last long. It may end in success, i.e., a decision satisfying the person and causing a surge of positive emotions. If the solution had not been found, the *depression* (loss of strength) occurs that could be associated with an energy overrun.

An extreme case of specific regimes is called a *panic*. Usually, panic is understood as a strong stress response to unexpected and frightening external phenomena. Moreover, a person's behavior in a state of panic is individual, unpredictable and usually *chaotic*, from febrile activity to falling into a stupor [7][8][23].

However, we consider not the reaction to a threat to life, but to the need to solve urgently certain cognitive (intellectual) problem. Here, the intensive (up to the stress regime) search for a solution could lead to increased stress up to the regime of *intellectual panic*, which is called also "*throes of creativity*". This regime is characterized by the same (may be not so pronounced) manifestations: chaotic emotional jumps from euphoria (when the solution seems to be found) to disappointment (if it appears to be incorrect), and again, from over-mobilization to complete decline and despair (*depression*).

Thus, negative emotions (anxiety, worrying) and the panic in particular can play both negative (destructive) and positive (constructive) role, if expressed in over-mobilization and does not result in deep depression.

III. MAIN FEATURES OF NCCA

The model NCCA has been elaborated in [11][12][13]. It is based on the dynamical theory of information [16][17][30], neuroscience [21][22], and neurocomputing [18] – [20]. Let us recall briefly its main features.

A. Mathematics and schematic representation of NCCA

The system is combined by two coupled hemi-subsystems, RH and LH, by analogy to the cerebral hemispheres of human brain. They represent complex multilevel block-hierarchical combination of neural processors of the Hopfield [16] type (***H***) and Grossberg [17] type (***G***), referring to description of neocortex. These equations could be written in the form:

$$\frac{dH_i^0(t)}{dt} = \frac{1}{\tau_i^H}[\Im_H\{H, \beta_i(G^R{}_{\{i\}})\} + \sum_{i \neq j}^{n} \Omega_{ij}^{Hebb} H_j^0 + \\ + \sum_k \Psi_{ik} \, G_k{}^{R,1} - \Lambda(t) \cdot H_i^{typ}] + \tfrac{1}{\tau^Z} Z(t) \cdot \xi_i(t), \quad (1)$$

$$\frac{dH_i^{typ}(t)}{dt} = \frac{1}{\tau_i^H}[\Im_H\{H, \beta_i(G^L{}_{\{i\}})\} + \\ + \sum_{i \neq j}^{n} \Omega_{ij}^{Hopf} \cdot H_j^{typ} + \sum_k \Psi_{ik} \cdot G_k{}^{L,1} + \Lambda(t) \cdot H_i^0], \quad (2)$$

where, $H^0{}_i$ (*raw* images) and $H^{typ}{}_i$ (*typical* images) variables (bistable elements) refer to Hopfield-type processors [18] for RH and LH, respectively. These processors correspond to the distributed memory (*images*), where each object is represented by certain chain of excited neurons, Ω_{ij} refer to connections between neurons within the processor; the functional $\Im_H$ describes the internal dynamics. The variable *Z(t)* in RH represents amplitude of the random self-excitation, with $0<\xi(t)<1$ being random function, and τ^Z being characteristic time of *Z(t)* variations.

$$\frac{dG_k^{R,\sigma}}{dt} = \frac{1}{\tau_G}[\Im_G\{G_k^R, \alpha^\sigma{}_k(\{\Psi_{ik}^{R,(\sigma-1)}\}, G_k^{R,(\sigma+\nu)})\} + \\ + \hat{\Upsilon}\{G_k^{R,\sigma}, G_l^{R,(\sigma+\nu)}\} - \Lambda(t) \cdot G_k^{L,\sigma}] + \tfrac{1}{\tau^Z} Z(t) \cdot \xi(t), \quad (3)$$

$$\frac{dG_k^{L,\sigma}}{dt} = \frac{1}{\tau_G}[\Im_G\{G_k^L, \alpha^\sigma{}_k(\{\Psi_{ik}^{L,(\sigma-1)}\}, G_k^{L,(\sigma+\nu)})\} + \\ + \hat{\Upsilon}\{G_k^{L,\sigma}, G_l^{L,(\sigma+\nu)}\} + \Lambda(t) \cdot G_k^{R,\sigma}]. \quad (4)$$

Here, $G^{R,\sigma}{}_k$ and $G^{L,\sigma}{}_k$ represents the *symbols* [19] in RH and LH, respectively. They are also bistable elements with internal dynamics described by the functional $\Im_G$; Ψ_{ik} correspond to the connections between image neurons and their symbol; the functional Υ describes interactions between symbols at various levels, that results in creating the *symbolic images* at the current level and their symbols at the next level (for details see [13]). The marker σ specifies the number of the symbol-processor level.

The hemi-systems RH and LH have different functional specialization. RH plays the main role in learning of *new* information and creativity, while LH is responsible for processing the well-known information. This specialization is secured by the presence of random factor (*noise*) in RH and *different* training rules for all the connections, i.e., Hebbian rule [29] for RH and Hopfield one [18] for LH, e.g.:

$$\frac{d\Omega_{ij}^{Hebb}(t)}{dt} = \frac{\Omega_0}{4\tau^\Omega} \cdot [H_i(t) + 1] \cdot [H_j(t) + 1], \quad (5)$$

that corresponds to gradual connection amplification with time in RH (the *choice*), and

$$\frac{d\Omega_{ij}^{Hopf}(t)}{dt} = -\frac{\Omega_0}{2\tau^\Omega} \cdot [1 - H_i(t) \cdot H_j(t)], \quad (6)$$

that corresponds to the *selection* of relevant connections ("redundant cut-off") in LH; Ω_0 being the characteristic (maximum, or "black") value of the connection. Due to this difference, LH stores only well-trained ("black") connections, while RH stores as well weak (or "grey") ones.

Finally, *Λ(t)* secures the interaction ("dialog") between hemi-systems so as $\Lambda = +\Lambda_0$ corresponds to RH→LH transfer of activity, while $\Lambda = -\Lambda_0$ corresponds to LH→RH.

The schematic representation of NCCA is shown in Figure 1.

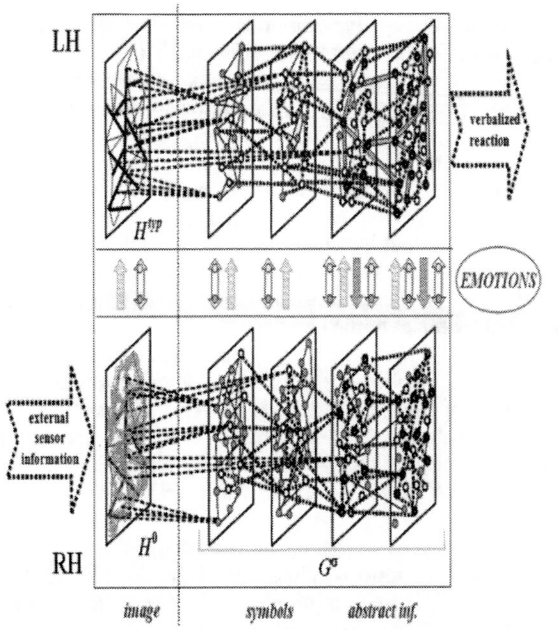

Figure 1. Schematic representation of NCCA.

The system evolves by self-development (in Figure 1 — from the left to the right). The ground (zero) level is represented by two ***H***-type processors (distributed memory) receiving the external information in the form of "raw" images (certain chains of excited neurons). Let us stress that the image plate H^0 (so called "*fuzzy set*") in RH does play key role in intuition and actions under the extreme conditions. Actually, it could be treated as an analogue to the human *sub-consciousness* filled with personal subjective associations, thus presenting the source for nontrivial solutions.

All other levels $\sigma = 1\ldots N$ are presented by ***G***-type processors carrying out the *symbolic* information, with each symbol concentrates (being a convolution) all the information of its image [11].

The high-level symbols correspond to *abstract concepts*, which are not based on any raw image of real object (such as "*science*", "*problem*", etc.). However, they do control all the "parent" symbols at lower levels and thus could control the activity of the whole system. According to neuro-physiological studies, these very functions are character for the *frontal lobes* of human brain [8][9][24][25].

B. Imitation of the extreme mode (panic)

Note that the system of equations (1) – (4) is not complete in math sense, since the variables $\Lambda(t)$ and $Z(t)$ are not specified as yet. In [12][13], we argued that they are tightly connected with emotions. The last are considered as a product of interaction between cortical and subcortical structures [21][22], which influence mainly the random factor in RH. Let us recall briefly the math background of this concept:

$$\frac{dZ(t)}{dt} = \frac{1}{\tau^Z}\left[a_{Z\mu}\cdot\mu + a_{ZZ}\cdot Z + F_Z(\mu,Z) + \Theta(Z,H,G_k^\sigma)\right], \quad (7)$$

$$\frac{d\mu}{dt} = \frac{1}{\tau^\mu}\left[a_{\mu\mu}\cdot\mu + a_{\mu Z}\cdot(Z - Z_0) + F_\mu(\mu,Z)\right], \quad (8)$$

$$\Lambda(t) = -\Lambda_0 \cdot th\left(\gamma\cdot\tau^Z\cdot\frac{dZ}{dt}\right). \quad (9)$$

Here, $Z(t)$ is the amplitude of random (stochastic) component (*noise*) presented in RH only. The functional $\Theta\{Z,H_i,G_k^\sigma\}$ refers to the influence of variables H_i and G^σ_i (associated with the neocortex structures). The value Z_0 represents "normal" value of $Z(t)$ necessary for regular system functioning, τ^Z corresponds to characteristic time of $Z(t)$ variation.

The variable $\mu(t)$ in (7), (8) corresponds to purely "emotional" component produced by subcortical structures; it represents the effective composition of neurotransmitters (the difference between stimulants and inhibitors); τ^μ being the characteristic time for $\mu(t)$ variation.

The variable $\Lambda(t)$ that is stitching together the equations (1)—(4), refers to the cross-hemi-system connections (like *corpus collosum* in brain), which provide the collaboration of two hemi-systems. The parameters τ^Z and γ control the pattern of $\Lambda(t)$ variation.

In [14][15], it was shown that typical pattern of $Z(t)$ behavior for recognition and prediction process represent dumping oscillations around normal value Z_0 (see Figure 2*a*).

Note that the prognosis represents a particular case of recognition problem (the recognition of the time-dependent process).

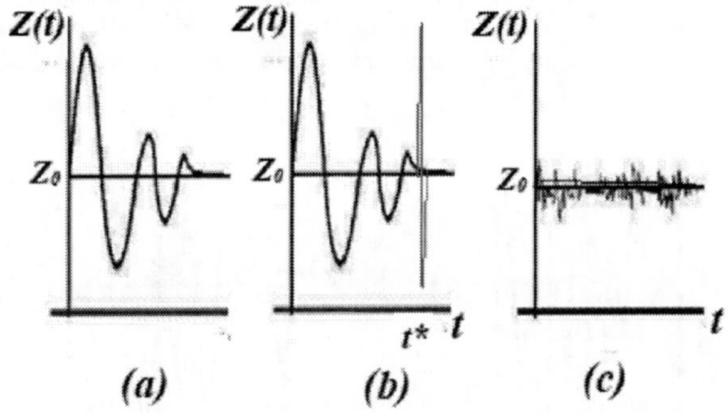

Figure 2. Typical patterns of the noise amplitude $Z(t)$ behavior in the cases of (a) recognition procedure; (b) incorrect prognosis with sense of humor manifestation, and (c) aesthetic emotions ("*goosebumps*").

Special case of incorrect prognosis, which activates the sense of humor has been discussed in [13][14]. It arises when the examinee process seems familiar up to some moment t^*, but the next bulk of information appears to be once unexpected, but still well-known. This switches the recognition process to the other, also familiar pattern. It corresponds to the specific reaction of the system, that is, sharp up-down jump ("spike") in the noise amplitude, which could be associated with human *laughter* (see Figure 2*b*).

In [15], it was shown that perception of art calling for bright but unformulated emotions (the *goosebumps*) could be imitated by small *trembling* of $Z(t)$ around Z_0 (see Figure 2*c*).

Note that two last examples represent in some sense a kind of stress behavior ("*smooth* stress"), which corresponds to somewhat extreme impressions.

In [14], the variation of $Z(t)$ under external load was considered. It was shown that extremely high load results in specific behavior: irregular high-amplitude oscillations of $Z(t)$ with high probability result in the fall to the abnormal stationary state $\{Z^*, \mu^*\}$, where $Z^* << Z_0$ and $\mu^* << 0$, that corresponds to deep depression or *coma*. These results coincide qualitatively with conclusions of [10].

Here, we put forward the following hypothesis. The panic mode could be imitated as follows. If the recognition process meets unexpected difficulties (without any external effect) while the problem should be solved *urgently*, $Z(t)$ at the first stage increases (without oscillations) up to some critical value $Z^{**} >> Z_0$. High level of noise corresponds to super-mobilization of all the resources including self-excitation of so called "sleeping" neurons (never involved into training process before). Thus, at this stage increasing $Z(t)$ value (negative emotions, i.e., anxiety, worrying, nervousness, etc.) does play positive (constructive) role. Then, this regime changes for chaotic "jumps" of $Z(t)$ around Z^{**} (see Figures 3*a*, 3*b*) that could be treated as *intellectual panic*. Indeed, if $Z(t)$ achieves the value $Z^{**} >> \Omega_0$ (the rough value of "black" connections), then these connections seem to be broken and the noise dominates in RH. It results in chaotic self-activation of the neocortex neurons (variables H^0 and G^R) independently of any already learned patterns. This corresponds to "free wandering thoughts" discussed in Section II. The jumps in $Z(t)$ correspond to the emotional (mood) jumps.

The decrease of $Z(t)$ down to zero at some moment t^{**} results in a deep long depression (see Figure 3*b*), which could be overcome only by external efforts (an analogue to medical intervention).

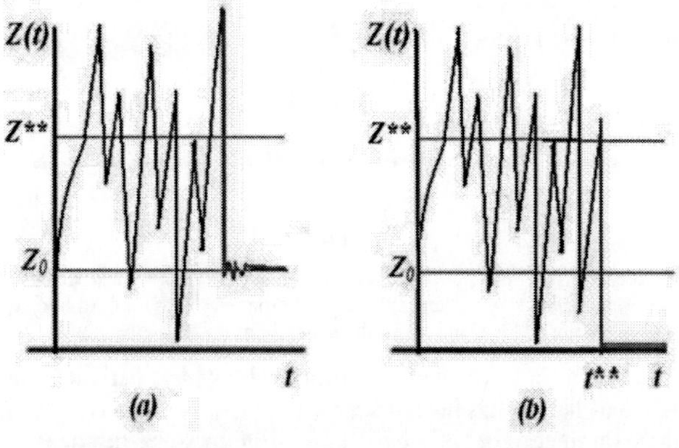

Figure 3. Typical behavior of $Z(t)$ under the "intellectual panic" in the case of (a) "aha moment" and (b) deep long depression.

However, such mode should require significant amount of energy and thus, could not last long. It could stop either by sharp drop in $Z(t)$ down to normal value Z_0, i.e., the peak of positive emotions (*aha!* moment, or *eureka!*) if rather "good" solution was found (Figure 3a), or by certain external (an analogue to *drug*) effect. Otherwise it could lead to deep depression as in Figure 3*b*.

IV. Conclusion and Further Work

Within NCCA, emotions are associated with the noise amplitude $Z(t)$ derivative dZ/dt: increasing $Z(t)$ ($dZ/dt>0$) corresponds to negative emotions (anxiety, worrying), while decreasing $Z(t)$ ($dZ/dt<0$) corresponds to positive ones (satisfaction, relax). Note that negative emotions in normal cognitive process (such as recognition, prognosis, decision making, etc.) do play positive role increasing the activity in RH for generating several hypotheses on the given problem solution. Here, positive emotions also play positive role activating LH for hypothesis testing.

It is shown that under certain extreme conditions (such as the necessity of urgent solving any complex cognitive intellectual problem), normal functioning mode could be replaced by the extreme one. In this mode, increasing $Z(t)$ up to some critical value Z^{**} actually plays positive role resulting in mobilization of the latent resources (self-excitation of "*sleeping*" neurons in RH). Further increasing $Z(t)$ up to values $Z(t) >> Z^{**}$ results in chaotic activation of neurons in RH, which provokes chaotic "jumps" of the noise amplitude $Z(t)$. This behavior could imitate the effect of *intellectual panic*, or "*throes of creativity*".

In this paper, we have not considered possible effects connected with ratio of characteristic times τ^Z and τ^Ω for variation of noise amplitude and connection training, respectively. This ratio should control the process of creation of new connections between the sleeping neurons in the "*fuzzy set*" $\boldsymbol{H^0}$ thus resulting in new nontrivial images and solutions.

Also, we have not considered here the behavior of the neurotransmitter composition $\mu(t)$ at the *panic* stage. Apparently, this component should also demonstrate certain chaotic behavior, but with some time shift with regard to the noise amplitude $Z(t)$. This dynamical process deserves special study.

Moreover, variation of ratio of parameters Λ_0, Z_0, Ω_0, and Z^{**} could lead to interesting effects and deserve additional study. In normal cognitive mode, these parameters are to be similar by the order of magnitude: $\Lambda_0 \sim \Omega_0 \sim Z_0$. Deviations from this ratio could result in some specific regimes as, e.g., "*mental rigidity*" [9] (poor dialog between hemi-systems) at $\Lambda_0 << \Omega_0$, or "*low creativity*" [24] at $Z_0 << \Lambda_0 \sim \Omega_0$, etc. Of course, all these effects require special study.

In addition, various combinations of parameters Z_0, τ^Z and μ_0, τ^μ could serve to reproduce the well-known Hippocrates classification of human temperaments (choleric, sanguine, melancholic, phlegmatic) and to reveal the correlation between the temperament and a tendency to a certain mode of panic behavior. But this is the subject for special study.

It should be noted that all typical patterns of $Z(t)$ behavior discussed here represent the results of theoretical simulations. Apparently, clinical verification is needed. Now, we plan certain collaboration with Dr. Dibsburry from PsychPress (Talent Management Psychology, Melburn, Australia) and Prof. Bykov from Irkutsk State Medical University (Russia) to verify our hypothesis by tests and questionnairs. Possible collaboration with Kurchatov Research Center (Russia) on fMRI study of the people in panic state is also considered. However, all these problems require further work.

References

[1] Y. Bengio and Y. Le Cun, Scaling Learning Algorithms towards AI. In: Large Scale Kernel Machines, ed. by L. Botton, O. Chapelle, D. DeCoste, and J. Weston, MIT Press, 2007.

[2] Y. Le Cun, Y. Bengio, and G. Hinton, "Deep learning," Nature, vol. 521, pp. 436 – 444, 2015.

[3] E. Goldberg, The New Executive Brain. Oxford University Press, 2009.

[4] A. Samsonovich, "Emotional biologically inspired cognitive architecture," BICA, vol. 6, pp. 109 – 125, 2013.

[5] E. Hudlyka, "Affective BICA: Challenges and open questions," BICA, vol. 7, pp. 98 – 125, 2014.

[6] J. Valerdu et al., "A cognitive architecture for the implementation of emotions in computing systems," BICA, vol. 15, pp. 34 – 40, 2016.

[7] S. M. Sarkis, Executive Function Difficulties in Adults, PSLI, 2017; ISBN-13: 978-1683730989.

[8] "The Human Frontal Lobes: Functions and Disorders", Ed. By B. L. Miller and J. L. Cummings, 2017;ISBN 9781462531837.

[9] "Executive Functions in Health and Disease", Ed. By E. Goldberg, Academic Press, 2017; ISBN 978-0-12-803676-1.

[10] S. Parin, A. Polevaia, and S. Polevaia, "A neurochemical approach to stress and the role of the endogenous opioid system in control of heart rate variability for cognitive load", the Ninth Int. Conf. on Advanced Cognitive Technologies and Applications (COGNITIVE), IARIA, Feb. 19 – 23, pp. 44–49, 2017.

[11] O. D. Chernavskaya, D. S. Chernavskii, V. P. Karp, A. P. Nikitin, and D. S. Shchepetov, "An architecture of thinking system within the Dynamical Theory of Information," BICA, vol. 6, pp. 147–158, 2013.

[12] O. D. Chernavskaya et al., "An architecture of the cognitive system with account for emotional component," BICA, vol.12, pp. 144–154, 2015.

[13] O. D. Chernavskaya and Ya. A. Rozhylo, "On the possibility to imitate the emotions and "sense of humor" in an artificial cognitive system," The Eighth Int. Conf. on Advanced Cognitive Technologies and Applications (COGNITIVE), IARIA, March 2016, pp. 42–48, 2016.

[14] O. D. Chernavskaya and Ya. A. Rozhylo, "The natural-constructive approach to representation of emotions and a sense of humor in an artificial cognitive system," IARIA Journal of Life Sciences, vol. 8(3&4), pp. 184–202, 2016.

[15] O. D. Chernavskaya and Ya. A. Rozhylo, "On the possibility to interpret aesthetic emotions and the concept of chef-d'oeuvre in an artificial cognitive system," the Ninth Int. Conf. on Advanced Cognitive Technologies and Applications (COGNITIVE), IARIA, Feb. 19 – 23, pp. 24—31, 2017.

[16] H. Haken, Information and Self-Organization: A macroscopic approach to complex systems. Springer, 2000.

[17] D. S. Chernavskii, "The origin of life and thinking from the viewpoint of modern physics," Physics-Uspekhi, vol. 43, pp. 151–176, 2000.

[18] J. J. Hopfield, "Neural networks and physical systems with emergent collective computational abilities," PNAS, vol. 79, p. 2554, 1982.

[19] S. Grossberg, Studies of Mind and Brain. Boston: Riedel, 1982.

[20] T. Kohonen, Self-Organizing Maps. Springer, 2001.

[21] L. F. Koziol and D. E. Budding, Subcortical Structures and Cognition. Implications for Neurophysiological Assessment. Springer, 2009.

[22] J. Panksepp and L. Biven, The Archaeology of Mind: Neuro-evolutionary Origins of Human Emotions. N.Y.: Norton, 2012.

[23] R. Solso, Cognitive psychology (5th ed.). Needham Heights, MA: Allyn & Bacon, 1998.

[24] E. Goldberg, Creativity: The Human Brain in the Age of Innovation. Carlisle & Co, NY, 2018.

[25] A. Dietrich, "The cognitive neuroscience of creativity," Psycho nomic Bulletin & Review, vol. 11, pp. 1011–1026, 2004.

[26] K. M. Heilman, "Possible brain mechanism of creativity," Arch. of Clinical Physiology, vol. 31, pp. 285 – 296, 2016.

[27] A. Kaufman et al, "The neurobiological foundation of creative cognition," in: The Cambridge Handbook of Creativity, Cambridge University Press, pp. 216 – 232, 2010.

[28] H. Quastler, The emergence of biological organization. New Haven: Yale University Press, 1964.

[29] D. O. Hebb, The Organization of Behavior. John Wiley & Sons, 1949.

Linking Computerized and Perceived Attributes of Visual Complexity

Kanaka Babshet

School of Electrical and
Information Engineering
University of the Witwatersrand
Johannesburg, South Africa
Email: kanaka.babshet@fnb.co.za

Vered Aharonson

School of Electrical and
Information Engineering
University of the Witwatersrand
Johannesburg, South Africa
Email: vered.aharonson@wits.ac.za

***Abstract*—Psychological studies explore visual complexity as perceived by humans. Image complexity is studied extensively in the mathematical, computational sciences. The two disciplines often define visual complexity differently and are thus disjointed. This is manifested in differences between subjective human-perceived complexity, and computer vision algorithms' performance in visual tasks. Our study investigates this discrepancy in the context of cognitive tests that employ visual stimuli to assess a subject's primal cognitive functions. A database of cognitive tests including visual recognition tasks and the performance of 403 subjects in terms of response times was used. Computer vision and information theory features were extracted from the images in these tasks. Inspired by cognitive psychology studies, the features were categorized into whole-image and object-specific features. A random forest classifier was used to map the computed features into three complexity labels in the tasks, labelled according to the subjects' performance. The classifier computationally captured the significant features for the human-perceived task complexity by mapping the occurrence of these features to the complexity labels of the subjects' performance. The whole-image features demonstrated greater visual significance than the object-specific features. The features' importance values could provide insights into the links between mathematical visual complexity definitions and visual complexity as perceived by humans.**

Keywords*– *Visual complexity; Cognitive assessments; Computer vision; Binary images.

I. INTRODUCTION

Human visual perception is the processing and interpreting of a visual environment, transmitted from the eyes via neural paths to the brain. The image properties extracted in this activity culminate in a decision or action [1]. The details of the translation or encoding entailed in this process are, however, unknown.

Cognitive tests are designed to challenge this brain process. These tests display visual stimuli, pose a task associated with these stimuli, and require a response or decision from the tested subject. The performance of cognitively intact individuals in these tests could thus provide insights into the characteristics of the process involved in visual perception. Specifically, the differences between different tasks in terms of complexity could be assessed.

Understanding task complexity allows us to better engineer the interface of these cognitive tests. Having a predefined complexity scale offers a platform for dynamic adaptation to a user's cognitive capabilities by adjusting the complexity of the set of tasks presented based on their previous task response times. This ensures that the subject is presented with a task of an appropriate difficulty level for them, rather than something that is too easy or too difficult, which could cause frustration or boredom, and limit the usefulness of the assessment. An evaluation of performance which takes into account response times can also be refined by considering the complexity of the task as a weighting component in the test score.

Visual perception and the complexity of images were studied in cognitive psychology [2]. Witkin et al. [3] proposed a field dependence concept, explaining how people assess their visual field by either separating and organising the visual information into clear-cut groupings, or assessing their visual field as a whole. Attneave et al. [4] studied the different ways in which the perceived visual complexity of an image is affected by the information distribution in the image. Equivalently, computer vision studies employed mathematical image processing to extract information from an image [5]. The complexity of visual stimuli or images can thus be computed using mathematical metrics and computer algorithms.

Both disciplines share similar concepts conceptually on visual attributes on the information of a full image and/or part of image. Both strive to define visual complexity. The relevance of computer features and metrics to the way humans perceived complexity according to the aforementioned psychological theories is, however, rarely assessed.

Computerised cognitive tests are a context where visual stimuli in the form of computer generated images and a large cohort of human subjects performance can be studied. This study employs computerised cognitive tests data and aims to find a set of computed attributes, or features, which could help explain the complexity of a task associated with visual stimuli.

This paper first presents a short background on the test data provided for this study, with the details of the subsequent algorithm development and implementation in Section 2. It is then followed by the feature results in Section 3, and a concluding analysis and discussion in Section 4.

II. METHODS

Test data from previously conducted cognitive tasks was made available for this study. This was used to find a set of computed visual attributes which could correlate to the tasks' perceived complexity based on the task results in the provided data. This Section presents the details of this process.

A. The Data: Visual Stimuli and Human Performance Data

The cognitive tasks and users' performance data were taken from NexSig's computerised cognitive testing studies [6]. The visual part of this dataset involves stimuli in the form of simple, black and white, four-by-four square images that can be described as 16-bit binary arrays, as illustrated in Figure 1. In this study, we focused on one type of visual task from this test battery: a recognition task. An example recognition task is illustrated in Figure 1: three images are presented on the screen, and the subject is required to recognise which of the three images is different.

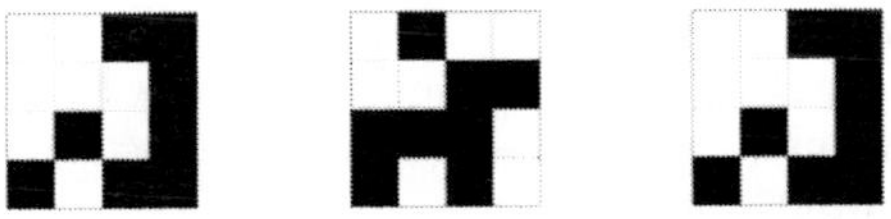

Figure 1. An example of a **recognition** task.

The computerized tests recorded and logged both response time and correctness of the subjects' responses for each of the tasks presented. All subjects in the studies were assessed by healthcare professionals prior to taking the cognitive tests. The database used in our study included tests of cognitively intact subjects only, who had no motor or vision impairment.

There were 5087 recognition tasks in the dataset. The data was stored in a table, where each row represented a task instance. The images presented in the tasks were coded as 16 bit arrays where a white square in the image is represented by a 0 and a black square by a 1. A binary array encodes the image starting at the top left and downwards row-by-row. For example, the first image in Figure 1 would be encoded as 0011000101011011. Following the 3 binary vectors of the 3 images presented in the task, each row contains the subject's response and response time in milliseconds. A separate table contains the demographics of the subjects: age, gender and computer proficiency.

B. *Algorithm Implementation*

Figure 2 depicts a flow diagram of the methodology employed in the study.

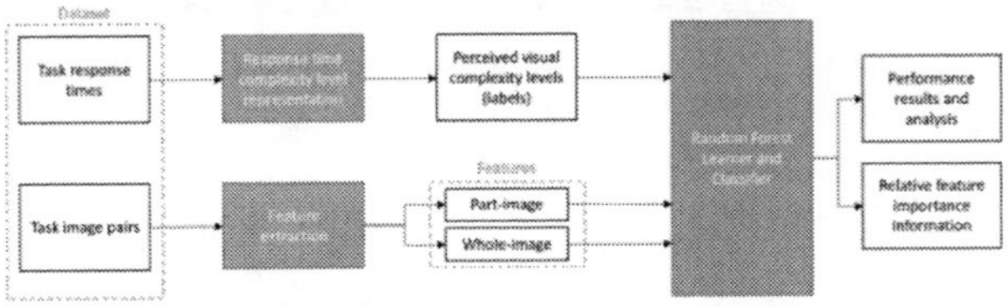

Figure 2. A flow diagram of the algorithm implementation

Each response time in the dataset was represented by a label corresponding to a human-perceived complexity. Concurrently, visual features of the cognitive tasks were extracted. The human perceived complexity labels and the features were the inputs to a random forest learner. The machine-learned selection process indicated which of the features were relevant in the human-perceived visual complexity prediction. The implementations of the blocks in Figure 2 are described below.

1) Human Visual Complexity Level Representation: An inherent assumption in this study, corroborated by the administrating neuropsychologists, was that the subjects' response times were associated with, or reflected in, the tasks difficulty level or complexity. Subject demographics - age, gender and computer proficiency - were examined to ensure that these factors did not distort the response-times distribution. Initial examination of the dataset response times yielded that their distributions were similar, and had a Gaussian shape with a longer right-hand tail, for all age groups, for male and female subjects and for groups of proficiency levels. The response-times' continuum was segmented into K segments from which a complexity labels scale was constructed, from "easy" to "hard," corresponding to the segments of short response times to the segments of long response times, respectively. Different segmentation paradigms, as well as different K values were applied and evaluated in different experiments, as labels for the random forest learner.

2) Computer-Vision Complexity Attributes: The algorithm was developed to discover which visual features could define the visual complexity in a recognition task. The study was performed on the pair of the 2 different images from the 3 images presented in the task. This choice was based on the assumption that the third image, identical to one of the images in the pair, does not significantly impact on the visual comparison.

3) Feature Extraction from the Image Pair: The features were either adapted from earlier image processing and computer vision studies, or were conceptually based on Attneave [4] and Witkin's [3] psychological theories on visual perception.

a) Object Type Definitions: The following visual object *types* are referred to in the subsequent feature descriptions. All object types are defined for both black and white blocks:

- **Adjacent Path:** Consecutive adjoining blocks of the same colour (directly next to each other, against one of the four **sides**) to form a path of its own. Black adjacent paths outlined in red in the example image (Figure 3).
- **Diagonal Path:** Consecutive blocks of the same colour diagonal to each other (against one of the four **corners**) to form a path of its own. Black diagonal path outlined in green in the example image (Figure 3).
- **Single block:** a block that is not part of an adjacent path or diagonal path. Black single block outlined in blue in the example image (Figure 3).

By these definitions, the image in Figure 3 has a white adjacent path, and a white single block as well.

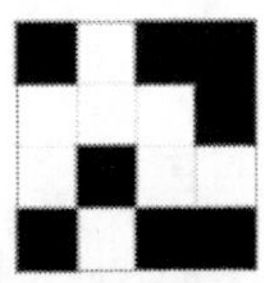

Figure 3. Example image to illustrate the object **types**.

b) Feature Extraction Paradigm: Quantifying a recognition task's complexity entails a consideration of a *relative* visual complexity of a pair of images, i.e., if one image is visually complex, while the other is simple, the recognition task will be relatively easy.

All features were computed for each image in the pair, and inserted into the machine learning model as two independent features. Additionally, features that pertain to a comparative nature were computed for the pair of the images and were used as a single feature. The latter, relative type of features are marked in the list below with a "(relative)" next to the feature name.

Inspired by the cognitive theories of Attneave [4] and Witkin [3], two categories of features were calculated: object-specific features, and whole-image features. Examples and illustrations for these features are described further.

c) Object-Specific Features:

- **Number of objects**: This feature is a count of the number of adjacent paths, diagonal paths, and single blocks respectively within each image, for both black and white objects. Table I presents an example of this count, computed for the image pair presented in Figure 4.

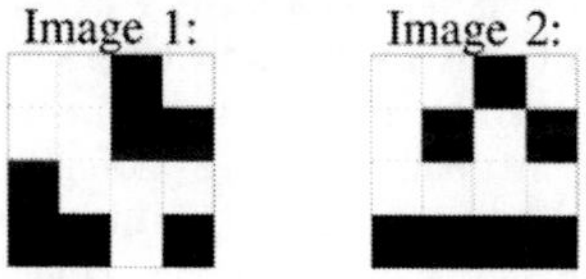

Figure 4. Example image pair to illustrate *number of objects*, *object path lengths*, *different objects present*, and *similar objects within an image*

TABLE I. NUMBER OF OBJECTS FOR THE IMAGE PAIR IN FIGURE 4

	Image 1		Image 2	
	Black	White	Black	White
Adjacent Paths	2	1	1	1
Diagonal Paths	0	0	1	0
Single Blocks	1	1	0	1

- **Object path lengths**: This feature is the total lengths of the adjacent paths and the diagonal paths, for both black and white objects, in an image. Table II presents an example for this feature, computed for the images of Figure 4.

TABLE II. OBJECT PATH LENGTHS FOR THE IMAGE PAIR IN FIGURE 4

	Object Path Lengths			
	Image 1		Image 2	
	Black	White	Black	White
Adjacent Paths	6	8	4	8
Diagonal Paths	0	0	3	0

- **Objects with similar angles (relative)**: This is the number of black or white objects that have either the same angle, or the inverse angle in a pair of two images, measured from the horizontal axis.
- **Objects with similar locations (relative)**: This feature indicates the number of objects that have **similar** locations. The locations are calculated as a centroid midpoint and points within half a square of each other are considered as similarly located objects. Only objects of identical type and colour, i.e., black adjacent paths, are checked for location similarity. Figure 5 illustrates similar locations for a pair black adjacent paths, a pair of white adjacent paths, and a pair of white single blocks in the two images.

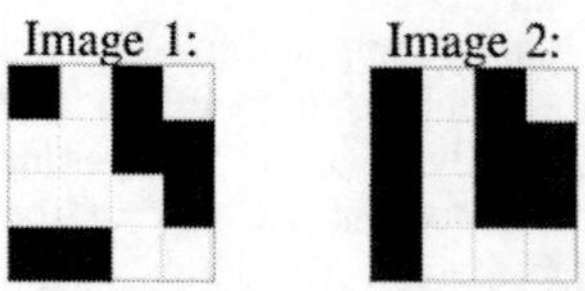

Figure 5. Example image pair to illustrate *objects with similar locations*

- **Different object types present (relative)**: This binary feature returns a one if any of the previous object types exists in one image, but not in the other. For example in Figure 4, Image 2 has a black diagonal path while Image 1 does not, while Image 1 has a black single block while Image 2 does not, which will produce a value of one.
- **Similar objects within an image**: This feature indicates the number of objects that have similar shape and size, regardless of angle, within an image. In Figure 4, for example, image 1 has two similar objects, while Image 2 has none.
- **Similar objects in an image pair (relative)**: This feature counts the number of objects that have similar shape and size, regardless of angle, in both images of the pair. For example, there is one similar object in the two images of Figure 6.

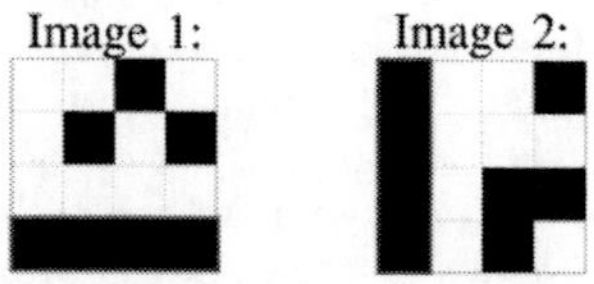

Figure 6. Example illustrating *similar objects found in an image pair*

d) Whole-Image Features:

- **Whole-image object spacing**: This feature is an average of the distances between objects of one colour in an image. In the example of Figure 7, the average distance for the black objects in Image 2 is larger than in Image 1.

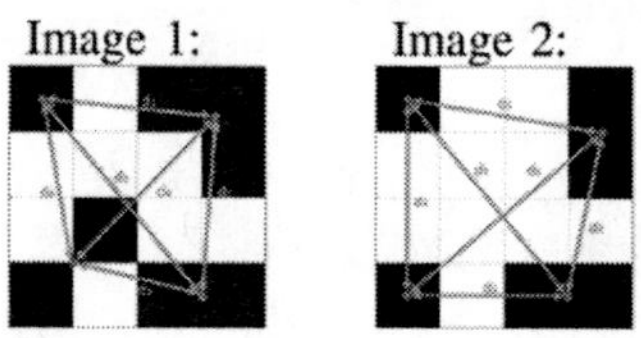

Figure 7. Example image pair showing the various object distances calculated for *whole-image object spacing*

- **Whole-image squares comparison (relative)**: This feature is a direct comparison of an image pair, where each square in the image is referred to as a bit; black represented by 1 and white by 0. The computation entails an XOR on the 16-bit array representations of the images and a summation of the resulting array.
- **Relaxed image symmetry**: This is a binary feature that indicates symmetry, defined across the horizontal axis, the vertical axis, and the two diagonals, including inverse colour symmetry as illustrated in Figure 8.

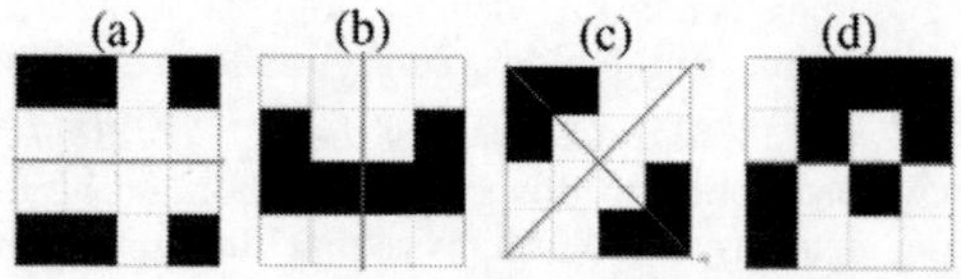

Figure 8. Example images which display the various definitions of symmetry

'Relaxed' symmetry, defined as one-block difference within the symmetrical image, is also considered as an occurrence of symmetry due to the low prevalence of exact symmetry in these images.

- **Features from Gabor filters**: Gabor filters are made up by sinusoidal planes modulated by a Gaussian envelope [7]. A 'filter bank' of Gabor filters models the first stage of the brain's visual processing (V1) [8]. In our implementation, a filter bank of Gabor filters at various orientations and frequencies was applied to each image in the pair, resulting in an output feature vector for each image. The features were the sum and standard deviation of the vector.
- **Fractal dimension features**: The ratio that indicates the level of visual detail in a fractal pattern at different levels of magnification was calculated using the box counting technique [9]. This technique estimates the number of boxes required to cover the non-zero parts of an image at different box sizes, and computes the fractal dimension as the slope between number of boxes and box sizes [10]. Two additional features were calculated: The range of the fractal dimension values across the total number of measurements taken, and the standard deviation of the different fractal dimension values across the various measurements taken.

All the above features were extracted for the image pairs in the recognition tasks from the dataset. These were then to be entered into the machine learning (random forest) classifier.

C. Random Forest Learner and Classifier

A random forest learner was implemented, with a 3-fold cross validation, to map the feature sets to the human-perceived complexity labels.

An important characteristic of the random forest method is that it yields feature importance information. The importance values were generated for each feature in Matlab as part of the *TreeBagger* function. Each value was calculated using the out of bag permuted predictor delta error, where a larger error corresponds to a more important feature for the mapping performance, in our case, to the complexity labels [11].

III. Results

The subsequent results, obtained from following the above methodology, are presented in this section through an analysis on the data provided, and the importance levels of the features extracted from the images.

The response-times distributions change with subjects' age, gender and computer skills are illustrated in Figures 9, 10, and 11, respectively. The graphs demonstrate that while the response time volumes vary within the factors, the distributions are similar across the age groups, between the genders, and across the computer skills. The response times could thus be assumed as an un-biased representation of the perceived complexity of the tasks performed by the subjects.

A. Feature Importance

The importance values of the features that provided the most insight are provided in Table III.

Table III implies that object-specific features have lower importance values compared to the whole-image features. The highest importance values of the whole-image features are those from the Gabor filter and fractal dimension calculations,

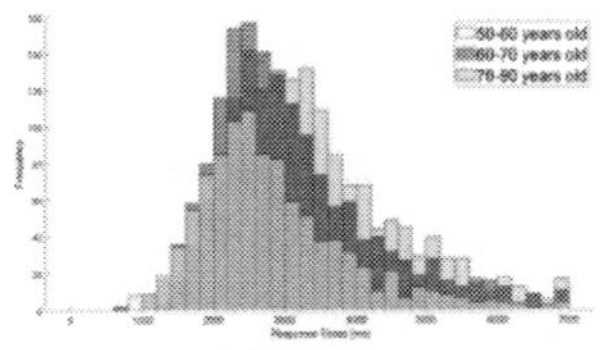

Figure 9. Frequency plot of the response times segmented by age

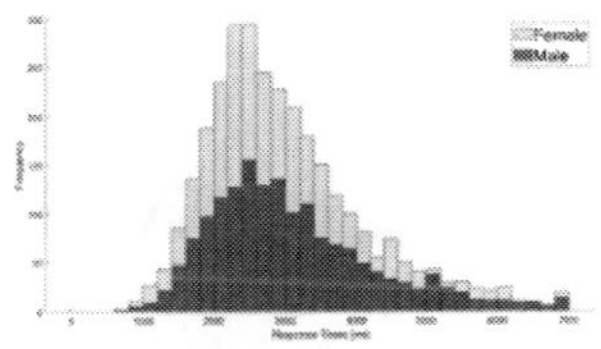

Figure 10. Frequency plot of the response times segmented by gender

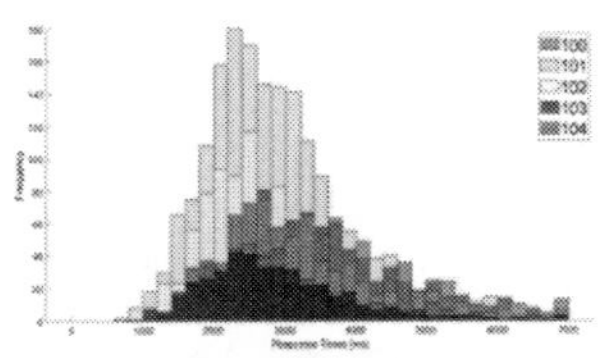

Figure 11. Frequency plot of the response times segmented by computer skill from 100 as computer illiterate to 104 as computer literate

as well as the white spacing feature and the symmetry. The strongest feature is the standard deviation of the Gabor filter. The smallest importance value for the whole image feature set, and one of the smallest in the entire feature set is the direct square comparison.

To illustrate the feature importance results of Table III, examples of recognition tasks from the dataset for which the complexity labels were correctly predicted by the algorithm are presented in Table IV. Three examples are given for each predefined complexity label: 1, 2 and 3.

1) Object-Specific Feature Importance: The black adjacent path/s length/s yielded the highest importance value among these features. This can be explained by examples 2 and 3 of Table IV, where only one of the two different images has one long black adjacent path, with no other black objects. This makes it easily distinguishable from the other image in the task, and justifies the "easy," label 1 mapping. The number of adjacent paths, which got low importance ranking, however, displays no specific trend in all tasks in Table IV across the three complexity labels. This visual trend can also be related to the relatively high importance value of the "Different black objects presence" feature: When one image in a pair has only one long black adjacent path and the other image has a variety of black features, the task was labelled as "easy" - label 1. The different white objects presence feature, however, does not display the same characteristic. Different white objects are present in several image pair examples of Table IV and across the various complexity labels, with no specific trend.

The importance values of the features for the objects' presence and locations are all relatively small. The only object type whose location yielded a positive importance value was

TABLE III. PROMINENT FEATURE IMPORTANCE RESULTS

Whole-Image Features		Object-Specific Features	
Feature	**Import-ance Value**	**Feature**	**Import-ance Value**
Gabor filter std. dev	1.00	Black adjacent path length/s	0.73
Gabor filter sum	0.95	Different black objects present	0.73
Fractal dimension range	0.92	Similar black adjacent path location	0.61
White object spacing	0.86	Black similar objects within an image	0.57
Relaxed symmetry	0.86	White similar objects within an image	0.55
Fractal dimension	0.76	Number of black adjacent paths	0.41
Fractal dimension std. dev.	0.56	Number of white adjacent paths	0.39
Black object spacing	0.53	Similar white diagonal path location	0.08
Black similar objects in an image pair	0.42	Different white objects present	0.00
White similar objects in an image pair	0.26		
Direct squares comparison	0.23		

the black adjacent path. In examples 5, 6 and 9 of Table IV, the presence of a similarly located black adjacent path in both images could have made them harder to distinguish between, thus increasing the perceived complexity in some way. Similarly, features related to similar shapes within an image yielded small importance values.

2) Whole-Image Feature Importance: The white object spacing feature had a much larger importance value compared to the black object spacing feature. In example 2 of Table IV, the average distance between the **white** objects of image 1, and image 3, is greater than that of image 2: There is only one long black adjacent path in the middle of image 1, whereas there are smaller black objects dispersed around image 2. This noticeable difference in the white spacing could have justified

TABLE IV. EXAMPLES WITH CORRECT COMPLEXITY LABEL PREDICTIONS

#	Image 1	Image 2	Image 3	Complexity Label
1				1
2				1
3		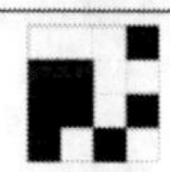		1
4	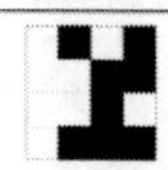	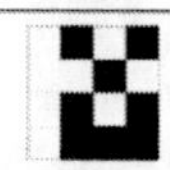	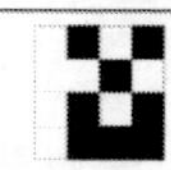	2
5	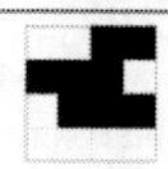	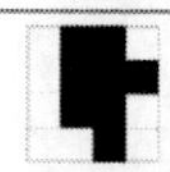	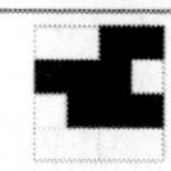	2
6				2
7	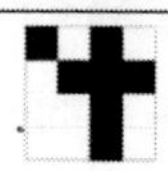	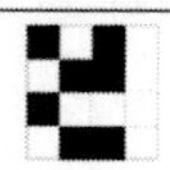	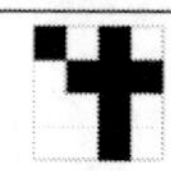	3
8	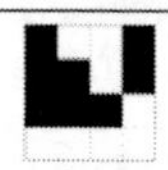	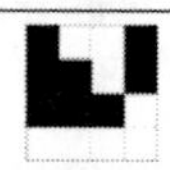	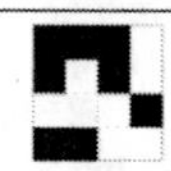	3
9	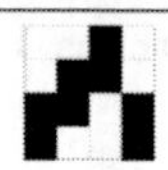	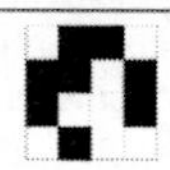	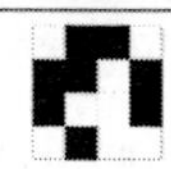	3

the 'easy', label 1, mapping.

The relaxed symmetry feature had relatively high importance value. In example 1 of Table IV, for instance, image 1 is symmetrical across the x axis, as well as the y axis, in inverted colours. This symmetry can explain the image as perceptually easy to discriminate in the recognition task, and could justify the "easy", label 1, mapping for that task.

The feature of the direct squares comparison had no importance in the complexity predictions. This feature had no correlation to the human complexity labels with values randomly ranging from 4 to 12 for the tasks in Table IV.

The mathematical models - Gabor filters and fractal dimensions yielded the largest importance values. In the recognition tasks of Table IV, the values of all five features associated with these models: fractal dimension, range of the fractal dimension, standard deviation of the fractal dimension, sum of the Gabor filters and standard deviation of this sum, consistently decrease with increasing complexity.

IV. Discussion

The feature importance analysis implies that whole-image features had greater significance than object-specific features. As per Witkin's [3] field dependence concept, individuals may assess their visual fields as a whole, making only loose partitions of an image. This observed trend in our data may, however, be also related to the small size and simplicity of the images used, where individuals may not need to look for finer details.

The high importance of the number of black adjacent paths is in line with Attneave's [4] theories on visual redundancy, where long strings of adjoining pixels of the same colour could constitute for a level of visual redundancy, thus simplifying the visual-field's perceived complexity.

The small size of the images may also explain the result that the black spacing feature had a small importance value: The probability of having only one black object in these images is large - a fact that was assessed by the square counting feature. In this case, the average black object spacing feature is reduced to zero, which may produce a bias in the image pairs' black object spacing calculations. The higher importance of the average spacing of the white objects may be explained by the presence of more white objects in the image and is illustrated in the examples of Table IV, in the higher perceived complexity.

All white object-specific features demonstrated low importance values. The highest importance value related to white objects was the white object average distance feature, which was similar in strength to the black object average distance. This may be explained by associating the white objects distances with the black objects placements. These findings may imply that the white objects are perceived as background space.

The only whole-image feature that showed no importance in the complexity mapping was the direct squares comparison. This suggests that this typical computer process of scanning an image and comparing images is alien to human perception.

The significant importance of image symmetry in the complexity predictions, is in line with Attneave's [4] premise on image symmetry representing another form of visual redundancy, thus reducing the visual observation's perceived complexity. It indicates that when subjects observe an image that has symmetry, the mirroring makes it simpler to distinguish against other, non-symmetrical images.

Finally, the positive importance values of the mathematical Gabor filter and fractal dimension features imply their relation to visual perception. These importance values, and the trends showed that the smaller the **difference** in the values of these features for each of the two images in the pair, the greater the perceived complexity. This is also in line with the assumption in this study, that the smaller the difference between the images in the task, the harder it is to recognise the odd one. The feature importance trends found in the study thus suggest a potential of linking human visual perception to computational models of complexity.

While one might argue that the feature importance results have been obtained for images that are too small or simple, the motivation behind this chosen image set is that the lack of colour, and size of the images would allow for a more objective visual analysis by the subject. The disadvantage with presenting elaborate and natural visual stimuli, is that objects in the images, or the images themselves, are likely to visually trigger past memories or associations for a subject. These triggers could distract their focus off the required objective comparison of the images, thus skewing the human results that the algorithm is trying to mimic. It could, however, be worthwhile to explore designing stimuli that apply to real-world situations while preventing distractions in the future.

Additionally, many of these feature observations have touched on either Attneave [4] or Witkin's [3] theories at a high-level to demonstrate correlation to psychological research. This was only done at a high-level since the primary scope of this study was in trying to understand how computational or mathematical aspects of these images could be used in defining their visual complexity. However, in future work, it could be useful to conduct further research into psychological studies that have relevance to this topic. Given this, there is also potential for collaboration with psychologists to try link these results to human psychological perception mechanisms, and gain some insight to contribute to psychological research.

V. Conclusion

A method for the computation of visual tasks complexity combining information theory, machine vision and human perception measures was developed and assessed by its relevance to human perception. The computational complexity features could explain human visual complexity perception in the context of cognitive tests where this complexity perception is assumed to be represented by subjects' response times to visual tasks. The feature importance values corroborated psychological studies of human visual perception. These findings indicate a potential to link computer-extracted features to human perception in their definition of complexity of visual tasks.

References

[1] S. M. Anstis, "What does visual perception tell us about visual coding," Handbook of psychobiology, 1975, pp. 269–323.

[2] J. Wagemans, J. H. Elder, M. Kubovy, S. E. Palmer, M. A. Peterson, M. Singh, and R. von der Heydt, "A century of gestalt psychology in visual perception: I. perceptual grouping and figure–ground organization." Psychological bulletin, vol. 138, no. 6, 2012, p. 1172.

[3] H. A. Witkin and D. R. Goodenough, "Field dependence and interpersonal behavior." Psychological bulletin, vol. 84, no. 4, 1977, p. 661.

[4] F. Attneave and M. D. Arnoult, "The quantitative study of shape and pattern perception." Psychological bulletin, vol. 53, no. 6, 1956, p. 452.

[5] R. Mahendran, G. Jayashree, and K. Alagusundaram, "Application of computer vision technique on sorting and grading of fruits and vegetables," J. Food Process. Technol, vol. 10, 2012, pp. 2157–7110.

[6] V. Aharonson and A. D. Korczyn, "Human–computer interaction in the administration and analysis of neuropsychological tests," Computer methods and programs in biomedicine, vol. 73, no. 1, 2004, pp. 43–53.

[7] J.-K. Kamarainen, "Gabor features in image analysis," in 2012 3rd International Conference on Image Processing Theory, Tools and Applications (IPTA). IEEE, 2012, pp. 13–14.

[8] S. Marčelja, "Mathematical description of the response of simple cortical cells," Journal of the Optical Society of America, vol. 70, 12 1980, pp. 1297–300.

[9] Y. Fisher, E. Jacobs, and R. Boss, "Fractal image compression using iterated transforms," in Image and text compression. Springer, 1992, pp. 35–61.

[10] M. Bouda, J. S. Caplan, and J. E. Saiers, "Box-counting dimension revisited: presenting an efficient method of minimizing quantization error and an assessment of the self-similarity of structural root systems," Frontiers in plant science, vol. 7, 2016, p. 149.

[11] W. Man, Y. Ji, and Z. Zhang, "Image classification based on improved random forest algorithm," in 2018 IEEE 3rd International Conference on Cloud Computing and Big Data Analysis (ICCCBDA), April 2018, pp. 346–350.

3D SpaceQuantumIndexation and Computation via VoxelNET to Enhance 3D Cognitive Systemisation

-Reasoning, Raycasting and GeoLoacted Voxels

Charlotte Sennersten
Mineral Resources
CSIRO
Australia
email: charlotte.sennersten@csiro.au

Craig Lindley
Data 61
CSIRO
Australia
email: craig.lindley@csiro.au

Abstract—**A global recursive equal-volume spatial quantization and indexation system can unify access to, use and perform volumetric computations across diverse fields to provide a volumetric evolution from the current 2D internet. A unifying spatial framework has been developed to demonstrate this alternative. The framework supports cognitive spatial analytics incorporating different datasets, advanced AI systems, human decision support, robotic and autonomous systems, and many other applications for which three-dimensional spatial structure is important. Domains in question can include a variety of sensor inputs, including environmental, physiological, neural, material, chemical, optical, locational (e.g. GPS and lidar), etc.. Sensor data in diverse domains is used to create domain-specific models for analytics and decision support, and for models of human cognitive performance amenable to automated, machine implementations. The system includes a unified, hierarchical spatial quantization system with time series data and fixed, locational, and mobile volumetric structures. The framework supports data, information and knowledge management and can also be used to manage the distribution of computational loads. It can also support new computing paradigms, e.g. tracking the spatial locations of geographically dispersed computations linked by quantum entanglement.**

Keywords-Spatial Cognition; Voxelisation; Computation; Sensor Integration.

I. INTRODUCTION

The main objective of this paper is to collate many years of work unifying and systemizing qualitative and quantitative data using a 3D spatial framework called the VoxelNET platform. The platform provides a 'digital twinned' world, a digitized replica of the volumetric physical world, a unified, hierarchical spatial quantization framework for location and movement tracking and volumetric computations across diverse fields. The main fields demonstrated over the years have been gaming, mining, space and robotics -where decisions mainly have been about volumetric comprehension, timing, and economy.

The goal of the computer and cognitive science research is to provide the software engineering implementation with requirements for a systemized volumetric infrastructure so people/users can share and understand otherwise siloed volumetric data.

An analogy might help to explain why all this is important. Imagine yourself scuba diving and navigating through water. You may not know what is 'up', 'down', 'left' or 'right' and available sensors do not capture the environmental, physiological or optical data in its 3D context. VoxelNET and its indexation helps to geo-index, cross-correlate, compute and contextualize the data in its global volumetric architecture. Our research purpose is to make sense of sensed and captured data in this 3D context.

The platform sits exemplifies Internet 4.0, Mining 4.0, Space 4.0, Industry 4.0 and other *X* 4.0 concepts representing the full integration of sensors, information and operations systems within the 3D and 4D structure of the world. This includes elements such as: cyber-physical systems (CPS), the internet of things (IoT), industrial internet of things (IIOT), cloud computing, cognitive computing, and artificial intelligence (AI). X 4.0 systems are characterized by the interpenetration of the physical world using data, computation, analytics and control systems. The result is an evolving large-scale infrastructure that includes the data interconnectivity required for integration, together with many diverse systems and components for modelling and analyzing the world. The total infrastructure hierarchy for control happens by a synthesis of human, automated and autonomous decision making at different levels. Decision making within such an integrated system is both heterogeneous and highly distributed. Raising the overall intelligence of X 4.0 systems requires higher levels of coordination. A critical element of this is the coordination of mapping and decision making regarding three-dimensional (3D) space. However, current internet concepts and technologies are neither inherently spatial nor three dimensional. Since X 4.0 is heavily concerned with data and computational integration of the physical world and its contents, which *are* inherently 3D and spatial, the deployment of a universal 3D spatial infrastructure can be a critical element in accelerating the evolution of these systems. A universal 3D spatial infrastructure can provide the 3D *spatial context* of X 4.0 data, models and computations, facilitating higher level cognitive functions that can process not only *what* is happening *when* (the current dominant paradigm for X 4.0), but also *where* it is happening. This amounts to the incorporation of spatial awareness and spatial cognition into X 4.0 systems for indexation, computation, analytics and display.

Previous work [1], [2]) has described the VoxelNET research prototype system, a 3D spatial indexation system and a computational infrastructure used to support volumetric representations and decisions. VoxelNET is a demonstrator for a broader concept of a universal 3D spatial data framework that can potentially provide the kind of spatial framework required for X 4.0.

VoxelNET quantizes the Earth into default 1 m^3 voxels that penetrate Air, Space, Water, Rock, and Soil so these natural continuous material distributions can be included in the Internet of Things (IoT), which otherwise tends to focus on separate artefacts or objects that are artificially produced [1] [2]. This allows the combination of representations of what is artificially made with what occurs naturally together with their respective locations, orientations and spatial distributions over time.

This can be extended beyond the Earth to include the Moon, Mars and other solar system objects. Of course, these objects have their own coordinate systems. This is catered for by the underlying mathematical formulations of coordinate systems, which can include alternate geometries (e.g. ellipsoidal, spherical, Cartesian) modelled as local coordinate systems within specified larger scale spatial coordinate reference frames within which they are situated and mapped by spatial transforms. The required transforms must specify a particular location (typically in 3 dimensions) and orientation (e.g., in terms of rotations around 3 axes) at a specific time (or epoch), together with a specification of velocity at a particular epoch. These parameters can be used by active functions to compute locations at different times.

The VoxelNET capacity for representing multiple coordinate systems can be used to locate objects and material masses within locational coordinate reference systems, as well as larger scale global reference frames within which local frames can be situated. Spatial reference frames are static, persisting over time, and voxels within the 3D structure are referred to as *location voxels*. The VoxelNET database allows data to be volumetrically indexed and associated with unlimited amounts of data for specific volumes. The volumetric indexation of locations is static. Objects and materials are represented using the concept of *material voxels*. These are volumetric representations of material masses and objects moving through static geolocated voxels. Representations of material voxels can be rescaled, combining multiple material voxels into larger scale voxels, or subdividing them into smaller scale and potentially mixed and/or materially/chemically transformed voxels, and aggregated or disaggregated into malleable shapes. This capacity has been used, for example, to map the removal of materials from a mineral resource block in the ground, through sequences of mixing and separating transforms via processes such as blasting, excavation, loading onto haulage, unloading, stockpiling, etc., to create provenance records for material entering a mineral processing plant.

This paper elaborates on a number of topics associated with this integrating vision of the VoxelNET system, including: general issues around spatial cognition, the integration and use of environmental and physiological sensors, management of distributed computation, understanding and integrating human cognition in a broader spatial context, and potential application in quantum computing. Section II. describes spatial cognition and associated concepts, while subsequent sections describe III. Sensors for Environment and Physiology, IV. Discretized Computation, V. VoxelNET, Brain, Gaze and Ray Casting - how to bind it together, and VI. Parallel Processing and Quantum Computing.

II. Spacial Cognition, Syntax, Awareness and Cognition

Spatial cognition involves not one but many specific abilities. These include locating points in space, determining the orientation of lines and objects, assessing location in depth, apprehending geometric relations between objects, and processing motion, including motion in depth. Building upon these details, spatial cognition includes awareness of locations and orientations in space, spatial relationships between and among objects and materials, how to navigate through an environment, and how to manipulate objects and materials by hand or machine for a large range of purposes. Zimring and Dalton [3] describe 'Linking objective measures of space to cognition' mainly focused on how people acquire, store, and represent information about directions, distances, and locations in the large-scale physical world. The authors also refer to Space Syntax in terms of "...rigorous measurement of the layout of physical settings and observation of people moving through it; environment and behavior studies have examined self-report behavior such as think-aloud protocols and sketch maps as well as movement in real-world settings; cognitive science has explored and modeled cognitive processes." [3].

Most researchers have found that cognitive representations, or their presumed externalizations such as sketch maps, are often distorted. Often people learn topology first and then develop more coordinated metric relationships later. For example, one might know that a shopping center is beyond the school but not know how far. People seem to have greater difficulty representing complex settings. In the realm of IoT and digitization, spatial navigation needs to be extended to digital 3D world representations, discretization, digital operations and digital 2D and 3D browsing in order to understand, design and optimize the operation of systems within their spatial context.

Moreover, as Thrift [4] puts it, "The fabric of space is open-ended rather than enclosing." and "we are increasingly a part of a 'movement-space' which is relative rather than absolute but which ... relies on an absolute space for its existence".

Spatial awareness is defined as "the ability to be aware of oneself in space. It is an organized knowledge of objects in relation to oneself in that given space and the relationship of these objects when there is a change of position." [5]. Spatial awareness is essentially a question of making a trade-off between local visual information (which can be seen from a single standpoint) and global spatial information, which includes visual data of the rest of the environment, but also haptics and symbolic representations of space such as maps. To be efficient, a person navigating must maximize their acquisition of global information while minimizing local information, achieved by recognizing when they already comprehend enough about their immediate surroundings and hence intuitively seek the next key location that permits a sudden increase in novel environmental data.

As thinking individuals, we are cognitively calculating ourselves through the physical and digital world i.e., the logic of the system. "The upper bound of human brainpower has been calculated to be 2 x 10^{16} calculations per second. If computational power continues to conform to Moore's Law, then by 2030 just an ordinary PC should compute at around 10^{16} instructions per second [6]. There is also an increasing ubiquity of hardware and software, which means that computing can take place in many locations" [4]. Moreover, islands of computational power analogous to individual human cognitive processing capacity are increasingly being integrated in seas of interconnectivity. This raises the need for collective cognitive frameworks for the unification of individual nodes of cognitive capability into larger scales of cognitive capability interconnected by much higher bandwidths than native human communication mechanisms (i.e., speech, non-verbal communication, technologies such as writing and drawing).

While navigating on and through Earth we can map physical reality using sensor data. Extending this to X 4.0 systems of systems, we need to be able to situate and index the information so we can translate context and invite people and machines to interact in a 'ground-truthed' collective digitized environment. A location method such as GPS is an estimate of a location, while the "ground truth" is the actual location on earth [7]. Ground truth refers to information collected on location, as opposed to information inferred from remotely sensed data. Ground truth allows image data, for example, to be related to real features and materials on the ground. The collection of ground truth data enables calibration of remote-sensing data, and aids in the interpretation and analysis of what is being sensed. Ground truth is a best representation of the geolocated information and its three dimensions of 360-degree landscape so we can share, interact and specify where we and things are, wayfinding ourselves by using various individual coordinate systems.

III. Cognition [Physiological Sensors] and Space [Environemntal Sensors]

How do we understand cognitive choices and how can we assist and design for our affordances versus shortcomings?

A. *Attention, Heart Rate, Arousal and Reasoning*

Human and animal intelligence is facilitated by several forms of memory, including a long-term semantic memory (SM) of abstract concepts and types, a short-term memory (STM) and a long-term episodic memory (LTM) of experiences. Humans also reason about their environment and use a so- called Memory SketchPad or working memory (WM) for active thinking processes that combines both new and old information to solve problems, such as finding a path, creating and negotiating a trajectory in the case of spatial reasoning [8].

Our eyes are the main physiological instrument that provides data for use by the cognitive system to navigate through a 3D space or a maze, and visual attention directs the eyes to features of interest in the visual field that are unconsciously selected for relevance to a problem-solving situation [9]. WM is used by cognitive processes to synthesize this kind of data into problem solutions.

Heart rate, heart rate variability, and other indicators of physiological arousal such as skin conductance are other unconscious responses to stimuli such as environmental and social factors.

All these physiological responses can be measured by physiological sensors such as infrared diode corneal reflection for eye gaze tracking to study visual attention, heart rate and its variability using pulse monitoring, and skin conductance measurements to study arousal [10] [11]. fMRI can be used to understand the spatial distribution of brain activity via increased blood flow.

Eye gaze tracking can be used to gain insight into the control of visual attention to gain data used by cognitive processes for problem solving, while unconscious physiological data can be used to infer emotional states relevant to cognitive goals and biases, e.g., as input to affective computing systems. The spatial context of these processes is crucial for understanding their details and a general external spatial reference frame can be used to locate measurements and external phenomena in relation to which cognitive processes are being performed.

B. *Lidar Pointclouds, Images and Objects*

Numerous environmental sensors measure different states of our environment and optical sensors such as lidar can map spatial details of local physical environments in detail and store the information to computer memory. A Lidar scan usually has a geolocated origin point such as a GPS point so the location of the Lidar scan can be situated in the world. Lidar gives the structure of a space, it's lay-out in 3D. RGBD and Photogrammetry combine image and depth. An image in a traditional sense is a 2D representation of the world providing inputs to image processing that can distinguish features via pixel color and contrast features to distinguish depth parameters [12]. A universal 3D spatial reference frame can be used to store all of these kinds of data for use both in real time and for retrospective analytical studies across agents and situations.

IV. COMPUTATION

Our brains and computers perform computation. Computation by definition means: I. the action of mathematical calculation, "methods of computation" and II. the use of computers, especially as a subject of research or study. In theoretical computer science and mathematics, the theory of computation is the branch that deals with how efficiently problems can be solved on a model of computation, using an algorithm. Humans, animals and robots use algorithms to perform tasks.

VoxelNET discretizes volumetric data in a systematic way and this can be used as a computational framework so we use computer/computing science as a baseline in parallel with cognition i.e., reasoning when looking into how to progress the design of the system for both machine and human benefit and comprehension.

Thrift writes "In a world in which numerical calculations are being done and redone continuously, static representation becomes subordinated to flow (not least because 'the image, in a traditional sense, no longer exists' [13], the nomadologic of movement becomes the natural order of thought. The world is reconfigured as a global trading zone in which network forms, which strive for coordination, are replaced by flow forms which strive for observation and projection.". He continues "Most importantly, I shall argue that the sheer amount of calculation that is now becoming possible at all points of so many spaces is producing a new calculative sense, which I will call 'qualculation' [14]." Thrift [4] includes factors like speed, faith in numbers and limited numerical facility available in the bodies of the population also involving a different sense of number and counting and series. It is important that the use of numbers varies with context and is not a discrete activity carried out for itself.

The computation field is divided into three major branches: automata theory and languages, computability theory, and computational complexity theory, which are linked by the question: *"What are the fundamental capabilities and limitations of computers?"*. To this we can add, what are the fundamental capabilities and limitations of the human brain and reasoning capability for computing and interpreting a holistic digital eco system?

A. *Computational Complexity Theory*

Computational complexity theory considers not only whether a problem can be solved at all on a computer, but also how efficiently the problem can be solved [15]. Two major aspects are considered: time complexity and space complexity, which are, respectively, how many steps it takes to perform a computation, and how much memory is required to perform that computation [16].

In order to analyze how much time and space a given algorithm requires, computer scientists express the time or space required to solve the problem as a function of the size of the input problem. For example, finding a particular number in a long list of numbers becomes harder as the list of numbers grows larger. If we say there are n numbers in the list, then if the list is not sorted or indexed in any way we may have to look at every number in order to find the number we're seeking, which will result in an average search time of $n/2$. We thus say that in order to solve this problem, the computer needs to perform a number of steps that grows linearly with the size of the problem.

B. *Discretisation*

In applied mathematics, discretization is the process of transferring continuous functions, models, variables, and equations into discrete counterparts. This process is usually carried out as a first step toward making them suitable for numerical evaluation and implementation on digital computers [17].

C. *Quantisation*

Quantization is the concept that a physical quantity can have only certain discrete values. Electrical charge, energy, light, angular momentum, and matter are all quantized on the quantum level. Also, the energy levels of electrons in atoms are quantized. In a computational system, quantization is typically the same as discretization, where the size of quanta involves a tradeoff between storage space and processing time on one hand, and the accuracy of physical simulation on the other; large quanta are easier to store and process, but less accurate for the simulation or representation of continuous physical phenomena. Quantization does not need to be linear, but can be a nonlinear map that partitions a numerical space and represents all of the values in each subspace by a single value [18].

Quantization errors are errors arising from the loss of information created by the mapping of continuous phenomena into discrete artificial quanta. The scalability of VoxelNET location and material voxels facilitates the optimization of voxel size in relation to the spatial frequency distributions of data, as well as the management of tradeoffs between quantization errors and computational space/time complexity.

D. *Size of Files*

To progress in a 3D world with sensors mapping real world environments we need to subdivide information in a discrete and quantized manner; this is a fundamental principle of digital computers, for which all continuous values must be represented in binary numbers. In many cases there are clear criteria for quantization scales. For example, to represent a varying phenomenon, basic sampling theory shows that samples of the phenomenon should be taken at a rate (i.e. the inverse of temporal or spatial quantum size) of at least twice the frequency, or half the wavelength, of the highest required frequency component of the sampled phenomenon. A lower rate than this will lose information, while a higher rate will add no new required information. For cognitive attention, the quantization scale is related to the importance of a sensory feature for the cognitive task at hand and its neural or computational transformation into a level of abstraction suitable to problem solving. E.g., in digital modelling of a Field of View (FoV), see Figure 1, we may need to represent digitized content supporting a task at high resolution, leading to large data sizes, while the background and middle ground of the FoV may be of less importance and therefore appropriately represented at a lower resolution.

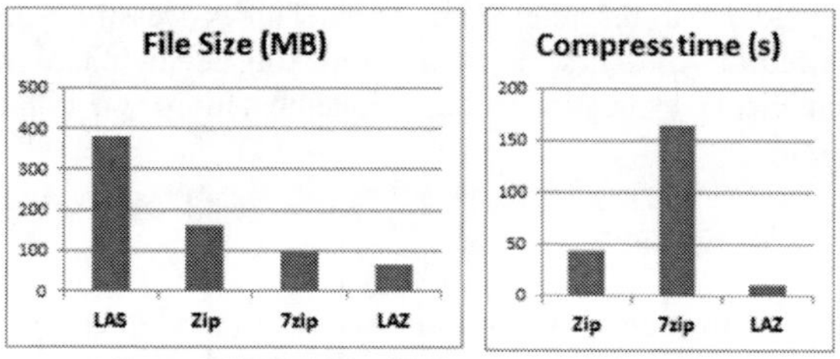

Figure 1. Typical lidar file sizes around 300-400MB.

Digitized content includes optical sensor information and computation for analytics and display.

V. VOXELNET, BRAIN, GAZE AND RAY CASTING

How do we bind together the external world with computation and human cognition in a coherent systemized way.

The technical solution to this described here is the VoxelNET system. By default, VoxelNET indexes and quantizes the Earth in equal volumetric computational units, see Figures 2, 3 and 4.

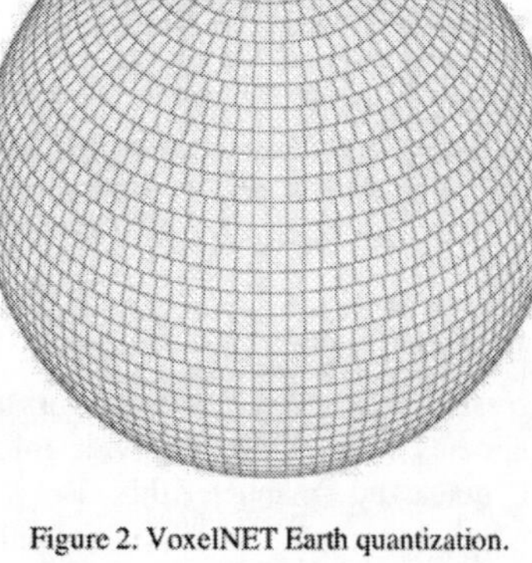

Figure 2. VoxelNET Earth quantization.

On one hand the VoxelNET database represents a linguistic interpretation and representation of the physical world while the client needs to replicate and represent the world in a direct 3D FoV manner. The VoxelNET infrastructure spatially parses all 3D objects and data in the world. The voxel indexation makes it possible to directly point towards a direct volume without lengthy descriptive relations in order to reduce time and space complexity. The volumetric context of a volume provides context information that points alone cannot. Equal volume quantization allows analyses to be conducted across numerous voxels which nevertheless have a comparable quantization of the world and therefore consistent and commensurable volumetric interpolation and averaging of data points.

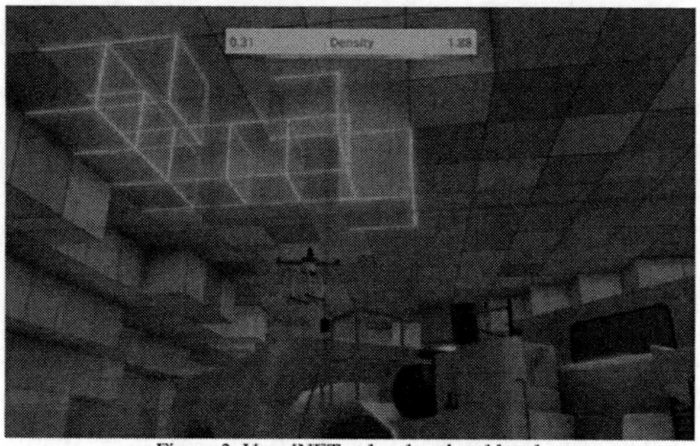

Figure 3. VoxelNET at local regional level.

A. *Gaze into the world -Ray Casting and Ray Tracing*

Ray casting is a rendering technique used in computer graphics and computational geometry making use of the same geometric algorithm as ray tracing. Ray tracing is a rendering technique that aims to simulate the way light bounces off objects, in turn creating more realistic shadows, reflections, and lighting effects. This ensures that the computer isn't wasting processing power on objects the camera doesn't see (compare FoV) while producing more realistic lighting effects. The ray casting method is used in addition to eye tracking, so it is possible to log what a user is looking at in the 3D digital/physical world.

B. *Eyetracking and Eyesteering via Ray Casting to connect with Human Intentions and Actions*

Corneal reflection and infrared light can be used to track the gaze behavior and therefore visual attention of a user interacting with computer content, revealing how things are operated, read, created, etc. to be tracked as an insight into ongoing cognitive processes. Gaze can also be used as an input device into the digital environment here via VoxelNET. The universal volumetric representation system demonstrated by VoxelNET can be used to generalize the use of this interaction and attention analysis technology.

C. *Real World Knowledge Systemisation and Indexation for Human Brains*

To connect the external world with the neural physiological foundations of human behaviors and cognition, we need a volumetric representation that can connect or link brain actions with contextual representations of the 3D world that make these meaningful.

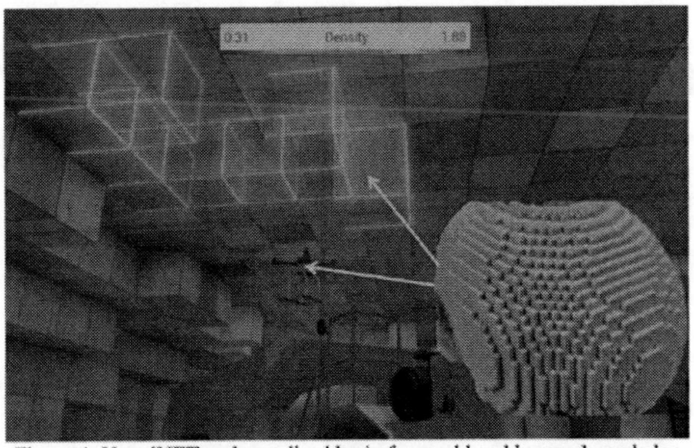

Figure 4. VoxelNET and voxelised brain for world and human knowledge systemization.

In times of neurological programming, machine learning and data mining, it becomes even more important to know and shape knowledge about how we look into the world', what brain regions we activate' and on what basis. Spatio- and spectro-temporal brain data (STBD) are the most commonly collected data for measuring brain response to external stimuli. However, Kasabov says "there is no unifying computational framework to deal with all these types of data in order to better understand this data and the processes that generated it." (2013) [19]. Kasabov's NeuCube model is based on a 3D evolving Spiking Neural Network (SNN) that is an approximate map of structural and functional areas of interest in the brain related to the STBD modeling that integrates various brain data, information and knowledge for a single person into one model.

In the VoxelNET world systemization the brain can be voxelised within a local coordinate system, allowing ray-casting via gaze to bind the two worlds together.

D. Brodmann Brain Areas

When our gaze is distributed across various external stimuli, our brain is processing incoming information in various functional volumes. As Kasabov puts it "The brain is a complex integrated spatio-temporal information processing machine. An animal or a human brain has a range of structural and functional areas that are spatially distributed in a constrained 3D space". The brain processes information, either triggered by external stimuli, or by inner processes, such as visual, auditory, emotional, environmental, social, or all of these stimuli together, complex spatio-temporal pathways are activated, and patterns are formed across the whole brain.

If we want to systemize digitized knowledge i.e., the human or the robot operating in the world and also execute 'compute on demand' with these methods we need to know what happens when, how and where. It is also a matter of how we have people and humans coexisting in the same digital twin world. We want to create a comprehensive digital twin where we create knowledge and not 'black boxes of algorithms/AI' no one understands.

Brodmann areas were originally defined and numbered by the German anatomist Korbinian Brodmann [20], see Figures 5 and 6. Brodmann split the cortex into 52 different volumetric areas and assigned each a number (many of these Brodmann areas have since been subdivided). He published his maps of cortical areas in humans, monkeys, and other species in 1909, along with many other findings and observations regarding the general cell types and laminar organization of the mammalian cortex.

Zilles reports that "A cited reference search in the Web of Science carried out in July 2018 resulted in over 170 000 citations of Brodmann's work, mainly of his monography (Brodmann, 1909). His publications on the cytoarchitectonic parcellation of the entire human cerebral cortex made him a founder of the field of anatomical brain mapping. The number of publications with references to different versions of his maps (Brodmann, 1908a, 1909, 1910, 1912, 1914) dramatically increased since the advent of neuroimaging using PET and MRI, and is still increasing ... The maps have become particularly popular in recent times for localization of activations using functional MRI and for meta-analyses of structural and functional relationships." [21].

The brain locations are of interest when also looking at Quantum Neural Networks (QNNs) as per what neurons are fired where, when and for what reason.

Brodmann's brain areas for humans and other primates are:

- Areas 3, 1 and 2 – Primary somatosensory cortex in the postcentral gyrus
- Area 4 – Primary motor cortex
- Area 5 – Superior parietal lobule

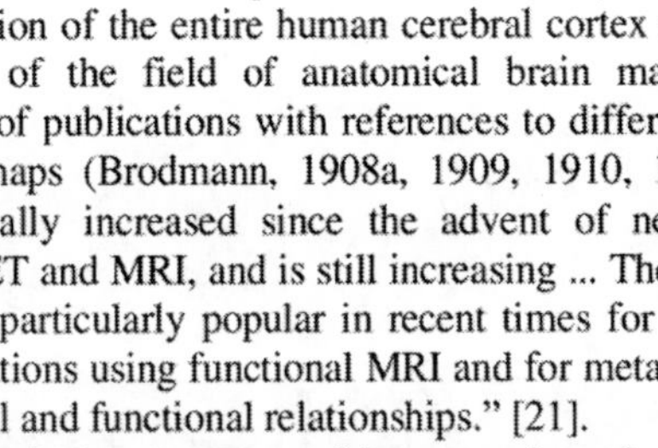

Figure 5. Inner brain 3D mapping [22].

- Area 6 – Premotor cortex and Supplementary Motor Cortex (Secondary Motor Cortex)
- Area 7 – Visuo-Motor Coordination
- Area 8– Includes Frontal eye fields
- Area 9 – Dorsolateral prefrontal cortex
- Area 10 – Anterior prefrontal cortex (most rostral part of superior and middle frontal gyri)
- Area 11 – Orbitofrontal area (orbital and rectus gyri, plus part of the rostral part of the superior frontal gyrus)
- Area 12 – Orbitofrontal area (used to be part of BA11, refers to the area between the superior frontal gyrus and the inferior rostral sulcus)
- Area 13 and Area 14* – Insular cortex
- Area 15* - Anterior Temporal lobe
- Area 16 – Insular cortex

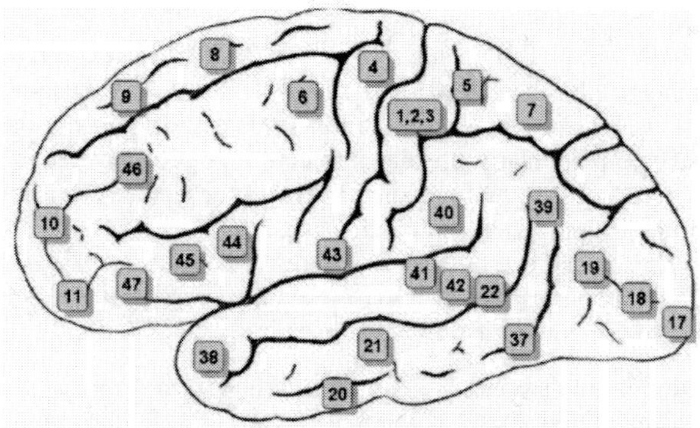

Figure 6. Outer brain volumes [22].

- Area 17 – Primary visual cortex (V1)
- Area 18 – Secondary visual cortex (V2)
- Area 19 – Associative visual cortex (V3, V4, V5)
- Area 20 -Inferior temporal gyrus
- Area 21 – Middle temporal gyrus
- Area 22 – Part of the superior temporal gyrus, included in Wernicke's area
- Area 23 – Ventral posterior cingulate cortex
- Area 24 – Ventral anterior cingulate cortex.
- Area 25 – Subgenual area (part of the Ventromedial prefrontal cortex)
- Area 26 – Ectosplenial portion of the retrosplenial region of the cerebral cortex
- Area 27 – Piriform cortex
- Area 28 – Ventral entorhinal cortex
- Area 29 Retrosplenial cortex
- Area 30 – Subdivision of retrosplenial cortex
- Area 31 – Dorsal Posterior cingulate cortex
- Area 32 – Dorsal anterior cingulate cortex
- Area 33 – Part of anterior cingulate cortex
- Area 34 – Dorsal entorhinal cortex (on the Parahippocampal gyrus)
- Area 35 – Part of the perirhinal cortex (in the rhinal sulcus)
- Area 36 – Part of the perirhinal cortex (in the rhinal sulcus)
- Area 37 – Fusiform gyrus
- Area 38 – Temporopolar area (most rostral part of the superior and middle temporal gyri)
- Area 39– Angular gyrus, considered by some to be part of Wernicke's area
- Area 40 – Supramarginal gyrus considered by some to be part of Wernicke's area
- Areas 41 and 42 – Auditory cortex
- Area 43 – Primary gustatory cortex
- Areas 44 and 45 – Broca's area, includes the opercular part and triangular part of the inferior frontal gyrus
- Area 46– Dorsolateral prefrontal cortex
- Area 47 – Orbital part of inferior frontal gyrus
- Area 48 – Retrosubicular area (a small part of the medial surface of the temporal lobe)
- Area 49 – Parasubicular area in a rodent

- Area 52 – Parainsular area (at the junction of the temporal lobe and the insula)

(*) Area only found in non-human primates.

The VoxelNET system is capable of representing the voxelised volumetric structure of the brain corresponding to the Brodmann areas in the form of a material voxel structure, as well as the voxelised spatial environment providing the perceptual, physical context of brain activations and the neural/cognitive functions that they represent (see figure 4). This can provide a much more ecologically valid method of studying neural function that the rarefied experimental structures more typically used in cognitive and neural sciences.

VI. Parallel Processing and Quantum Computing

To be able to process vast amounts of data, parallel processing or parallel computing is a method of simultaneously breaking up and running program tasks on multiple microprocessors resulting in reduction of processing time. Large problems can often be divided into smaller ones, which can then be solved at the same time and not sequentially. As an example: we may gaze into the world and direct attention towards complex scenes and need to calculate both optical sensors input and other operational calculations at the same time. A 3D infrastructure such as VoxelNET can be used to subdivide and direct computing to save/distribute computational resources while also displaying information/parts of scenes. Parallel processing can be accomplished via one computer with multiple cores and expanded via a computer network.

A. *Quantum Computers, Quantum Computing and Quantum Computational Intellgence*

Quantum computers aren't limited to two states; they encode information as quantum bits, or qubits, which can exist in superposition. Qubits represent atoms, ions, photons or electrons and their respective control devices can work together to act as computer memory and a processor. Quantum computing is a non-classical model of computation. Whereas a classical computer encodes data into fundamental units called bits, where each bit represents either a one or a zero, a quantum computer encodes data into bits that can represent a one, a zero, or some combination.

a. Quantum Qubit

A qubit, Qubit or Qbit, see Figure 7, can have 2-bit states at the same time. Therefore, a qubit is equal to a bit, but also equal to 2^Q bits. The two most relevant aspects of quantum physics are the principles of superposition and entanglement. A Qbit can be thought of as an electron in a magnetic field.

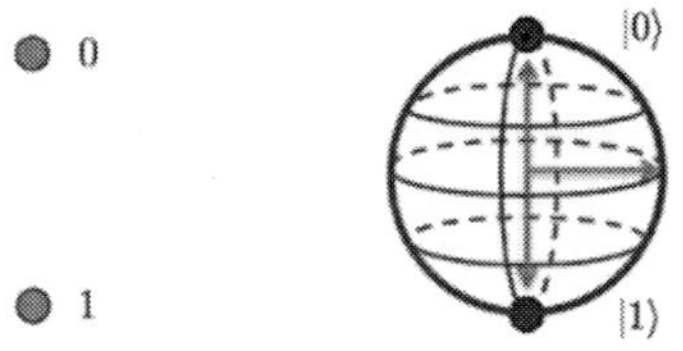

Figure 7. A classical bit and a Quantum Qbit comparison.

The 'Bloch sphere' is a geometrical representation of the pure state space of a two-level quantum mechanical system (Qubit), named after the physicist Felix Bloch, see Figure 8.

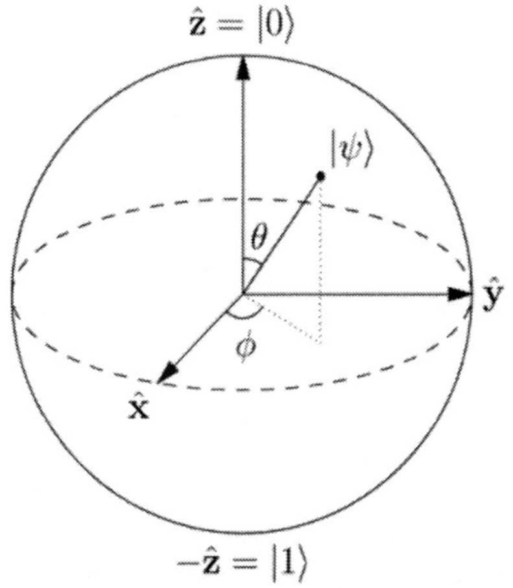

Figure 8. The quantum Bloch sphere, a geometrical representation of a quantum state space.

The bottom line of Quantum Computing (QC) is the existence of correlations between different Qbits as superposition states which when destroyed by measurement or any other means, the proper correlation is instantaneously communicated between the Qbits. Researchers have proposed some models where the neuron is modeled like a Qbit and organized into networks in the form of Quantum Associative Memory (QAM).

Here in regard to VoxelNET, we suggest that the indexed voxels can compute content in a discretized, quantized and spatially distributed way and therefore function as a quantum computational infrastructure. Every voxel can include one or several bloch spheres for computation purposes.

The interest in QC -physically based computation founded on quantum-theoretic concepts - has grown since the early 90's in the computer and cognitive sciences as a result of claims by Deutsch [23] 1985, [24] 1989 and Shor [25] 1994 that problems regarded by computer scientists as NP-hard or NP-complete can be solved by a quantum computer. [26] "Since it is regarded that if a computational solution can be found to one of the problems in the NP-complete class then a solution can be found to all problems in this class. These claims raise deep questions for computer scientists as to the nature of computational and algorithmic processes as well as the relation between computation and physical processes. Penrose [27] claimed in 1994 that solving the quantum measurement problem is a prerequisite to understand the human mind, and Hameroff's [28] proposal the same year that consciousness emerges as a macroscopic quantum state from a critical level of coherence of quantum-level events in and around cytoskeletal microtubules within neurons, raise important questions for the scientific foundations of cognitive science and the appropriate level for a computational account of mind/brain [29].".

An exhaustive survey made in 2012 [30] included various applications of Quantum inspired Computational Intelligence (QCI) techniques and proposed to lay out the landscape for researchers on Quantum computing as a young discipline. The introduction lays out "Computational Intelligence (CI) as an offshoot of artificial intelligence which involves the study of adaptive mechanisms to enable or facilitate intelligent behaviors in complex and changing environments. CI consists of collective efforts in emerging, fundamental computational paradigms, unlike intelligent systems (IS), which covers all aspects of artificial intelligence (AI) and focuses on the development of the latest research into practical, fielded applications. CI depends upon numerical data supplied by manufacturers and does not rely on "knowledge". AI, on the other hand, uses knowledge derived from human experts. The knowledge or intelligence exhibited from CI is self-emerging and spontaneous as opposed to manmade and artificial from AI.".

The theory of QC is related to a theory of reversible computing, which brings together ideas from classical information theory, computer science, and quantum physics.

Mapping brain regions and running a variety of Neural Network (NN) methods such as Back Propagation NN, Training Algorithms, Hamiltonian NN, Hopfield NN, Self-Organizing Map, Radial Basis Function NN, Recurrent NN, Stability Analysis, Support Vector Machines, Spiking NN, Quantum Inspired Fuzzy System, Quantum Inspired Evolutionary Methods must be based upon systemizations of environmental, human and robotic action, sensor data and computational power so that the background world representation is sufficiently systematic to support synthesis or comparison of CI results.

VII. Conclusion

This paper has presented a number of functions for which integration has been based upon a coherent unifying system of spatial and volumetric indexing and representation. The paper has emphasized the particular relevance of representing both the spatial structure of the physical world and that of neural information processing in order to study and leverage the response of human cognitive/neural systems to external situated 3D structures and events. The use of a unifying 3D location voxel structure has also been considered as a framework for managing computation on a spatial basis, where computing load can be managed and distributed on a spatial volumetric basis, and also potentially support quantum computing.

The overall conclusion is that 3D spatial structure is inherent in many kinds of data, information, knowledge and processes, and this can be used to integrate and coordinate distributed processes having diverse primary functions. The current internet, based upon abstract links and document-style interfaces, does not intrinsically provide this kind of coherent 3D spatial structure.

The main author and her 4D Internet team are currently implementing and progressing VoxelNET from Technology-Readiness-Level (TRL) 4 to 6 and next year (2021) progressing it further towards TRL 7-8.

Acknowledgment

Thanks to CSIRO Mineral Resources and the Hard Rock Mining Program for supporting this research.

References

[1] C. Sennersten, A. Davie and C. Lindley, "Voxelnet - An Agent Based System for Spatial Data Analytics", short paper, *Eighth International Conference on Advanced Cognitive Technologies and Applications (COGNITIVE 2016)*, March 20 - 24, Rome, Italy.

[2] C. Sennersten, C. Lindley, and B. Evans, "VoxelNET's Geo-Located Spatio Temporal Softbots -including living, quiet and invisible data", *The Eleventh International Conference on Advanced Cognitive Technologies and Applications (COGNITIVE 2019)*, May 05- 09 May, 2019, Venice, Italy.

[3] C. Zimring and R. Conroy Dalton, "Linking Objective Measures of Space to Cognition" in Environment and Behaviour, Vol. 35 No. 1, January 2003, pp. 3-16 DOI: 10.1177/0013916502238862.

[4] N. Thrift, "Movement-space: The changing domain of thinking resulting from the development of new kinds of spatial awareness, Economy and Society, 33:4, 582-604, (2004), DOI: 10.1080/0308514042000285305.

[5] https://www.google.com/search?client=firefox-b-e&q=spatial+awarness+definiton+%5C

[6] W. Sharpe, Cognitive Systems Project: Applications and Impact London DTI/Foresight (2003)

[7] https://www.researchgate.net/post/what_do_you_mean_ground_truth_dataset_or_images

[8] D. Norris, "Short-Term Memory and Long-Term Memory are Still Different", Psychological Bulletin, Vol. 143, No. 9, 992–1009, 2017.

[9] C. Sennersten and C. A. Lindley, "Real Time Eye Gaze Logging in a 3D Game/Simulation World", Measurement Technology and Intelligent Instruments IX, Key Engineering Materials, Vol. 437. Initially presented at The 9th International Symposium on Measurement Technology and Intelligent Instruments (ISMTII-09), June 29 - July 2, 2009, Saint-Petersburg, Russia.

[10] P. Jercic, C. Sennersten, and C. Lindley, "The Effect of Cognitive Load on Physiological Arousal in a Decision Making Serious Game", 9th International Conference on Virtual Worlds and Games for Serious Applications (VS-Games), UK, 2017.

[11] C-A. Wang, T. Baird, J. Huang, J. D. Couitinho, D. C. Brien and D. P. Munoz, "Arousal Effects on Pupil Size, Heart Rate,

and Skin Conductance in an Emotional Face Task", Frontiers in Neurology, 03 December, 2018 https://doi.org/10.3389/fneur.2018.01029

[12] F. Azhari, C. Sennersten, and T. Peynot, "Evaluation of Vision-based Surface Crack Detection Methods for Underground Mine Tunnel Images" (pap129s1), to Australian Conference on Robotics and Automation (ACRA 2019), Australia.

[13] L. Manovich (2001) The Language of New Media Cambridge MA MIT Press

[14] Callon, M and Law, J. (2004). 'Guest Editorial'. Environment and Planning D: Society and Space, 22: 3–11.

[15] Computational Complexity Theory, Stanford Encylopedia of Philosophy, USA (2015/16), https://plato.stanford.edu/entries/computational-complexity/

[16] Algoritmic Complexity https://www.cs.cmu.edu/~adamchik/15-121/lectures/Algorithmic%20Complexity/complexity.html

[17] https://www.definitions.net/definition/discretization

[18] W-K. Ling, "Quantisation", Non Linear Digital Filters, High Dynamic Range Video, 2016.

[19] N. K. Kasabov, "NeuCube: A spiking neural network architecture for mapping, learning and understanding of spatio-temporal brain data", Neural Networks (52) 2014, pp 62-76, http://dx.doi.org/10.1016/j.neunet.2014.01.006.

[20] R. Olry, "Korbinian Brodmann (1868–1918)", Journal of Neurology, Pioneers in Neurology, 257 , pp. 2112–2113, 2010.

[21] K. Zilles, "Dorsal Column, Grey Matter, Brodmann: a pioneer of human brain mapping—his impact on concepts of cortical organization", BRAIN – a Journal of Neurology, 2018: 141; 3262–3278, Oxford University Press on behalf of the Guarantors of Brain, 2018, doi:10.1093/brain/awy273.

[22] https://www.researchgate.net/figure/The-Brodmann-areas-map-of-the-cortex-taken-from-126_fig2_262216540

[23] D. Deutsch, Quantum theory, the Church-Turing principle and the universal quantum computer, Proceedings of the Royal Society of London, A 400, 97-117 (1985).

[24] D. Deutsch, Quantum computational networks, Proceedings of the Royal Society of London A 425, 73-90 (1989).

[25] P.W. Shor, Algorithms for quantum computation: Discrete logarithms and factoring, Proceedings of the 35th Annual Symposium on the Foundations of Computer Science, IEEE Press (1994).

[26] T. Menneer and A. Narayanan, "Quantum-inspired Neural Networks", Tech. Rep. R329, Department of Computer Science, University of Exeter, 1995.

[27] R. Penrose, Shadows of Mind: A Search for the Missing Science of Consciousness, New York: Oxford University Press, 1994.

[28] S. Hameroff, Quantum coherence in microtubes: A neural basis for emergent consciousness? Journal of Consciousness Studies, 1(1), 91-118, 1994.

[29] A. Narayanan, Biomolecular cognitive science, Proceedings of the Foundations of Cognitive Science Workshop, AISB95, Sheffield, UK, Available through ftp: atlas.ex.ac.uk, Research Report 325, 1995.

[30] A. Manju and M. J. Nigam, "Applications of quantum inspired computational intelligence: a survey", Artif Intell Rev (2014) 42:79–156, DOI 10.1007/s10462-012-9330-6, Springer, 2014.

Induced Acyclic Subgraphs With Optimized Endpoints

Moussa Abdenbi
Département d'informatique
Université du Québec à Montréal
Québec, Canada
Email: abdenbi.moussa@courrier.uqam.ca

Alexandre Blondin Massé
LACIM
Université du Québec à Montréal
Québec, Canada

Alain Goupil
Université du Québec à Trois-Rivières
Québec, Canada

***Abstract*—Given a lexicon, can we build a strategy for learning specialized vocabulary? If so, how to minimize its cost while maximizing its efficiency? We provide elements of answers to these questions, by using graph theory. A lexicon is represented by a directed graph of the *defining* relation between words and a *strategy* is an ordered sequence of vertices. We focus on two graphs properties, *acyclicity* which helps us to avoid words with cyclic definitions and *induced* to consider all the arcs between chosen words. We are interested in the *induced* and *acyclic* subgraphs of a directed graph containing a fixed set of vertices. To model cost minimization, we consider an optimization criteria based on the difference between the number of *sinks* and the number of *sources* of the subgraph, which represents words which appear in several definitions. We start with a study of the complexity of finding these subgraphs and we prove that it is a Non-deterministic Polynomial-time hard (NP-hard) problem. This observation leads us to provide two approximate solutions: a *greedy heuristic* and a local search enriched with *tabu restrictions*. Finally, we evaluate the efficiency of this graph based strategy comparing with psycholinguistic based strategies, on three digital dictionaries.**

***Keywords*–Directed graphs; learning strategies; computational linguistics.**

I. INTRODUCTION

Acquiring specialized vocabulary, as well as learning a new language, often involves different types of learning approaches [1]. One such strategy is *dictionary look-up*, *i.e.*, learning new words by reading definitions from a dictionary or having someone explain, describe, characterize the new words with already known other words. Another complementary strategy is *direct sensorimotor experience*, *i.e.*, learning by seeing, hearing, smelling, tasting, touching, or interacting in any other way with the object referenced by the words. The effort of learning a word directly seems more *costly* than the one of learning a word by definition, since it involves trial and error [2]. Therefore, it is important to carefully choose the words to be learned directly to reduce the effort required to assimilate their meaning. In particular, psycholinguistic and pedagogical provide some criteria to determine these words [3]–[7].

In this paper, we are interested in a better approach based on computational linguistics to extract these subsets of words for different specialized vocabularies. The relation between the words in a lexicon or a dictionary definition and the meaning of the defined word, is modeled by a directed graph or *digraph*. So, it is quite natural that we turn to graph theory and the study of subgraphs, which has attracted constant interest and lead to several applications [8]–[11].

A *lexicon* can be described as a digraph, where a vertex is a node containing a word and the directed "defining" relation between words is represented by arcs. A *strategy* is an ordered sequence of vertices [2] [12]. We focus our attention on *induced and acyclic* subgraphs of digraphs, and we consider an optimization criterion based of the difference between the number of *sinks* vertices and the number of *sources* vertices. In [13], we produced a brief study of the subgraphs satisfying the constraints above and proved that finding these subgraphs is an NP-hard problem. In this paper, we expand this problem and add the constraint that the subgraphs must contain a fixed and arbitrary set of vertices from the digraph. This supplementary constraint provides a larger and more interesting family of problems. We believe that the subgraphs under investigation here are optimal learning strategies, according to the strategy cost defined in [2]. Indeed, the acyclicity constraint models the absence of circular definitions between words and the induced constraint mean that all links between selected words in the dictionary are to be considered. Beyond these natural interpretations, the choice of a fixed set of vertices allow to focus learning on a specific set of words or jargon. Therefore, unlike a complete learning strategy [2], a grounding kernel [14] or psycholinguistic strategies [3] [5], which aims at learning an entire dictionary, our subgraphs lead to targeted learning strategy. Indeed, through the constraint of a set of fixed words that we add, we can restrict and direct the learning strategy towards a specialized jargon. This will therefore reduce the learning of superfluous words. Which leads to effective and low cost learning strategies.

This paper is divided as follows. In Section II, we introduce definitions and notation about directed graphs. In Section III, we prove that the problem of finding subgraphs under the constraints described above is NP-hard. In Section IV, we present two metaheuristics to solve this problem: a *greedy heuristic* and a local search enriched with *tabu restrictions*. In Section V, we describe an experiment that supports the conjecture on learning strategies formulated above that gives affirmative and encouraging results. In Subsection V-B, we implement and test these algorithms on sets of digraphs. The performance of these algorithms is discussed and analyzed. Concluding remarks are presented in Section VI.

II. PRELIMINARIES

We recall some definitions from graph theory. See [15] for more details.

A *digraph* is an ordered pair $D = (V, A)$, where V is its set of *vertices* and $A \subseteq V \times V$ is its set of *arcs*. Given a vertex $u \in V$, its set of *predecessors* is defined by $N^-(u) = \{v \in V \mid (v,u) \in A\}$ and its set of *successors* is $N^+(u) = \{v \in V \mid (u,v) \in A\}$. The *indegree* of

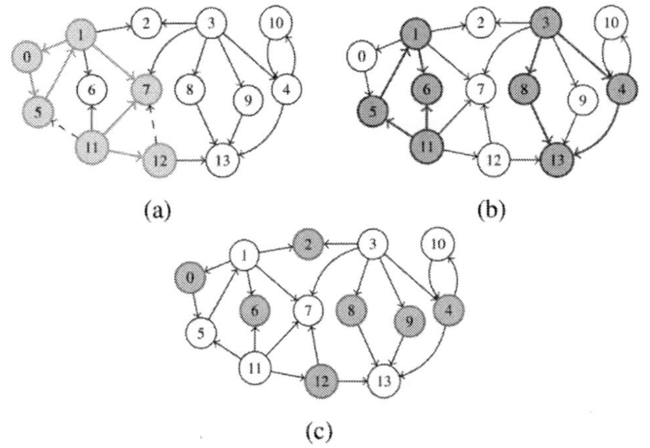

Figure 1. (a) In orange, a subgraph with a circuit $P = (0, 5, 1, 0)$. This subgraph is not induced because it does not contain the dashed arcs $(11, 5)$ and $(12, 7)$, despite that vertices $11, 5, 12, 7$ are contained in the subgraph. (b) In blue, a disconnected induced acyclic subgraph with an indirected path $P = (4, 3, 8, 13)$. Vertices 3 and 11 are sources, 6 and 13 are sinks. (c) In red, an independent set of size 7.

u is defined by $\deg_D^-(u) = |N^-(u)|$ and its *outegree* by $\deg_D^+(u) = |N^+(u)\}|$, where $|.|$ denotes set cardinality. An *(undirected) path* p from a vertex u_0 to a vertex u_k in D is a sequence of vertices $p = (u_0, u_1, \dots, u_k)$ such that, for $0 \le i \le k-1$, $(u_i, u_{i+1}) \in A$ or $(u_{i+1}, u_i) \in A$. The path p is *directed* if $(u_i, u_{i+1}) \in A$, for every $0 \le i \le k-1$. We say that a directed path $p = (u_0, u_1, \dots, u_k)$ is a *circuit* or a *cycle*, if $u_0 = u_k$. A digraph D is called *acyclic* if it does not contain any circuit, and it is called *connected* (or *weakly connected*) if there exists an undirected path between every pair of its vertices. A digraph $I = (V_I, A_I)$ is a *subgraph* of D, if $V_I \subseteq V$ and $A_I \subseteq (V_I \times V_I) \cap A$. For $U \subseteq V$, the *subgraph of D induced by U* is the subgraph $D[U] = (U, A_U)$, where $A_U = (U \times U) \cap A$. In words, for all vertices u and v in U, if we have an arc $(u, v) \in A$ then we must have $(u, v) \in A_U$. A vertex u is called a *source* of a subgraph I if $\deg_I^-(u) = 0$. Similarly, if $\deg_I^+(u) = 0$ then u is called a *sink* of I. We denote by $s(I)$ the number of sources in I and $t(I)$ its number of sinks. Finally, a set of vertices S of a digraph $D = (V, A)$ is called an *independent set*, if the induced subgraph $D[S] = (S, A_S)$ has $A_S = \emptyset$. In other words, for each $u \in S$, we have $\deg_{D[S]}^+(u) = \deg_{D[S]}^-(u) = 0$. Examples of induced and non-induced subgraphs appear in Figure 1, as well as an example of an independent set.

For the purposes of the next section, we state the following well-known NP-complete independent set problem,

Problem 1 ([16]): Given a specific digraph $D = (V, A)$ and a specific positive integer $i \le |V|$, is there an independent set $S \subset V$ such that $|S| = i$?

III. Decision Problem and NP-Completeness

As mentioned before, we are interested in induced and acyclic subgraphs of digraphs. In order to identify these subgraphs, we define the following optimization criteria.

Definition 1: Given a digraph $D = (V, A)$ and a subset $M \subseteq V$, let $\mathcal{P}(V)$ be the set of all subsets of V and $\mathcal{I}_D(M, i)$ the family of all induced and acyclic subgraphs of D of size i containing M. We define the function Δ_D, with domain $\{0, 1, 2, \dots, |D|\}$, by

$$\Delta_D(M, i) = \max\{t(I) - s(I) \mid I \in \mathcal{I}_D(M, i)\} \quad (1)$$

with the convention $\max \emptyset = -\infty$. Given $I \in \mathcal{I}_D(M, i)$ we say that I has *optimized endpoints*, if $\Delta_D(M, i) = t(I) - s(I)$. We are interested in induced and acyclic subgraphs with optimized endpoints of D.

Remark 1: The case $M = \emptyset$ is a specialization of the problem introduced in [13].

Now, we consider the following decision problem.

Problem 2: Given a digraph $D = (V, A)$, a set of vertices $M \subset V$ and two integers i and δ, does there exist an induced and acyclic subgraph of D of size i containing M, such that $t(I) - s(I) = \delta$?

We naturally associate with Problem 2 the following optimization problem.

Problem 3: Given a digraph $D = (V, A)$ and a set $M \subset V$ of vertices, what is the maximal value $\Delta_D(M, i)$ that can be realized by an induced and acyclic subgraph I of D of size i and containing M, for $i \in \{|M|, |M| + 1, \dots, |D|\}$?

Before we go further, it is worth discussing the dual problem of maximizing the difference $s(I) - t(I)$. Consider the following optimization function:

$$\Lambda_D(M, i) = \max\{s(I) - t(I) \mid I \in \mathcal{I}_D(M, i)\}$$

It turns out that this optimization criterion is equivalent to that of Definition 1 under a slightly modified digraph. Proposition 1 formalizes the relationship between the functions $\Lambda_D(M, i)$ and $\Delta_D(M, i)$. We omit the proof because it is quite simple.

Proposition 1: Given a digraph $D = (V, A)$, for any subset $M \subset V$ and $i \in \{0, 1, \dots, |D|\}$, we have

$$\Lambda_D(M, i) = \Delta_{D'}(M, i)$$

where $D' = (V, A')$ and $A' = \{(v, u) \mid (u, v) \in A\}$.

Now, we illustrate Problem 2 with an example. Let D be the digraph of size 14 illustrated in Figure 2 and let $M = \{1, 3, 11\}$, a subset of vertices of D depicted in gray. Positive instances of Problem 2 appear in (a) and (b) for respectively $i = 10$, $\delta = 4$ and $i = 11$, $\delta = 4$. It is not hard to prove that $\Delta_D(M, 10) = \Delta_D(M, 11) = 4$ so that $(10, \delta_1)$ and $(11, \delta_2)$ are negative instances of Problem 2 for $\delta_1, \delta_2 > 4$. Because of the two circuits $P_1 = (0, 5, 1, 0)$ and $P_2 = (4, 10, 4)$, the maximum size of an induced acyclic subgraph is $i = 12$. Therefore, there are only two solutions. Figure 2 (c) shows the first positive instances of Problem 2 with $i = 12$ and $\delta_1 = 2$. The second is obtained by replacing vertex 10 by vertex 4. Observe that $\Delta_D(\emptyset, 10) = 5 > \Delta_D(M, 10)$. This situation is depicted by the subgraph in blue in Figure 2 (d). It is easy to see that $\Delta_D(M, i) \le \Delta_D(\emptyset, i)$ for any M and i. Exhaustive inspection shows that the function Δ_D of the graph in Figure 2 is given by Table I. Obviously, for $i < |M|$ we have $\mathcal{I}_D(M, i) = \emptyset$, thus, $\Delta_D(M, i) = -\infty$.

A. NP-completeness

Now, we state and prove the following theorem.

Theorem 1: Problem 2 is NP-complete.

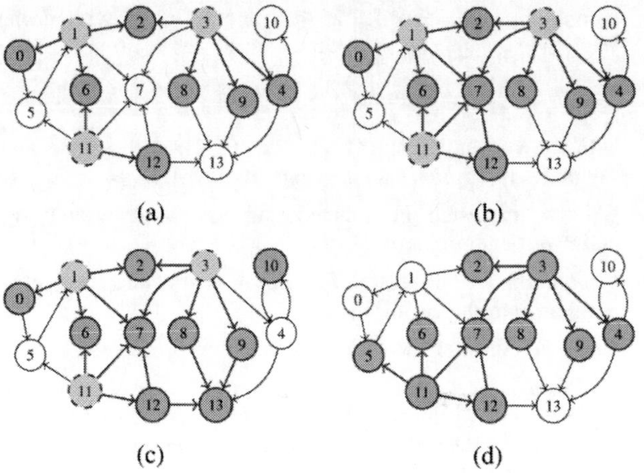

Figure 2. Induced acyclic subgraphs answering Problems 3 (a-c) with the set $M = \{1, 3, 11\}$ and (d) with the set $M = \emptyset$.

TABLE I. THE FUNCTION $\Delta_D(M, i)$ FOR THE DIGRAPH IN FIGURE 2 WITH $M = \{1, 3, 11\}$.

i	0	1	2	3	4	5	6	7	8	9	10	11	12	13	14
$\Delta_D(M, i)$	$-\infty$	$-\infty$	$-\infty$	0	0	1	2	2	3	3	4	4	2	$-\infty$	$-\infty$

Proof: It is clear that Problem 2 is in the class NP. To show that it is NP-complete, we reduce Problem 1 to it.

We represent an instance of Problem 1 by the tuple (D, i) where $D = (V, A)$ is a digraph and $1 \leq i < |V|$ is an integer. An instance of Problem 2 is represented by the tuple (D, M, i, δ) where $D = (V, A)$ is a digraph, M is a set of m fixed vertices of D, i is the number of vertices parameter and δ is the sinks−sources difference parameter.

Consider the map f that associates with an instance (D, i) of Problem 1, the instance $(D', M, i+m, i-m)$ of Problem 2, where the digraph $D' = (V', A')$ is defined by

$$V' = V \cup M \quad \text{and} \quad A' = A \cup (M \times V)$$

Clearly, the map f is computable in polynomial time. Figure 3(a) and Figure 3(b) show an example of construction, using the map f, of the digraph $D' = (V', A')$ for a digraph $D = (V, A)$ and a set $M = \{m_1, m_2\}$.

For a positive instance (D, i) of Problem 1, there is a set $S \subset V$ with $|S| = i$ such that $D[S]$ contains no arcs. We consider the subgraph $I = D'[S \cup M] = (V_I, A_I)$ of D' induced by vertices of $S \cup M$. Obviously, I contains M and all vertices of M are sources, which makes all vertices of S sinks in I. Because there is no arc between vertices in M and also no arcs between vertices of S in I, therefore I is acyclic. Finally, $s(I) = m$ and $t(I) = i$, which makes $(D', M, i+m, i-m)$ a positive instance of Problem 2. Now, let $(D', M, i+m, i-m)$ be a positive instance of Problem 2. There is an induced and acyclic subgraph $I = (V_I, A_I)$ of D', such that $M \subset V_I$ with $|I| = i+m$ and $t(I) - s(I) = i - m$. It is easy to see that $s(I) > 0$ and $t(I) > 0$. Since I contains M, it is clear that only vertices from M can be sources, so, $s(I) = m$. Otherwise, there exists $v \in V_I - M$ such that $\deg_I^-(v) = 0$, which is impossible. Indeed, by construction, we have arcs from M towards v in D' and since I is induced and contains both M and v, these arcs are in I and so $\deg_I^-(v) > 0$. Therefore, the remaining i vertices are necessarily sinks in I and are contained in V. Indeed, since $t(I) - s(I) = i - m$ and $s(I) = m$, then $t(I) = i$. So, we construct an independent set S of size i by considering only sinks of I and so $S = V_I - M$. Indeed, we are sure that there is no arc between vertices of S. Otherwise, if there exist $u, v \in S$ with $(u, v) \in A'$, that is mean that u is not a sink ($\deg_I^+(u) > 0$ and $\deg_I^-(u) > 0$ because $u \notin M$). Which leads to a contradiction $t(I) - s(I) < i - m$. Finally, S is an independent set of size i in $D = (V, A)$, which makes (D, i) a positive instance of Problem 1. See Figure 3(c) and Figure 3(d) for the construction of positive instances between Problem 1 and Problem 2.

Therefore, Problem 1 $\leq$ Problem 2 and Problem 2 is NP-complete. ∎

Remark 2: In virtue of Proposition 1 and the fact that the construction of D' from D takes a polynomial time (exactly, $\Theta(|A|)$), if we replace the optimization criterion by the difference between the number of sources and the number of sinks, the problem remains NP-complete.

IV. ALGORITHMS

Now that we have proved that Problem 2 is NP-complete, we conclude that Problem 3 is NP-hard and a polynomial algorithm to solve it is unlikely to exist. This motivates the use of approximate approaches among other resolution techniques. Thus we consider a *greedy algorithm* and a *tabu search* [17], two metaheuristics, to solve Problem 3.

In the following, let $D = (V, A)$ be a digraph, with $|V| = n$, $|A| = m$, and $M \subset V$ a subset of vertices of V. Let $I = (V_I, A_I)$ be an induced acyclic subgraph of D with $M \subseteq V_I$ and let $i = |V_I|$. Before presenting the algorithms, we assume that the following functions are implemented:

- DELTA(I) returns $t(I) - s(I)$, whose complexity is $\mathcal{O}(i + |A_I|)$.
- INDUCEDSUBGRAPH(D, E) returns the subgraph of D induced by the vertices of set E and has complexity $\mathcal{O}(n + m)$.
- NEIGHBORSVERTICES(D, I) returns all vertices u such that $u \in D - I$ and there exists $v \in V_I$ such that $(u, v) \in A$ or $(v, u) \in A$. This can be done in $\mathcal{O}(n + m)$.
- NEIGHBORHOOD(D, I, M, u) returns a set of induced and acyclic subgraphs by replacing, in turn, each vertex of $V_I - M$ by u. The complexity in that case is $\mathcal{O}((n + m) \times (i - |M|) \times (i + |A_I|))$.

The greedy strategy adopted is to add the most *interesting* vertices. Starting with the subgraph induced by M, $I = D[M]$ until we reach the desired size $|I| = i$. The function RANKVERTICES(D, I) assigns a score to each vertex $u \in D - I$ according to the variation they bring to the function DELTA(I) if we add them to I. Thus, the greater the value of DELTA(I) a vertex brings, the greater its interest. If two vertices bring the same variation, we choose the one with the greatest outdegree, which provides greater potential to generate sinks. Due to lack of space, we don't present the pseudo-code of algorithm, but we provide a full implementation of the greedy approach in [18].

For the tabu search algorithm, the main idea is to browse *neighborhoods* of an induced and acyclic subgraph I containing M, to increase the value DELTA(I). A *neighbor* of I is

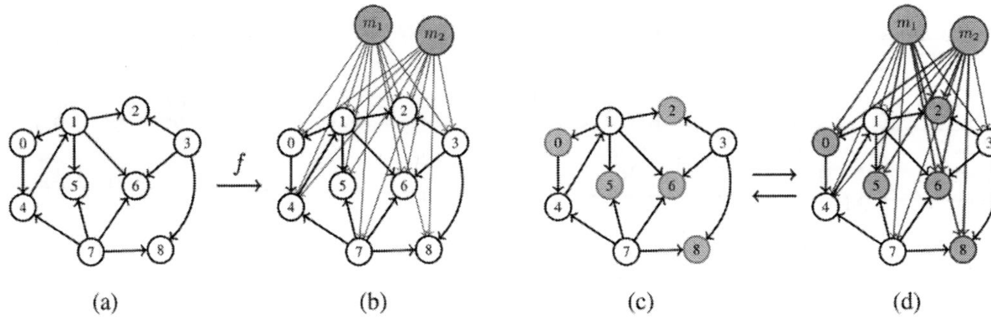

Figure 3. (a) A digraph $D = (V, A)$. (b) Construction of digraph $D' = (V', A')$ through the map f. (c) In red, a set S which makes $(D, 5)$ a positive instance of Problem 1. (d) In blue, an induced and acyclic subgraph which makes $(D', M, 7, 3)$ a positive instance of Problem 2. To build the digraph $D' = (V', A')$, we add vertices of $M = \{m_1, m_2\}$ to V to have V'. To build A', we add all possible arcs (u, v) to A, where $u \in M$ and $v \in V$. It's easy to see how we can build a positive instance of Problem 2 from a positive instance of Problem 1 and vice-versa.

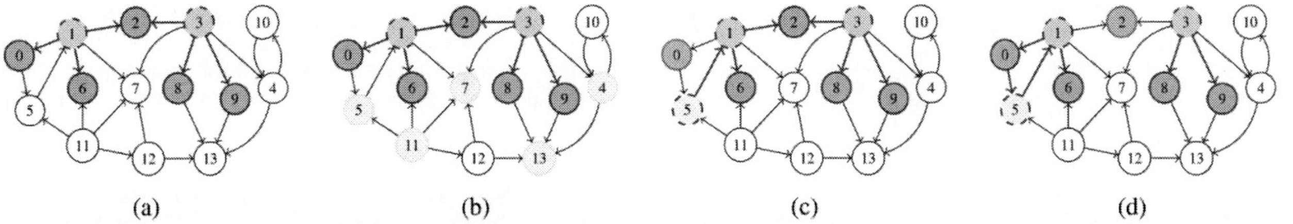

Figure 4. Let $D = (V, A)$ be the digraph represented above and $M = \{1, 3\}$ a subset of V. (a) In blue, an induced and acyclic subgraph $I = (V_I, A_I)$ of D containing M. Note that DELTA$(I) = 3$. (b) In yellow, vertices returned by NEIGHBORSVERTICES(D, I). The call to NEIGHBORHOOD$(D, I, M, 5)$ for example, will return I' the blue subgraph in (c) by switching vertices 5 and 0. Switching 5 and 2 results in the induced subgraph (d) which is rejected because it contains the circuit $P = (0, 5, 1, 0)$ so that NEIGHBORHOOD$(D, I, M, 5)$ will not consider this case. The remaining subgraphs built by replacement of vertices 6, 8 and 9 by 5 are all rejected because of the circuit $P = (0, 5, 1, 0)$.

an induced and acyclic subgraph I', such that $M \subset V_{I'}$, with $|I| = |I'| = i$ and a symmetric difference between V_I and $V_{I'}$ of exactly 2 vertices.

To generate some of these neighbors, we start by finding the neighboring vertices of I. The function NEIGHBORSVERTICES(D, I) finds these vertices. See Figure 4(b) for an example. For each neighbor u, we call NEIGHBORHOOD(D, I, M, u), which returns a set of induced and acyclic subgraphs by replacing each vertex $v \in V_I - M$ by u. In other words, it returns the subgraph INDUCEDSUBGRAPH$(D, (V_I - \{v\}) \cup \{u\})$ when it is acyclic.

See Algorithm 1 for the pseudo-code of this approach. Note that vertex returned by NEIGHBORSVERTICES(D, I) and the one inverted by the function NEIGHBORHOOD(D, I, M, u), are considered as our *tabu restriction*. We limit the number of prohibited vertices to two, thus this restriction does not penalize in the search for a better solution. It's implemented in Algorithm 1 by the queue T and lines 7 and 11. Note that, lines 12-15 are for the *aspiration criteria*. See Figure 4 for an illustrated example with a single call to NEIGHBORHOOD(D, I, M, u).

The complexity of Algorithm 1 is basically the complexity of the three functions DELTA(I), NEIGHBORSVERTICES(D, I) and NEIGHBORHOOD(D, I, M, u), which is $\mathcal{O}(n \times (i - |M|) \times (n + m)^2 \times (i + |A_I|)^2)$. The parameter *max_iterations* is the maximum number of loop laps allowed, and is an arbitrary multiple of n.

Algorithm 1 Tabu Search

```
1:  function TABUSEARCH(D, I : graph, M : set) : integer
2:      B, I' ← I let T be a queue with capacity 2
3:      repeat
4:          for u ∈ NEIGHBORSVERTICES(D, V_I') − T do
5:              for I'' ∈ NEIGHBORHOOD(D, I', M, u) do
6:                  if DELTA(I') < DELTA(I'') then
7:                      I' ← I'' add the removed vertex to T
8:                      if DELTA(B) < DELTA(I'') then
9:                          B ← I''
10:                     Exit from loop in line 5
11:             Add u to T
12:         v ← T.HEAD()
13:         for I'' ∈ NEIGHBORHOOD(D, I', M, v) do
14:             if DELTA(B) < DELTA(I'') then
15:                 B ← I''
16:     until B ≠ I' and max_iterations is reached
17:     return DELTA(B)
```

V. Applications

We now turn back to our initial motivation in computational linguistics, by showing that the resulting structure drives a learning strategy in comparison with other psycholinguistic strategies. Then we evaluate the quality of the metaheuristics in terms of error, compared to an exact solution.

Note that we use algorithms with $M = \emptyset$ because the primary goal is to measure the correlation between cost of a strategy and our optimization criterion Δ_D. Also, the psycholinguistic strategies below are designed for learning an entire language, which differs from a targeted learning strategy when $M \neq \emptyset$.

A. Computational linguistics

To reinforce the hypothesis stated in Section I, we conducted an experiment to compare costs of learning strategies. We consider three digital dictionaries from the Wordsmyth linguistical educational project [19]. The Wordsmyth Learner's Dictionary-Thesaurus (WLDT), the Wordsmyth Illustrated Learner's Dictionary (WILD) and the Wordsmyth Children's Dictionary-Thesaurus (WCDT). And we use some computational linguistics definitions taken from [2] [20]. We construct a

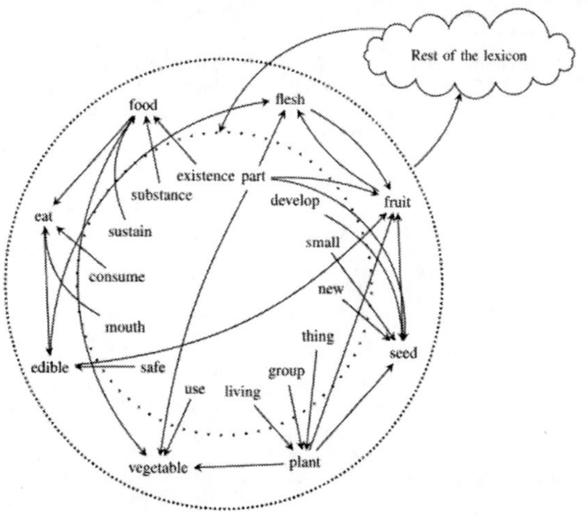

Figure 5. A partial subgraph of a digraph representing a dictionary [2].

digraph from a dictionary by considering each word as a vertex and we have an arc from word w_1 to word w_2 if and only if w_1 appears in the definition of w_2. Figure 5 depicts a subgraph of a digraph representing a dictionary. On a given dictionary D, we define a *learning strategy* of D as any *ordered sequence* S of words from D. We consider two ways of learning a new word,

- *Learning by definition.* We suppose that, if we already know the meaning of all the words occurring in the definition of word w, then we can learn the meaning of w simply by reading its definition. We consider the cost of such learning process to be 0.
- *Direct learning.* On the other hand, if we do not know the meaning of some words in the definition, we have the possibility to learn it *directly* with a cost of 1. For example, by seeing, hearing, smelling, tasting, touching, or interacting in any other way with the object referenced by the word.

In other words, the effort of learning a word directly, is more costly than the one of learning a word by definition.

Finally, we make the assumption that learning a dictionary efficiently amounts to learn its complete set of words at a minimal cost. This implies that a learning strategy is efficient if its associated cost is minimal, which is realized exactly when the number of words learned directly is minimal. Which is represented by the following two parameters in the Table II,

- *cost* : the total number of words learned directly.
- *effic.* : the efficiency, which is the ratio of the total number of words learned over the number of words learned through direct learning.

TABLE II. THE LEARNING COST AND EFFICIENCY OF STRATEGIES.

Dictionary		Subgraph strategy	Childes AOA	Freq. NGSL	Brysbaert AOA	Brysbaert Concret.	Brysbaert Freq.
WILD	size	50	1981	1169	1369	2417	1188
	cost	**3013**	3174	3079	3079	3207	3059
	effic.	**1.40**	1.33	1.37	1.37	1.32	1.38
WLDT	size	200	1580	697	1277	2366	957
	cost	**917**	1803	1088	1530	2485	1296
	effic.	**6.58**	3.34	5.54	3.94	2.42	4.65
WCDT	size	300	3316	1122	2879	5974	1995
	cost	**2431**	4366	2777	4016	6616	3315
	effic.	**12.23**	6.81	10.70	7.40	4.49	8.96

Under those definitions and assumptions, we implemented the algorithm *cost of a complete learning strategy* from [2] to compare strategies. We represented WILD dictionary by a graph with 4244 vertices and 59478 arcs, WLDT dictionary with 6036 vertices and 29735 arcs and WCDT dictionary with 20128 vertices and 107079 arcs. We focus our comparison on psycholinguistic strategies, from a database made available by Brysbaert [5] and the Child Language Data Exchange System (CHILDES) project [3]. Strategies are constructed [3]–[6] according to the following psycholinguistic criteria:

- Brysbaert-AOA: a set of words ordered according to the age of their acquisition.
- Brysbaert-Concreteness: a set of words ordered following their concreteness, from the most concrete to the most abstract.
- Brysbaert-Frequency: a set of words ordered by their rate of occurrence in a given corpus.
- Childes-AOA: a set of words from Child Language Data Exchange System (CHILDES) project are ordred following the age of their acquisition.

A last strategy that we considered, called NGSL/Frequency, is obtained from the NGSL [7],

- Frequency-NGSL: a set of words that are designed and ordered to help students learning English as a second language.

We compute some induced acyclic subgraphs with optimized endpoints on the three digital dictionaries. We consider vertices from the resulting subgraphs as a strategy. We order those vertices according to their outgoing degree, from the highest to the lowest to maximize the potential number of words learned by definition.

Since the size of the dictionary digraphs is important, it takes more computing time to obtain exact solutions. Therefore, to get as close as possible to the exact solution, we use algorithms above with the greedy solution as an initial subgraph input to tabu search.

Table II gives the results of cost computation. It is clear that the subgraphs strategies are better (values in bold) in terms of low cost and high efficiency. Moreover, the initial number of words (strategy size) required to learned in subgraphs based strategies are significantly smaller than the words in psycholinguistic strategies. Note that the acyclic constraint ensure that there is no cyclic words definition and so, no word appears in the definitions of the words that define it. The low cost and high efficiency support our assumption that our induced acyclic subgraphs with optimized endpoints are minimal directed learning strategies in a lexicon.

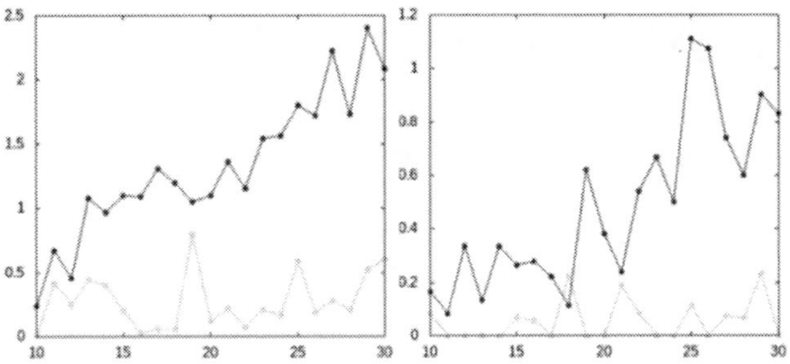

Figure 6. Average error for the greedy algorithm (in green) and the tabu search (in blue) for $M1$ (left) and $M2$ (right). X-axis is for digraphs sizes and Y-axis is for average error. The error is computed by subtracting the value of $\Delta_D(M,.)$ given by greedy or tabu algorithm from the exact value given by the naive algorithm. See [18] for more details.

B. *Metaheuristics evaluation*

Obviously, since Problem 2 is NP-complete, it is probable that all exact solutions to the associated optimization problem take at least an exponential time to be obtained. That being said, it is necessary to have an exact solution in order to calculate the error of metaheuristics and it is always interesting to observe the execution times of an exact solution. Therefore, we have implemented an exact algorithm based on a naive approach. Namely, we enumerate all possible subsets of V, then we construct the corresponding induced subgraphs and finally we verify the acyclicity. For each subgraph of size $|M| \leq i \leq |V|$, we choose the ones with the largest DELTA().

For sizes $10 \leq n \leq 30$ we generated 3 weakly connected digraphs. For each graph size n we generated two random sets $M1$ and $M2$ of sizes $n/3$ and $2n/3$ respectively.

Unsurprisingly, the heuristics are faster than the naïve algorithm, especially for small sets M. When the size of M is close to the size of D, the difference between the $\Delta_D(.,.)$ values given by the heuristics and the exact values is small. We explain this observation by the fact that a large part of the vertices is fixed by M, restricting the remaining choices and the error made by the heuristics.

Figure 6 (a) shows the average error for two random sets $M1$ and $M2$, with sizes $1/3 \times |D|$ and $2/3 \times |D|$ respectively.

For more details and a full Python implementation of the previous two algorithms, with benchmarks, see the GitLab repository [18]. Due to lack of space, these implementations are not included here.

VI. CONCLUSION

The problem studied in this paper is new. It is therefore difficult to compare our results to similar work in the literature. The results of linguistics experiment in Subsection V-A, show that, even if solutions given by tabu algorithm are approximate, they are best and lowest cost learning strategies. This result encourages us to further investigate linguistic applications. Mainly to push the experimentation on other digital dictionaries to establish the effectiveness of induced acyclic subgraphs with optimized endpoints as a learning strategy. Thereafter, extract targeted strategies with subsets M of vocabularies specialized in different fields. From graph theory point of view, we will also be interested in specializing to digraphs that satisfy one of our constraints: acyclicity. We believe that the solution to Problem 2 then becomes polynomial. It is also natural to investigate other optimization functions based on the number of sources and sinks, such as the ratio $t(I)/s(I)$ which provides additional information to those obtained from the difference $t() - s()$. We strongly suspect, in that case, that the problem remains NP-complete.

REFERENCES

[1] S. Harnad, "The symbol grounding problem," Physica D: Nonlinear Phenomena, vol. 42, no. 1, 1990, pp. 335 – 346.

[2] J.-M. Poulin, A. Blondin Massé, and A. Fonseca, "Strategies for learning lexemes efficiently: A graph-based approach," in The Tenth International Conference on Advanced Cognitive Technologies and Applications COGNITIVE 2018. Barcelona, Spain, 02 2018, pp. 18–22.

[3] B. MacWhinney, "The childes project: Tools for analyzing talk: Transcription format and programs," Child Language Teaching and Therapy, vol. Vol. 1, 3rd ed, no. 4, 2000, p. 366.

[4] M. Brysbaert and B. New, "Moving beyond kucera and francis: A critical evaluation of current word frequency norms and the introduction of a new and improved word frequency measure for american english," Behavior research methods, vol. 41, no. 4, 11 2009, pp. 977–990.

[5] V. Kuperman, H. Stadthagen-Gonzalez, and M. Brysbaert, "Age-of-acquisition ratings for 30,000 english words," Behavior Research Methods, vol. 44, no. 4, 12 2012, pp. 978–990. [Online]. Available: https://doi.org/10.3758/s13428-012-0210-4

[6] M. Brysbaert, A. Warriner, and V. Kuperman, "Concreteness ratings for 40 thousand generally known english word lemmas," Behavior research methods, vol. 46, no. 3, 10 2014, pp. 904–911.

[7] C. M. Browne, "A new general service list: The better mousetrap we've been looking for?" Vocabulary Learning and Instruction, vol. 3, no. 2, 2014, pp. 1–10.

[8] A. Boukerche, X. Cheng, and J. Linus, "A performance evaluation of a novel energy-aware data-centric routing algorithm in wireless sensor networks," Wireless Networks, vol. 11, no. 5, 2005, pp. 619–635.

[9] P. Erdős, M. Saks, and V. T. Sós, "Maximum induced trees in graphs," Journal of Combinatorial Theory, Series B, vol. 41, no. 1, 1986, pp. 61–79.

[10] L. Székely and H. Wang, "On subtrees of trees," Advances in Applied Mathematics - ADVAN APPL MATH, vol. 34, 01 2005, pp. 138–155.

[11] A. Blondin Massé, J. de Carufel, and A. Goupil, "Saturated fully leafed tree-like polyforms and polycubes," Journal of Discrete Algorithms, vol. 52-53, 2018, pp. 38 – 54, combinatorial Algorithms – Special Issue Devoted to Life and Work of Mirka Miller.

[12] M. Aronoff and J. Rees-Miller, The Handbook of Linguistics. John Wiley & Sons, 2002.

[13] M. Abdenbi, A. B. Massé, and A. Goupil, "Induced DAGs with maximal sinks-sources difference," Bordeaux Graph Workshop, 2019, accepted.

[14] G. Chicoisne, A. Blondin-Masse, O. Picard, and S. Harnad, "Grounding abstract word definitions in prior concrete experience," in Sixth Annual Conference on the Mental Lexicon, 2008, p. 1498, university of Alberta.

[15] R. Diestel, Graph theory, 4th ed., ser. Graduate Texts in Mathematics. Springer, Heidelberg, 2010, vol. 173.

[16] R. M. Karp, Reducibility among Combinatorial Problems. Boston, MA: Springer US, 1972, pp. 85–103.

[17] T. F. Gonzalez, Handbook of Approximation Algorithms and Metaheuristics (Chapman & Hall/Crc Computer & Information Science Series). Chapman & Hall/CRC, 2007.

[18] M. Abdenbi, Algorithms implementation, (accessed 2020), https://gitlab.com/moussa.abdenbi/implementation-cognitive.

[19] Wordsmyth Illustrated Learner's Dictionary and Wordsmyth Learner's Dictionary-Thesaurus, (accessed 2018), https://www.wordsmyth.net.

[20] A. B. Massé, G. Chicoisne, Y. Gargouri, S. Harnad, O. Picard, and O. Marcotte, "How is meaning grounded in dictionary definitions?" in Proceedings of the 3rd Textgraphs Workshop on Graph-Based Algorithms for Natural Language Processing, ser. TextGraphs-3. USA: Association for Computational Linguistics, 2008, p. 17–24.

Reproducing Fine Textures on Touch Displays Using Band-Limited White Noise Vibrations

Ugur Alican Alma

Centre for Tactile Internet
with Human in the Loop (CeTI)
Chair of Acoustic and Haptic Engineering
Dresden, Germany 01069
Email: ugur_alican.alma@tu-dresden.de

Ercan Altinsoy

Centre for Tactile Internet
with Human in the Loop (CeTI)
Chair of Acoustic and Haptic Engineering
Dresden, Germany 01069
Email: ercan_altinsoy@tu-dresden.de

***Abstract*—In this paper, perceived roughness of different band-limited white noise vibrations was evaluated on a tactile display. In the previous study, white noise vibrations without a specific cut-off frequency were found suitable while rendering fine textures. In that study, some participants reported that low frequency content of the noise vibrations were not plausible when they were touching the fine textures to rate the similarity between them. Therefore, the motivation of this work is to improve the perceptual capacity of white noise vibrations by adjusting its character according to the surface roughness of fine textures. Two essential factors can be used to adjust the character of noise vibrations: Frequency content and intensity level. In this study, a perceptual test is conveyed to scale the congruence between fine textures and band-limited noise vibrations with different high pass filters and intensities. In total, four cut-off frequencies (30 Hz, 60 Hz, 90 Hz and 120 Hz) and three intensity levels were tested to seek their best combination with respect to three fine textures with the grit sizes of 0.05 mm, 0.1 mm and 0.2 mm. Based on the analysis of the collected data, cut-off frequency is found as a primary factor to create plausible fine texture sensation on a display. On the other hand, vibration intensity has no significant effect on perceived similarity when the vibration intensity changes less than 3 dB.**

Keywords–Haptic; Texture; Rendering.

I. Introduction

The field of haptic augmented reality has experienced rapid growth using touch displays recently. Touch displays are rapidly emerging apparatus since they are programmable input devices. Besides their programmability, integration of haptic feedback to touch displays made them indispensable devices for users. With the enhancement of haptic feedback, not only blind [1], but also old or young people can have easier control on touch surfaces [2]. In the last decade, haptic touch devices have been already prototyped using different surface actuation mechanisms [3], [4], and there is even a commercialized touch product [5]. Thanks to haptic feedback, humans can experience cues, such as texture, shape and stiffness [6]-[9]. Particularly, texture cues provide fundamental haptic information about the objects on 2-D space. Hence, texture rendering has been considered as the first step on enhancing haptic dimension of touch devices.

So far, immense amount of researches have been conducted to produce texture sensation on displays by reproducing different texture dimensions, such as roughness and friction. These two cues have been simulated on touch displays using different approaches, such as electrostatic force, ultrasonic vibrations and vibrotactile feedback [8]-[10]. On the other hand, in recent years, some of the researchers introduced significant studies on measurement-based rendering techniques which enabled creating realistic haptic textures [9]. However, since such methods simply plays back the captured immense data from the surfaces, limited capabilities of tactile receptors [11] is unavoidably ignored [12]. Besides that, perception mechanisms of fine and coarse textures are different from each other as explained in the duplex theory of tactile texture perception [13]. Based on this theory, vibrations occurring from the spatial pattern of a surface can be only perceived when texture is not too fine. For fine textures, the effect of induced vibrations on the perception is not clear, but vibrotactile encoding ability of sensory receptors take place to perceive them [14], [15]. Based on the study of Tiest [16], it was reported that complex vibrations induced when a finger moves over fine textures are not identical to surface roughness while it is identical for coarse textures. In the seventies, the studies of Lederman [17]-[20] and Johnson [21]-[23] brought significant contributions to texture perception. According to their studies, spatial cues can contribute to roughness perception if the spatial size of bumps are larger than 0.1/0.2 mm. Afterwards, Bensmaia and Hollins asserted that waveform variations on complex vibrotaction can change the perception of texture, and vibrotactile encoding is sufficient itself to perceive fine textures [24]. Furthermore, another study claimed that active surface exploration with finger with varying speed can activate different tactile receptors with different selective frequencies [13].

As mentioned, the data-driven approach (playing back captured surface data) proposes tactile vibration for fine and coarse textures with similar complexity resolution. Moreover, played back recorded vibrations can contain non-perceivable frequency components, which are below the human vibration detection threshold. According to the former study [12], it was observed that recorded texture vibrations were too complex for coarse textures while fine textures were simulated best with complex vibrations. However, actual physical representation was not necessary to render fine textures since white noise vibrations were found as efficient as recorded vibrations. So far, not enough researches have been done on perception-based texture modelling [25], [26]. Accordingly, the aim of this study is to propose a simple and perceptually efficient fine texture rendering strategy. Therefore, white noise vibrations will be elaborated based on perceived roughness of fine textures which have different spatial densities. This elaboration procedure will be explained in section 2. With the proposed strategy, capturing surface data process, which is cumbersome and time consuming process, can be eliminated. This aim will be investigated by assessing the congruence between several sand papers and band noise vibrations with different cut-off frequencies and intensities. The fine sand papers are selected so as to have grit sizes of 0.05 mm, 0.1 mm and 0.2 mm. For the perceptual investigation, four cut-off frequencies and three intensity levels (reference, -3 dB reduced and +3 dB increased levels) were tested. Investigation process will be described in detail in Section 3. Before the main experiment session, perceived intensities of the band noise vibrations were equalized via a preliminary test to investigate the effect of the frequency clearly. Based on the results of the evaluation, cut-off frequency is found as a significant factor to have an effect on perceived roughness. On the other hand, changing the intensity level as much 3 dB is not found as a significant factor on the suitability of the band-limited white noise vibrations. In the following section, creation process of tactile stimuli, experimental setup and experimental method are explained.

II. Experimental Setup

A. Creation of Vibrotactile Feedback

The band-limited white noise vibrations were produced at MATLAB with the sampling frequency of 44100 Hz. In total, 4 different high pass filters were applied to the white noise signals with the order of 6. The cut-off frequencies are 30 Hz, 60 Hz, 90 Hz and 120 Hz. In addition, a low pass filter with 1000 Hz cut-off frequency was applied to the band-limited noise signals to eliminate non-perceivable high frequencies. Note that the cut-off frequencies were selected considering the just noticeable difference of frequency [11]. During the preliminary research phase, 150 Hz cut-off frequency was also tested, but it was found similar with the vibration with Fc 120 Hz. The profiles of four types of band noise signals are schematically illustrated in Figure 1.

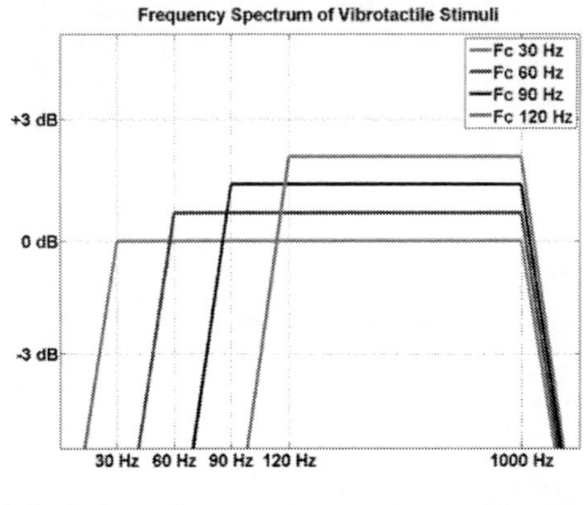

Figure 1. In the figure, frequency spectrum of prepared band-limited white noise signals are illustrated to show the spectral characteristics of each band noise vibrations.

Furthermore, intensity levels of the vibrations with different Fc values were equalized based on perceived vibration intensity. This process was done by conducting a preliminary test in which 5 subjects tuned the power amplifier until 4 types of vibrations have same perceived intensity. Thus, the peak magnitude difference between the signals are explicitly illustrated in Figure 1. After equalizing the perceived intensities of the vibrations, four types of vibrations were also produced at reduced (-3 dB) and increased (+3 dB) intensity levels.

B. Test Setup

To carry out a similarity evaluation on a display, an experimental apparatus was built as seen in Figure 2. A touch display monitor (Gechic HD 1102H) was assembled on top of an electrodynamic shaker (RFT Messelektronik), and the control interface was designed to contain scaling bar and play button for driving the vibrotactile stimuli. The tactile feedback was played for 5 seconds after the subjects clicked the play button on the interface, and a closed-back headphone (beyerdynamics DT-770) was used to prevent the potential interference of the sound of the electrodynamic shaker.

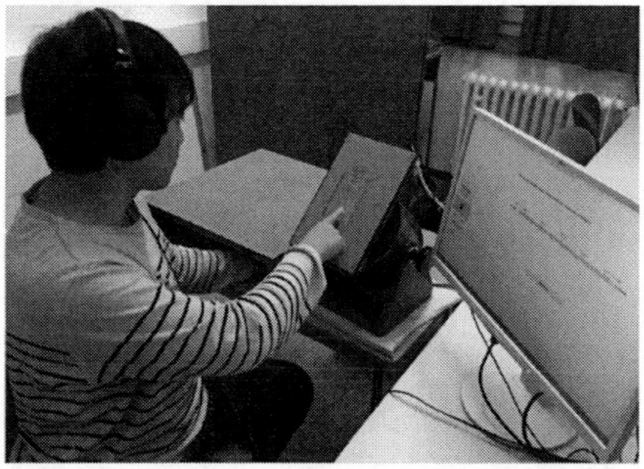

Figure 2. The experimental setup and the evaluation interface are seen above. During the evaluation, the participants touched the sand papers under the wood cover.

As shown in Figure 3, three sand papers with different grit sizes were utilized in the perceptual study to examine the relation between the spatial density of fine textures and the frequency content of white noise. The image demonstrates the sand papers from left to right with increasing grit sizes. Note that the sand papers have regular spatial distributions.

Figure 3. From left to right, the sand papers have 0.05 mm, 0.1 mm and 0.2 mm grit sizes.

Before the experiment started, tactile feedback generation system was validated as follows: Intensity level of the band noise vibrations at actual intensity on the display was perceptually set to be similar with the perceived roughness magnitude of 0.1 mm sand paper by tuning the power amplifier. This process was repeated for each participant. Therefore, the effect of altering the intensity level on the perceived roughness similarity can be examined. Moreover, the subjects were told to move their fingers in the central area of the display where the characteristic of vibrations was calibrated. In addition, the participants were requested to slide their fingers gently over the touch screen to avoid changing vibration intensity on the display considerably.

III. Experimental Method

In the evaluation, similarity tests were conducted based on Rohrmann scaling method [27] since it is a practical approach to evaluate similarity of a stimuli on linear one dimensional scale. In total, four band-limited white noise vibrations with cut-off frequencies of 30 Hz, 60 Hz, 90 Hz, and 120 Hz were judged in three different intensity levels. It means that there are 36 stimulation cases (4 vibrations x 3 intensity levels x 3 sand papers) when the subjects evaluate the vibrotactile stimuli for each texture. In total, 12 subjects, 9 male and 3 female aged between 24 and 39 years, participated in the experiment.

The evaluation consists of two consequent steps which are exploring the vibrations and textures, and the rating process. When the participants clicked the play button from the evaluation interface, the vibrations were driven one by one on the touch display. Then, the participants were requested to move their fingers on the display at a constant speed during the stimuli inspection. Also, the participants were allowed to repeat each vibrotactile stimulus until they are ready for the rating process. Afterwards, the subjects scaled the similarity of the each vibrotactile feedback with respect to each sand paper using verbal labels. The verbal labels are "not at all", "little bit", "middle", "very much" and "fully", placed on the continuous equal interval scale from 0 to 100 at the experiment interface. Also, the participants were allowed to rate anywhere in between two labels using the slider. Furthermore, before the main rating process, training session took place so that the subjects were trained to be familiar with the evaluation procedure and the types of vibrotactile stimuli before the main experiment. The data of the training session were not used for analysis of the test. The main test aimed to collect the subjective evaluation data with respect to all combinations of the vibrotactile stimuli and the textures. All participants completed the evaluation including the training session below 30 minutes.

IV. Results

In the perceptual test, the similarity of the vibrotactile stimuli were judged by the subjects. The collected data for each vibrotactile stimulus were normally distributed. To begin with the investigation of the experimental data, similarity ratings of the vibrotactile stimuli were plotted for each texture as seen in Figure 4. In the figure, it is observed that there is a distinct differences between the ratings of the vibrations with different cut-off frequencies. In addition, when intensity level of the vibrotactile stimuli was reduced and increased, the ratings of the vibrations increased for 0.05 mm and 0.2 mm textures, respectively. This shows that the participants well-tuned the perceived intensity of the vibrations according to 0.1 mm sand paper. To analyze the effect of each factor (Cut-off frequency, intensity and texture) on the perceived roughness similarity, a three-way ANOVA test was performed. This test was carried on for 432 values (4 types of vibrations x 3 intensity levels x 3 sand papers x 12 subjects) using all similarity ratings as the dependent value. In conclusion, the cut-off frequency ($F(3, 431) = 19.351$, $p = .0001$) and the grit sizes of the fine textures ($F(3, 431) = 5.268$, $p = .005$) were found to have significant effects on the perceived similarity.

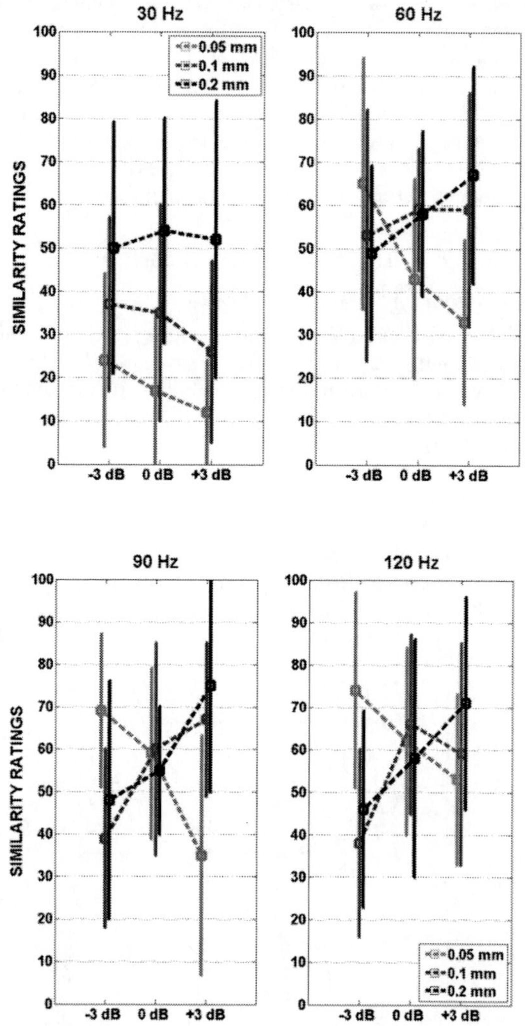

Figure 4. Similarity ratings of three texture vibrations are concluded as above. On the top, the ratings of fc = 30 Hz and fc = 60 Hz, on the bottom, fc = 90 Hz and fc = 120 Hz cases are plotted.

Apart from individual analysis of the independent factors, significant interaction effects were found between the factors of cut-off frequency and texture ($F(3, 431) = 5.346$, $p = .0001$), the intensity and the texture ($F(3, 431) = 20.079$, $p = .0001$), and all three together ($F(3, 431) = 1.691$, $p = .045$). The interaction among the three factors demonstrates that creating plausible band noise vibrations for fine textures depends on all three factors together, but primarily frequency content. On the other hand, although intensity was not found to have a significant effect on the ratings, it might have been significant if intensity level would have been altered more than 3 dB. Furthermore, Post-hoc t-tests with a Bonferroni procedure was performed to make pairwise comparisons for each factor. As a result, significant differences were found for 5 pairwise comparisons out of 12 comparisons: " fc = 30 Hz - fc = 60 Hz", "fc = 30 Hz - fc = 90 Hz", "fc = 30 Hz - fc = 120 Hz", "0.05 mm texture - 0.2 mm texture" and "0.1 mm texture - 0.2 mm texture".

V. DISCUSSION

In this study, the suitability of the band-limited white noise vibrations are evaluated according to three different fine textures. The goal of this evaluation was to detect the most plausible frequency band and the vibration intensity level according to grit sizes of the fine textures. Therefore, a perception-based fine texture rendering model can be attained as an alternative to data driven method. With this method, data capturing process can be discarded, and texture rendering process can be simplified. This idea was developed after testing the suitability of white noise vibrations, recorded vibrations and simple sinusoids with respect to the fabric textures in the previous study. Since suitability ratings of white noise were found similar with the recorded vibrations for fine textures, it was considered that plausibility of white noise can be augmented by removing redundant frequency components. In addition, different vibration intensity levels were tested in the evaluation so that the roles of both cut-off frequency and vibration intensity on perceived similarity can be figured out in one test. According to the results, the cut-off frequency was found as a primary factor to create congruent texture vibrations. However, it is likely that vibration intensity could have had more impact on the similarity ratings if the intensity level would be increased or decreased more than 3 dB.

According to the collected similarity ratings, the band noise vibrations with 30 Hz cut-off frequency was found as the most unsuitable vibrotactile stimuli for the fine textures, as expected. Even altering the vibration intensity did not increase the ratings considerably. However, when the cut-off frequency was 60 Hz, the similarity ratings for the finest and the mid-fine textures increased with the confidence interval of 95%. This event demonstrates the effect of cut-off frequency on the suitability of the white noise vibrations. When the cut-off frequency of the tactile stimuli became 90 Hz, the mean ratings were maximum for 0.1 mm and 0.2 mm textures (at increased intensity level) with the confidence interval of 80%. For 0.05 mm texture, The maximum mean rating was attained when the cut-off frequency became 120 Hz (at reduced intensity level). For the Fc 90 and 120 Hz cases, altering vibration intensity changed the means of the ratings with the confidence interval of 95%. This demonstrates that the effect of vibration intensity on perceived roughness can be only observed if frequency content of the vibration is set to be congruent with respect to a reference texture.

Another point attained from the statistical analysis is that 0.05 mm and 0.1 mm textures were found significantly different than the 0.2 mm texture, but they were not found significantly different from each other. Possibly, it shows that different cutaneous perception processing might have occurred for 0.2 mm texture compared to 0.05 mm and 0.1 mm textures. This outcome agrees with the previous studies conducted by Lederman and Johnson arguing that spatial cues can contribute to roughness perception if the spatial size of a surface is more than 0.1/0.2 mm.

The perceived intensity of four band-limited noise vibrations were equalized at the preliminary test. It is because the human vibration detection threshold depends on the frequency of the vibration. Balancing the perceived intensity allowed to perform a reliable judgment on the effect of the cut-off frequency. Furthermore, the reason why the grit sizes of the sand papers were chosen as 0.05 mm, 0.1 mm and 0.2 mm is to analyze relation between the roughness of fine textures and the the factors comprehensively.

The maximum ratings of the vibrotactile feedback, which are resembling the roughness, were clustered between 70% and 80%. The reason why the ratings did not reach 100% is because the tactile texture perception consists of four main dimensions, and roughness is one of the dimension in texture perception. Therefore, lacking of other dimensions (hardness, friction and heat capacity) might have limited the subjective evaluation.

VI. CONCLUSION

With the results of this study, the effect of frequency and vibration intensity on the perceived magnitude of roughness is investigated. Hence, the primary and second factors affecting the suitability of created texture vibrations is figured out. On the other hand, the state of art for reproducing textures has been measurement-based approaches, but perception-based rendering algorithms will likely draw more attention in near future. It is because perception-based methods can provide plausible texture sensation on displays with simpler vibrations and rendering processes, as observed in the previous study [12]. These advantages can be particularly crucial for tactile internet technology, which aims rapid data transmission between smart haptic devices for extremely low latency [28]. Namely, texture rendering approaches which drive only perceptually perceivable amount of data with high perceptual capacity can be the most useful technique. As a future work, an extended study will be conducted to compare the perceptual capacities of perception-based and data-driven approaches, and this test will be carried out with more participants for more reliable statistical analysis.

ACKNOWLEDGMENT

Funded by the German Research Foundation (DFG, Deutsche Forschungsgemeinschaft) as part of Germany's Excellence Strategy - EXC 2050/1 - Project ID 390696704 - Cluster of Excellence "Centre for Tactile Internet with Human-in-the-Loop" (CeTI) of Dresden Technical University.

REFERENCES

[1] A. Bateman, O. K. Zhao, A. V. Bajcsy, and M. C. Jennings, "A user-centered design and analysis of an electrostatic haptic touchscreen system for students with visual impairments", International Journal of Human-Computer Studies, 109, 102-111, 2018.

[2] D. Cingel and A. M. Piper, "How parents engage children in tablet-based reading experiences: An exploration of haptic feedback", In Proceedings of the 2017 ACM Conference on Computer Supported Cooperative Work and Social Computing, pp. 505-510. 2017.

[3] O. Bau, I. Poupyrev, A. Israr, and C. Harrison, "TeslaTouch: electrovibration for touch surfaces", In Proceedings of the 23nd annual ACM symposium on User interface software and technology, pp. 283-292. 2010.

[4] J. Mullenbach, C. Shultz, A. M. Piper, M. Peshkin, and J. E. Colgate, "Surface haptic interactions with a TPad tablet", In Proceedings of the adjunct publication of the 26th annual ACM symposium on User interface software and technology, pp. 7-8. 2013.

[5] M. Cherif, E. J. Colgate, M. A. Peshkin, M. F. Olley, and G. Topel, "Materials and structures for haptic displays with simultaneous sensing and actuation", U.S. Patent Application 14/931,209, filed May 5, 2016.

[6] S. C. Kim, A. Israr, and I. Poupyrev, "Tactile rendering of 3D features on touch surfaces", In Proceedings of the 26th annual ACM symposium on User interface software and technology pp. 531-538. ACM, 2013.

[7] S. Saga and R. Raskar, "Simultaneous geometry and texture display based on lateral force for touchscreen", In World Haptics Conference (WHC), pp. 437-442, IEEE, 2013.

[8] G. Ilkhani, M. Aziziaghdam, and E. Samur, "Data-driven texture rendering with electrostatic attraction", In International Conference on Human Haptic Sensing and Touch Enabled Computer Applications, pp. 496-504, Springer, Berlin, Heidelberg, 2014.

[9] H. Culbertson, J. Unwin, and K. J. Kuchenbecker, "Modeling and rendering realistic textures from unconstrained tool-surface interactions", IEEE transactions on haptics, pp. 1-1, 2014.

[10] L. Winfield, J. Glassmire, J. E. Colgate, and M. Peshkin, "T-pad: Tactile pattern display through variable friction reduction", In EuroHaptics Conference, 2007 and Symposium on Haptic Interfaces for Virtual Environment and Teleoperator Systems, World Haptics 2007, Second Joint pp. 421-426, IEEE, 2007.

[11] M. Rothenberg, R. T. Verrillo, S. A. Zahorian, M. L. Brachman, and S. J. Bolanowski Jr, "Vibrotactile frequency for encoding a speech parameter", The Journal of the Acoustical Society of America, pp. 1003-1012, 1977.

[12] U. A. Alma and E. Altinsoy, "Perceived Roughness of Band-Limited Noise, Single, and Multiple Sinusoids Compared to Recorded Vibration", In IEEE World Haptics Conference (WHC), pp. 337-342, IEEE, 2019.

[13] D. Katz, "The world of touch", Psychology press, 2013.

[14] M. Hollins, S. J. Bensmaa, and R. Risner, "The duplex theory of tactile texture perception", In Proceedings of the 14th annual meeting of the international society for psychophysics, pp. 115-121, the International Society for Psychophysics Quebec, Canada, 1998.

[15] M. Hollins and S. R. Risner, "Evidence for the duplex theory of tactile texture perception", perception & psychophysics, 62(4), pp.695-705, 2000.

[16] W. M. B. Tiest and A. M. Kappers, "Haptic and visual perception of roughness", Acta psychologica, 124(2), pp.177-189, 2007.

[17] S. J. Lederman, "Tactile roughness of grooved surfaces: The touching process and effects of macro-and microsurface structure", Perception & Psychophysics, 16(2), pp. 385-395, 1974.

[18] S. J. Lederman, "The callus-thenics of touching", Canadian Journal of Psychology, 30(2), p. 82, 1976.

[19] S. J. Lederman and M. M. Taylor, "Fingertip force, surface geometry, and the perception of roughness by active touch", Perception & Psychophysics, 12(5), pp. 401-408, 1972.

[20] S. J. Lederman, "Tactile roughness of grooved surfaces: The touching process and effects of macro-and microsurface structure", Perception & Psychophysics, 16(2), pp. 385-395, 1974.

[21] C. E. Connor and K. O. Johnson, "Neural coding of tactile texture: comparison of spatial and temporal mechanisms for roughness perception", Journal of Neuroscience, 12(9), pp. 3414-3426, 1992.

[22] K. O. Johnson and G. D. Lamb, "Neural mechanisms of spatial tactile discrimination: neural patterns evoked by braille like dot patterns in the monkey", The Journal of physiology, 310(1), pp. 117-144, 1981.

[23] J. R. Phillips and K. O. Johnson, "Tactile spatial resolution. II. Neural representation of bars, edges, and gratings in monkey primary afferents", Journal of neurophysiology, 46(6), pp. 1192-1203, 1981.

[24] S. J. Bensmaïa and M. Hollins, "The vibrations of texture", Somatosensory & motor research, 20(1), pp. 33-43, 2003.

[25] R. F. Friesen, R. L. Klatzky, M. A. Peshkin, and J. E. Colgate, "Single pitch perception of multi-frequency textures", In Haptics Symposium (HAPTICS), pp. 290-295, IEEE, 2018.

[26] S. Okamoto and Y. Yamada, "Lossy data compression of vibrotactile material-like textures", IEEE transactions on haptics, pp. 69-80, 2013.

[27] B. Rohrmann, "Verbal qualifiers for rating scales: Sociolinguistic considerations and psychometric data", Project report, p.68, 2007.

[28] E. Steinbach, M. Strese, M. Eid, X. Liu, A. Bhardwaj, and Q. Liu, "Haptic codecs for the tactile internet", Proceedings of the IEEE 107, no. 2, pp. 447-470, 2018.

Cognitive Science Approach to Achieve SDGs

Muneo Kitajima

Nagaoka University of Technology
1603-1 Kamitomioka Nagaoka
Niigata, Japan
Email: mkitajima@kjs.nagaokaut.ac.jp

***Abstract*—The UN report, "The Future is Now: Science for Achieving Sustainable Development," expressed expectations for contributions from cognitive science for the achievement of the Sustainable Development Goals (SDGs). This is because achievement of the SDGs can be regarded as an extension of problem-solving activities in individuals' daily behavior choices. However, as categorized in Newell's "time scale of human action," the SDGs belong to the SOCIAL BAND, while individuals' daily problem-solving belongs to the COGNITIVE BAND, which makes it difficult to construct predictive models. In other words, it is impossible to define a well-defined problem space that spans between the non-linearly connected BANDs. As an alternative approach, this paper proposes an adapted version of the Cognitive Chrono-Ethnography (CCE), a study methodology integrating cognitive science and ethnography, for understanding individuals' daily behavior and specifying their action selection activities that would eventually lead to the achievement of some of the SDGs.**

Keywords–Sustainable Development Goals (SDGs); Cognitive Chrono-Ethnography (CCE); real world problem-solving; adaptive problem-solving; happiness goals.

I. INTRODUCTION

The Sustainable Development Goals (SDGs) are a blueprint for achieving a better, more sustainable future for all. They are aimed at addressing the global challenges we face, including those related to poverty, inequality, climate change, environmental degradation, peace, and justice. Under the SDGs, 17 interconnected goals, and 169 targets under these goals, have been defined. For instance, "Goal 3: Ensure healthy lives, and promote well-being for all at all ages" is associated with 13 targets, such as "3.9 By 2030, substantially reduce the number of deaths and illnesses from hazardous chemicals and air, water and soil pollution and contamination." In the report entitled "The Future is Now: Science for Achieving Sustainable Development," which is the first quadrennial Global Sustainable Development Report prepared by an independent group of scientists [1], the cognitive capacity required for sustainable development choices has been explained as follows:

> During the long period of human evolution, humans have overcome multiple complex challenges, and remained highly adaptive. There is therefore reason to hope that we will also overcome the current challenges to sustainability that are faced on a societal – indeed global – scale. Evolutionary adaptation is most often based on tangible experiences, short-term outcomes and relatively straightforward theories of change. Several aspects of the transformation towards sustainability can be different.
> (···)
> Changing behaviours towards evolutionary adaptation in such a context can therefore be different from other contexts in which humanity has had to deal with society-wide challenges. Individuals will play a pivotal role in driving the necessary transformations. Understanding how people – as consumers and engaged citizens – make choices and decisions in that regard can help to further motivate such action [2]. Cognitive science, psychology, behavioural economics, neurobiology and brain research can provide important insights in that regard [3]. They might indicate, for example, what is going on in our brains when we hear science-based information about sustainability challenges, and consequently make decisions and choices.

Thus, the United Nations (UN) report [1] has clearly outlined the need for contributions from cognitive science. At first sight, the kinds of activities involved in achieving any of the SDGs may be considered as problem-solving activities; hence, the knowledge concerning problem-solving that has been accumulated in cognitive science should prove to be of due relevance in achieving SDGs. However, as shown in the next section, the band structure of human action, [4, page 122, Fig. 3-3] when incorporated into the problem space, which includes both SDGs and real world problem-solving, makes the application of predictive models, such as production systems (e.g., Adaptive Control of Thought - Rational (ACT-R) cognitive architecture [5][6], and Soar [7]), and the Goals, Operators, Methods and Selection rules (GOMS) approach to user modeling [8] less useful than it would be under situations tailored to bolster the effectiveness of these prediction systems.

Accordingly, the rest of this paper explores the issue of appropriate treatment and utilization of cognitive science for contributing to the achievement of SDGs. Section II describes how problem-solving activities are related to achieving SDGs. Section III describes how the Cognitive Chrono-Ethnography (CCE) can be applied for specifying individuals' problem solving activities that would eventually lead to the achievement of some of the SDGs. The acknowledgement and conclusions are provided at the end.

II. PROBLEM SOLVING FOR ACHIEVING THE SDGS

Efforts to achieve the SDGs ultimately translate into individual human efforts. In some cases, an individual may seek to achieve any of the SDGs *directly*, while in other cases, he or she may seek to achieve any of the SDGs *indirectly*, through activities within the organization or the community to which the individual belongs. In either case, such an activity on the part of an individual can be considered as an activity oriented toward achieving one or more SDGs.

A. Societal SDGs vs. Individual Level Goals

Activities to achieve any of the SDGs have to be implemented as problem-solving activities conducted in the real world context, which is called "real world problem-solving" [9]. However, as pointed out in the UN report [1], it would be difficult for a majority of people to concretely envisage the situations wherein any of the SDGs can be achieved, and ascertain the relevance of using real-world problem solving on an individual level to achieve these goals. An example from the UN report is as follows:

> Carbon dioxide emissions, for example, are not seen, smelled or directly experienced as harmful, and their negative impacts will occur relatively far into the future, while they are often associated in the present with behaviours that are immediately useful or pleasurable. Their likely impacts and delayed risks are inferred from science-based models rather than immediate individual experience, although that may currently be changing.

This difficulty can be easily understood by considering Newell's time scale of human action [4, page 122, Fig. 3-3]. As shown in Table I, it identifies non-linearly connected four bands: SOCIAL, RATIONAL, COGNITIVE, and BIOLOGICAL. The claim that human action should be structured in terms of these four discrete bands, suggests that it should be possible to build predictive and explanatory models for activities that happen within a single band, and at the same time, it should be impossible, or inappropriate, to build predictive models that include activities that happen in multiple bands with inter-band interactions. The impossibility of constructing predictive models for inter-band activities comes from the existence of non-linear inter-band connections, which would also make the predictive and/or explanatory models non-linear. Even if a model is deterministic, it will suffer from Sensitive Dependence on Initial Condition (SEDIC), a primary feature of such a non-linear system, and consequently, become unpredictable.

As also shown in Table I, the SDGs exist in the SOCIAL BAND, whereas the goals for real world problem-solving exist in the COGNITIVE BAND or RATIONAL BAND. Problem solving activities that are conducted in one band should not be linearly connected to those activities conducted in a different band because there are gaps between different bands. Activities within a band, however, can be linearly connected to each other, and it is possible to perform problem-solving activities in a well-defined problem space, if the problem-solver has sufficient knowledge to represent the problem space. However, it is impossible for a problem-solver to represent a problem space as a well-defined one if goals exist in different bands, i.e., some goals are in the SOCIAL BAND and others in the COGNITIVE BAND, because of the unpredictable nature of such a non-linear system.

Problem-solvers can identify a top-level goal that belongs to any of the SDGs and lower level goals that belong to the BAND where their real-world problem-solving activities are carried out. These lower level goals would effectively contribute as sub- or sub-sub- goals, and so on, in the entire hierarchical goal structure. However, the problem thus constructed, should have the features of ill-defined problems

TABLE I. NEWELL'S TIME SCALE OF HUMAN ACTION. (ADAPTED FROM NEWELL [4, PAGE 122, FIG. 3-3]).

Scale (sec)	Time Units	System	World (Theory)
10^7	months		
10^6	weeks		SOCIAL
10^5	days		BAND
10^4	hours	Task	
10^3	10min	Task	RATIONAL
10^2	minutes	Task	BAND
10^1	10sec	Unit Task	
10^0	1sec	Operations	COGNITIVE
10^{-1}	100ms	Deliberate Act	BAND
10^{-2}	10ms	Neural Circuit	
10^{-3}	1ms	Neuron	BIOLOGICAL
10^{-4}	100μsec	Organelle	BAND

because even if the state the problem-solver is currently in is well-specified, and the moves associated with the current state toward the states belonging to a different band are defined, i.e., the what and how to do is clearly specified, it is not possible to anticipate the result of the execution of the selected move due to the non-linear relationships between the goals in the different bands.

B. Real World Problem-Solving

Any activities that eventually lead to the achievement of any of the SDGs have to be implemented as problem solving activities that are conducted in the real-world context [9]. Skills necessary for performing these problem solving activities can be acquired through adaptive problem-solving activities [10] that have been studied thoroughly in an effort to implement the second cycle of the Programme for the International Assessment of Adult Competencies (PIAAC) survey. Note that the PIAAC is a program focusing on the assessment and analysis of adult skills. The major survey conducted as a part of PIAAC is the Survey of Adult Skills. This survey measures adults' proficiency in key information-processing skills – literacy, numeracy, and problem solving – and gathers information and data on how adults use their skills at home, at work, and in the wider community. This international survey is conducted in over 40 countries/economies, and measures the key cognitive and workplace skills needed for individuals to participate in society, and for economies to prosper.

A problem-solving task requires a problem solver to execute appropriate Perceptual-Cognitive-Motor (PCM) processes that are expected to be effective for accomplishing that task. Figure 1 illustrates how problem-solving activities happen at the interface between tasks and PCM processes. They could become diverse depending on the nature of the tasks, and how people carry out the PCM processes. External tasks impose time constraints on people's problem-solving activities, and people's PCM processes are carried out under the limitations (or possible ranges) of their specific PCM capabilities.

In general, individuals show a mixture of conscious and unconscious processes depending on the situation. Individuals' behavior is not always in alignment with their intentions residing in the RATIONAL BAND and the higher COGNI-

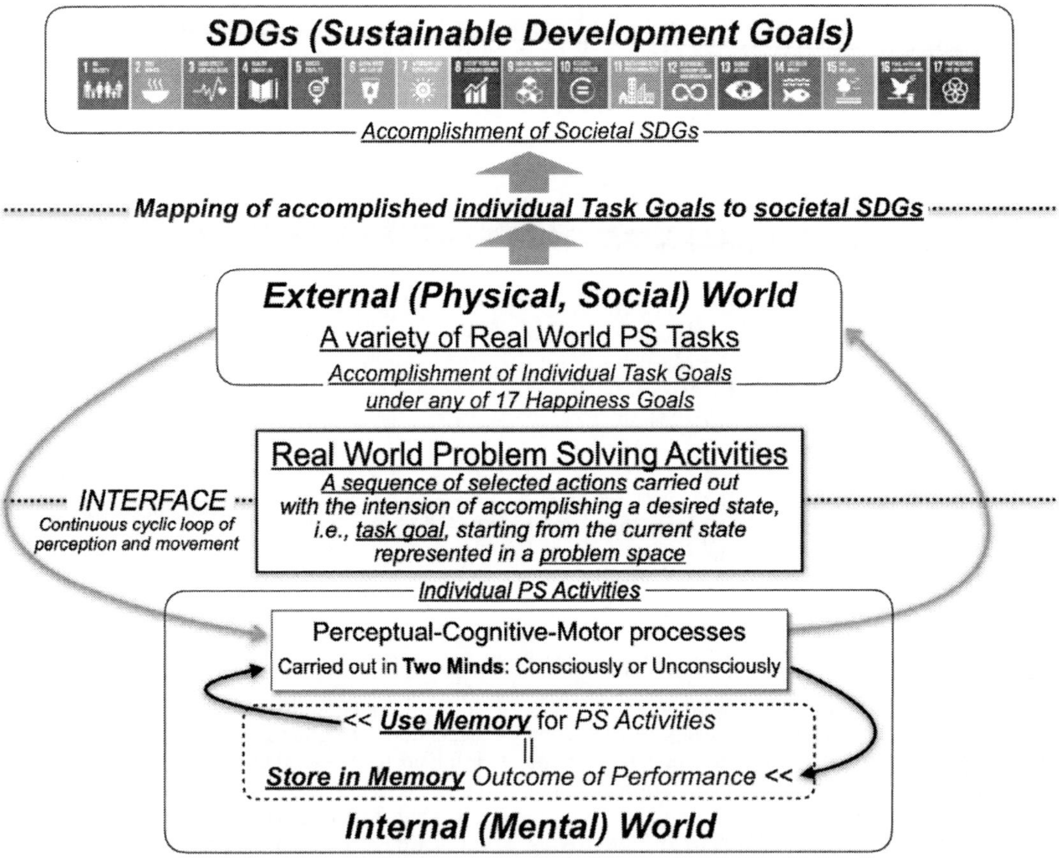

Figure 1. Accomplishing SDGs through individual real world problem solving activities for accomplishing individual task goals under happiness goals.

TIVE BAND, but is often carried out as activities in the lower COGNITIVE BAND at the order of hundreds of milli seconds. The former corresponds to System 2, and the latter to System 1. Kahneman [11][12] calls "System 1 and System 2" Two Minds, and describes System 1 as fast, automatic, and highly susceptible to environmental influences; and System 2 as slow-processing, reflective, and taking into account explicit goals and intentions. In this way, problem-solving activities are necessarily adaptive to the tasks people have to deal with. Adaptation is carried out within the range of PCM capabilities. As pointed out by Greiff et al. [10], "Adaptive Problem Solving" skill is one of the critical competencies people must have in order to achieve well-being in the contemporary multi-valued, networked, diverse, and heterogeneous society.

The interactions between the tasks that people encounter, and the PCM processes that people carry out to accomplish those tasks have a significant influence on people's development of problem-solving abilities. Therefore, people's past experiences significantly affect the actual action sequences for solving problems that are observed when some tasks to be performed are given to them. The bottom part of Figure 1 illustrates the relationships between real world problem-solving tasks and an individual's activities for accomplishing the goals. There are cognitive architectures available in the cognitive science society that are capable of simulating individuals' real world problem-solving activities (e.g., ACT-R [5][6], Soar [4], Model Human Processor with Realtime Constraints (MHP/RT) [13][14][15] , and so on).

C. Individual Level Achievement of SDGs

In some cases, individual activities performed in the COGNITIVE BAND or the RATIONAL BAND ultimately lead to the achievement of the SDGs belonging to the SOCIAL BAND. Banerjee et al. [17] reported such a case. They ran two Randomized Controlled Trials. Note that a Randomized Controlled Trial (RCT) is an experimental form of impact evaluation in which the population receiving the program or policy intervention is chosen at random from the eligible populations, and a control group is chosen at random from the same eligible populations. This method tests the extent to which specific, planned impacts are being achieved. The distinguishing feature of an RCT is the random assignment of units (e.g., people, schools, or villages) to the intervention or control groups. One of its strengths is that it provides a very powerful response to questions of causality, helping evaluators and program implementers ensure that the achieved outcome is a result of only the intervention, and not anything else.

Banerjee et al. [17] utilized this method and showed that vital information regarding vaccination was spread by using people who were considered gossips as information sources,

TABLE II. HAPPINESS GOALS [16] AND THEIR RELATION TO SOCIAL LAYERS. +'S DENOTE THE DEGREE OF RELEVANCE OF EACH GOAL TO EACH LAYER, I.E., INDIVIDUAL, COMMUNITY, AND SOCIAL SYSTEM, RESPECTIVELY. +++: MOST RELEVANT, ++: MODERATELY RELEVANT, AND +: WEAKLY RELEVANT.

	Name of Happiness	Types	Social Layers		
			Individual layer	Community layer	Social system layer
1	Target Happiness	The Achiever	+++	+++	+++
2	Competitive Happiness	The Winner		+++	+++
3	Cooperative Happiness	The Helper		+++	+++
4	Genetic Happiness	The Relative	+++	+++	
5	Sensual Happiness	The Hedonist	+++	+++	
6	Cerebral Happiness	The Intellectual	+++	+++	++
7	Rhythmic Happiness	The Dancer	+++	+++	
8	Painful Happiness	The Masochist	+++		
9	Dangerous Happiness	The Risk-taker	+++	++	+
10	Selective Happiness	The Hysteric	+++	++	
11	Tranquil Happiness	The Mediator	+++		
12	Devout Happiness	The Believer		+++	++
13	Negative Happiness	The Suffer	+++	++	
14	Chemical Happiness	The Drug-taker	+++		
15	Fantasy Happiness	The Day-dreamer	+++		
16	Comic Happiness	The Laugher	+++	+++	
17	Accidental Happiness	The Fortunate	+++	+++	+++

and it eventually led to an increase in the vaccination rate. They proposed a research framework that can handle information propagation in situations where individuals cannot grasp the network structure through which information propagates. For their work, they received the Nobel Prize in Economics in 2019. In their study, the RCT method was used for verifying whether gossips, who had no knowledge about the structure of the information network, and had been nominated by people in the area, really worked toward spreading information. However, what the gossips did could be re-interpreted from the viewpoint of problem-solving activities as follows:

> The gossips did not necessarily work toward achieving any of the SDGs but their efforts for the fulfillment of their personal goals – that were likely to belong to the COGNITIVE BAND – led to the achievement of Goal 3 of the SDGs, "Good health and well-being for people" as a by-product.

Similar mechanisms could be implemented by using the concept of "nudge" in behavioral economics, which is any aspect of the choice architecture that alters people's behavior in a predictable way without forbidding any options or significantly changing their economic incentives [18][19]. In situations where the local decisions made in the COGNITIVE BAND do not take into consideration the consequences of the SOCIAL BAND (bounded rationality), actions are selected based on the principle of satisficing [20]. Currently, the coronavirus disease 2019 crisis requires large-scale behavior change. Bavel et al. [21, page 463] point out in their paper entitled "Using social and behavioural science to support COVID-19 pandemic response" that "nudges and normative information can be an alternative to more coercive means of behaviour change or used to complement regulatory, legal and other imposed policies when widespread changes must occur rapidly."

D. Problem Solving for Achieving Happiness Goals

Real world problem-solving is carried out within the COGNITIVE BAND. The actions taken by the gossips to spread information in the study by Banerjee et al. [17] can be understood using the PCM and memory processes, as depicted in Figure 1, by simulating their activities based on appropriate cognitive architectures. But what were the actual behavioral goals the gossips pursued?

It would be reasonable to assume that the goal of the gossips in their real world problem-solving is likely to have been providing useful information to their listeners. Morris [16] has characterized such goals as happiness goals and has listed 17 of them. The left portion of Table II shows these goals, including such goals as "the inherent happiness that comes with the love of a child," "the competitive happiness of triumphing over your opponents," "the sensual happiness of the hedonist," and so on.

Kitajima et al. [22] proposed the "Maximum Satisfaction Architecture (MSA)." MSA consists of three parts: 1) human brain characterized by System 1 and System 2; 2) society consisting of the three layers of Individual, Community, and Social system; and 3) happiness goals. MSA assumes that the human brain pursues one of the 17 happiness goals defined by Morris [16] at every moment, and switches to another goal when appropriate, by evaluating the current circumstances. Each of the happiness goals is associated with one or multiple layers of society. These layers have evolved from the history of human beings. Each layer is associated with its own value reflecting historical development, and thus, it relates to different sets of happiness goals.

The right portion of Table II shows tentative assignments of the degree of relevance of each goal to each layer. The middle portion of Figure 1 suggests that any real world problem-solving activities for achieving specific task goals would be conducted by individual persons in the pursuit of any of the 17 happiness goals in the social layers suggested in the right portion of Table II. The happiness goals would define a value structure of the problem-solver when he or she makes decisions by running the PCM and memory processes under specific circumstances while selecting his or her next actions. As such,

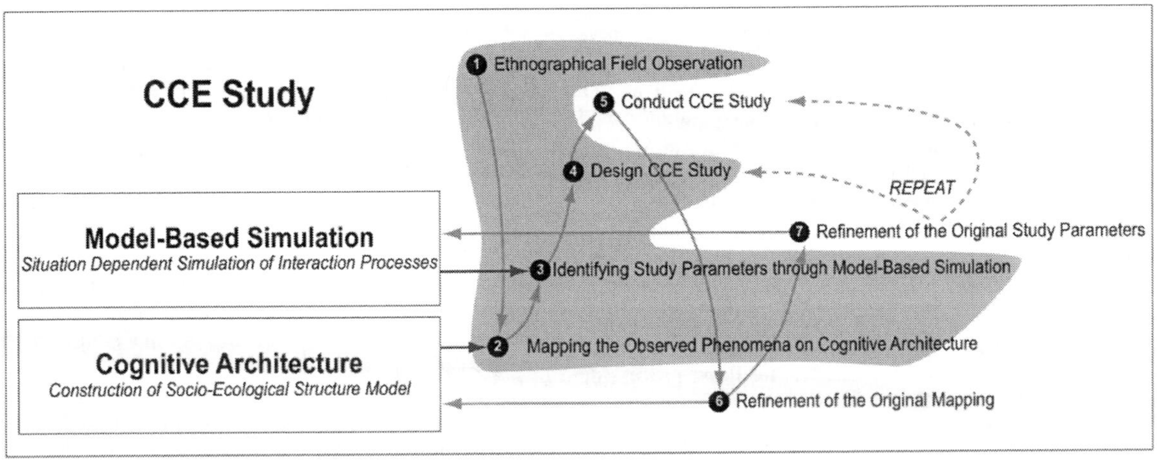

Figure 2. The CCE procedure [15, Figure 5.1].

it is vital to assume the correct happiness goal when simulating a problem-solver's next action selection processes.

III. Achieving SDGs by Applying CCE

The gossips in Banerjee et al.'s study [17], who pursued a certain happiness goal while selecting the appropriate next actions to be performed as real-world problem-solving activities, happened to contribute to achieving one of the SDGs. The upper portion of Figure 1 depicts this as "Mapping of accomplished individual Task Goals to societal SDGs." Banerjee et al. [17] hypothesized that those persons who were nominated by villagers as people who would be good at transmitting information in a network would be highly central individuals; and that sending information via such nominated individuals would lead to significantly wider diffusion of information than sending it via randomly chosen people, or even respected ones. They tested this hypothesis by conducting RCT studies, and succeeded in bridging the gap between achievement of any of the SDGs and accomplishment of individual task goals by selecting the appropriate individuals for making this possible. This section describes a cognitive scientific approach to what Banerjee et al. [17] did by integrating all the portions shown in Figure 1.

A. Cognitive Chrono-Ethnography (CCE)

This paper focuses on the particular study methodology of the CCE [23]. CCE is helpful in building an understanding of people's daily action selection processes by combining three concepts. "Cognitive" declares that CCE deals with interactions between consciousness and unconsciousness in the PCM cycles. "Chrono(-logy)" suggests that CCE concerns itself with the time dimension for characterizing human behavior, including not only short-term action sequences, but also relatively long-term behavioral changes, ranging from ~ 100 msec to days, months, and years, i.e., spanning through the COGNITIVE, RATIONAL, and SOCIAL bands. "Ethnography" indicates that CCE takes ethnographical observations as a concrete study method because in daily life, people's Two Minds tend to re-use experientially effective behavioral patterns, which is called "cognitive biases." Ethnographical field observations are essential for understanding each person's biases in his or her daily life. In order to conduct a CCE study, study participants (elite monitors) are selected. Each point in the parameter space defining the study field has values. The study question is "what such-and-such people would do in such-and-such way in such-and-such circumstance (not an average behavior)." Therefore, elite monitors, i.e., such-and-such persons, are selected by consulting the parameter space. In this process, it is necessary that the points in the parameter space, which correspond to the elite monitors, are appropriate for analyzing the structure and dynamics of the study field. Monitor selection is conducted by purposive sampling rather than by random sampling, similar to the RCT methodology.

B. CCE Procedure Adapted to SDGs Achievement

This subsection shows the steps for conducting a CCE study adapted for understanding people who are practicing daily real world problem-solving activities, leading to accomplishment of the SDGs, as shown in Figure 1. This understanding can be used for exporting such people's activities to potential followers who can then contribute to the achievement of the SDGs in the future [24]. Figure 2 shows the seven steps to conduct a CCE study [15, Figure 5.1]. Described below are the CCE steps adapted to the problem of SDGs achievement. Necessary additions appear after the general descriptions of the CCE procedure.

(1) *Ethnographical Field Observation:* Use the basic ethnographical investigation method to clarify the outline of the structure of social ecology that underlies the subject to be studied.

> Here, the study's focus would be any social ecology that has achieved or is approaching accomplishment of any of the UN defined targets associated with one of the 17 SDGs. The purpose of the CCE is to understand how this goal accomplishment is possible in the social ecology in question. Therefore, the enabling condition for a CCE study is the existence of such a social ecology, i.e., there is an ecologically valid solution for achieving the target under the SDGs.

(2) *Mapping the Observed Phenomena on Cognitive Architecture:* With reference to the behavioral characteristics of

people, which have been made clear so far, and the cognitive architectures, consider what kind of characteristic elements of human behavior are involved in the investigation result in (1).

The emphasis is on identifying a plausible happiness goal that might be held by the people in question. This step is particularly important, because the happiness goal is normally different from the target of the SDGs, each of which resides in different bands.

(3) *Identifying Study Parameters through Model-Based Simulation:* Based on the consideration of (1) and (2), construct an initial simple model with the constituent elements of activated memories, i.e., meme, and the characteristic PCM processing to represent the nature of the ecology of the study space.

The focus would be to identify classes of behaviors that are distinguishable from each other due to different functioning of their PCM and memory processes. The bottom part of Figure 1 is achieved by using appropriate cognitive architecture, such as MHP/RT [13][14][15] by assigning plausible ranges of values for the model parameters, which would result in a number of distinguishable behavioral patterns. For example, in the case of spreading information concerning vaccination, the cognitive processes might differ depending on the nature of information to be spread. This means that a more sophisticated treatment of spreading information could be carried out than that attempted by Banerjee et al. [17], by taking into account the underlying PCM and memory processes.

(4) *Design a CCE Study:* Based on the simple ecological model, identify a set of typical behavioral characteristics from a variety of people making up the group to be studied. Then formulate screening criteria of elite monitors who represent a certain combination of the behavioral characteristics, and define ecological survey methods for them.

(5) *Conduct CCE Study:* Select elite monitors and conduct an ethnographical field observation. Record the monitors' behavior. The elite monitors are expected to behave as they normally do at the study field. Their behavior is recorded in such a way that the collected data is rich enough to consider the results in terms of the parameter space, and as un-intrusively as circumstances allow.

(6) *Refinement of the Original Mapping:* Check the results of (5) against the results of (2) for appropriateness of the mapping. If inappropriate, go back to (2) and restart the process from there.

(7) *Refinement of the Original Study Parameters:* If the result of (5) is unsatisfactory, go back to (4) and redesign and conduct a revised CCE study, otherwise go back to (3) to redo the model-based simulation with a set of refined parameters.

On completion of a CCE cycle, the existing social ecology that has contributed to the achievement of any of the SDGs is understood as a feasible scenario that could be transferred to another social ecology that is similar to the existing one, but has still not achieved the goal.

IV. Conclusion

This paper discussed the contribution of cognitive science to the achievement of the SDGs, taking as an example, the communication of vaccination information that lead to the achievement of health goals. There is room for consideration as to whether the targets set to achieve all SDGs can be advanced in the same way. However, as stated in the UN report [1], it is impossible to achieve the targets without human involvement. In that regard, cognitive science, dealing with human behavior is destined to make a significant contribution. This paper first linked social-level goals of the SDGs to their associated individual-level happiness goals, and then associated the latter with human behavior. This association shows that inducing actions that lead to individuals working toward their happiness goals can lead indirectly to the achievement of the SDGs. In this way, scenarios for achieving the SDGs have been and can be created.

For instance, concerning the goal of attracting tourists to tourist destinations, CCE has proven to be effective in understanding tourists' activities in a previous study [25]. The tourists had different happiness goals organizing their behavior; these happiness goals were sorted into combinations of Target Happiness goal with one or two goals out of Sensual, Cerebral, and Chemical Happiness goals. The total number of combinations was six. Each of the combined happiness goals were found to be associated with characteristic tourists' behavior, i.e., eating, strolling, bathing, shopping, playing, and relaxing. The social level goal that was indirectly achieved by the tourists' behavior was the revitalization of the economy of tourist destinations. Although this is not one of the social goals under the SDGs, it nonetheless shows the feasibility of the CCE study methodology in the context of the achievement of SDGs.

Acknowledgments

This work was supported by JSPS KAKENHI Grant Number 20H04290. The author would like to thank Editage (www.editage.com) for English language editing.

References

[1] P. Messerli and E. Murniningtyas, Global Sustainable Development Report 2019: The Future is Now – Science for Achieving Sustainable Development, New York, 2019, written by Independent Group of Scientists appointed by the Secretary-General of UN.

[2] German Advisory Council on Global Change (WBGU), "World in Transition – A Social Contract for Sustainability," Tech. Rep., 2011.

[3] R. Hertwig and T. Grüne-Yanoff, "Nudging and boosting: Steering or empowering good decisions," Perspectives on Psychological Science, vol. 12, no. 6, 2017, pp. 973–986, pMID: 28792862.

[4] A. Newell, Unified Theories of Cognition (The William James Lectures, 1987). Cambridge, MA: Harvard University Press, 1990.

[5] J. R. Anderson and C. Lebiere, The Atomic Components of Thought. Mahwah, NJ: Lawrence Erlbaum Associates, 1998.

[6] J. R. Anderson, How can the Human Mind Occur in the Physical Universe? New York, NY: Oxford University Press, 2007.

[7] J. E. Laird, A. Newell, and P. S. Rosenbloom, "Soar: An architecture for general intelligence," Artificial Intelligence, vol. 33, 1987, pp. 1–64.

[8] S. K. Card, T. P. Moran, and A. Newell, The Psychology of Human-Computer Interaction. Hillsdale, NJ: Lawrence Erlbaum Associates, 1983.

[9] V. Sarathy, "Real World Problem-Solving," Frontiers in human neuroscience, vol. 12, 2018, p. 261.

[10] S. Greiff et al., "Adaptive Problem Solving, Moving Towards a New Assessment Domain in the Second Cycle of PIAAC," OECD Education Working Papers, no. 156, 2017.

[11] D. Kahneman, "A perspective on judgment and choice," American Psychologist, vol. 58, no. 9, 2003, pp. 697–720.

[12] D. Kahneman, Thinking, Fast and Slow. New York, NY: Farrar, Straus and Giroux, 2011.

[13] M. Kitajima and M. Toyota, "Decision-making and action selection in Two Minds: An analysis based on Model Human Processor with Realtime Constraints (MHP/RT)," Biologically Inspired Cognitive Architectures, vol. 5, 2013, pp. 82–93.

[14] M. Kitajima and M. Toyota, "Simulating navigation behaviour based on the architecture model Model Human Processor with Real-Time Constraints (MHP/RT)," Behaviour & Information Technology, vol. 31, no. 1, 2012, pp. 41–58.

[15] M. Kitajima, Memory and Action Selection in Human-Machine Interaction. Wiley-ISTE, 2016.

[16] D. Morris, The nature of happiness. London: Little Books Ltd., 2006.

[17] A. Banerjee, A. G. Chandrasekhar, E. Duflo, and M. O. Jackson, "Using Gossips to Spread Information: Theory and Evidence from Two Randomized Controlled Trials," The Review of Economic Studies, vol. 86, no. 6, 02 2019, pp. 2453–2490.

[18] R. Thaler and S. Benartzi, "Save More Tomorrow^{TM}: Using Behavioral Economics to Increase Employee Saving," Journal of Political Economy, vol. 112, no. S1, 2004, pp. S164–S187.

[19] R. H. Thaler and C. R. Sunstein, Nudge: Improving Decisions About Health, Wealth and Happiness. Penguin, 3 2009.

[20] H. A. Simon, "Rational choice and the structure of the environment," Psychological Review, vol. 63, 1956, pp. 129–138.

[21] J. J. V. Bavel et al., "Using social and behavioural science to support COVID-19 pandemic response," Nature Human Behaviour, vol. 4, no. 5, 2020, pp. 460–471.

[22] M. Kitajima, H. Shimada, and M. Toyota, "MSA:Maximum Satisfaction Architecture – a basis for designing intelligent autonomous agents on web 2.0," in Proceedings of the 29th Annual Conference of the Cognitive Science Society, D. S. McNamara and J. G. Trafton, Eds. Austin, TX: Cognitive Science Society, 2007, p. 1790.

[23] M. Kitajima, "Cognitive Chrono-Ethnography (CCE): A Behavioral Study Methodology Underpinned by the Cognitive Architecture, MHP/RT," in Proceedings of the 41st Annual Conference of the Cognitive Science Society. Cognitive Science Society, 2019, pp. 55–56.

[24] M. Kitajima, "Cognitive Chrono-Ethnography (CCE): a methodology for anticipating future user needs," in Work: A Journal of Prevention, Assessment and Rehabilitation (IEA 2012: 18th World congress on Ergonomics - Designing a sustainable future), vol. 41. Amsterdam, The Netherlands: IOS Press, 2012, pp. 5251–5258.

[25] M. Kitajima, H. Tahira, S. Takahashi, and T. Midorikawa, "Understanding tourist's *in situ* behavior: a Cognitive Chrono-Ethnography study of visitors to a hot spring resort," Journal of Quality Assurance in Hospitality and Tourism, vol. 12, 2012, pp. 247–270.

The Concept of Resonance: From Physics to Cognitive Psychology

Jérôme Dinet

Université de Lorraine
91 avenue de la libération
54000 Nancy, France
Email: jerome.dinet@univ-lorraine.fr

Muneo Kitajima

Nagaoka University of Technology
1603-1 Kamitomioka Nagaoka
Niigata, Japan
Email: mkitajima@kjs.nagaokaut.ac.jp

***Abstract*—There are very few connections between physics and cognitive psychology. But in this paper, we assume that recent models inspired by concepts issued from physics and problem-solving cognitive processes like the Model Human Processor with Real Time Constraints (MHP/RT) model (Kitajima and Toyota, 2012) [1] allow to better describe and predict human behaviors especially in complex and dynamical environments where interactions between several bands and space-time constraints exist. After presenting the importance of the concept of resonance in physics and in cognitive psychology, the deterministic chaos in human action and behavior will be described, by focusing on an innovative model directly inspired by models issued from physics and problem-solving cognitive processes, Model Human Processor With Real Time Constraints (MHP/RT). If nowadays, the distance between physics and psychology is very prominent, the main goal of this paper is to defend the necessity to (re-)create strong relationships between physics and psychology to better understand and predict human behaviors because these situations are the majority of situations where an individual takes actions (such as walks, reads, stops, watching the other pedestrians' behavior in complex buildings or in street, etc.).**

Keywords*–*Physics; Resonance; Deterministic chaos; Cognitive modelling

I. Introduction

The human mind is endowed with innate primordial perceptions such as space, distance, motion, change, flow of time, and matter. Nevertheless, nowadays, there is very few connection between physics and cognitive psychology. Can physics offer anything to the cognitive sciences? The primary goal of this paper is to demonstrate why the answer to this question is in positive.

Physics is science that deals with the structure of matter and the interactions between the fundamental constituents of the observable universe. Psychology is scientific discipline that studies mental processes and behavior in humans (and animals). Physics (the basic natural science) elucidates the simplest fundamental questions in nature. Psychology is intimately related to the humanitarian sciences. Physics is concerned with all aspects of nature. Psychology is the science of individual or group behavior. Despite fundamental differences, there are the same problems even in so completely different disciplines. Interdisciplinality is best seen as bringing together distinctive components of two or more disciplines [2].

From a historical point of view, physics and psychology were strongly related [3]. For instance, in Wilhelm Wundt's (1832–1920) Leipzig laboratory and at numerous other research sites, procedures, techniques and tools issued from physics were used to conduct reaction time experiments. In the same way, the purpose of Wheatstone (1802–1875), one of the most famous English physicist, was to test his theory of stereo vision and for investigations into what would now be called experimental psychology.

But nowadays, the distance between physics and psychology is important: first, very few courses of fundamental sciences (biology, physiology, etc.) exist in psychology curriculum; second, no psychology course is proposed in science curriculum except for some hours in specific curricula (e.g., curricula in cognitive sciences). From an epistemological point of view, one of the main determinant factors was the division of the human being into a soul and a body which are united but separated [4]. This division, which corresponded to the Aristotelian classification of substances (Metaphysics XII), posed the problem of the unity of the science of the soul and its place alongside other fields [5] and explain the absence of connection between physics and psychology in teaching. Yet, the experimental methods in cognitive sciences have physics as their basis.

In this paper, we assume that a majority of interactions, including psychological interactions between humans and and environment (social or physical environment), can be derived from physical processes and thus, be apprehended by using concepts issued from physics such as resonance.

II. Resonance in Physics and in Cognition

This part is aiming to investigate the relationships between physics and psychology about the common concept of resonance.

A. *Resonance in Physics*

Initially, the term resonance originates from the field of acoustics, particularly observed in musical instruments, e.g., when strings started to vibrate and to produce sound without direct excitation by the player. Today, because this type of synchronization between two elements in a same environment (with the same constraints) is observed in other areas, resonance phenomena occur with all types of vibrations or wave (e.g., mechanical resonance, acoustic resonance, electromagnetic resonance, nuclear magnetic resonance, and so on).

The phenomenon of resonance is known and observed for a long time. For instance, In 1665, the Dutch physicist Christiaan Huygens, inventor of the pendulum clock, was lying in his bed with a minor illness and watching two of his clocks hanging on a wall. Huygens noticed something odd: No matter how the pendulums on these clocks began, in 10 minutes, they ended up swinging in exactly the opposite direction from each other. The cause of this effect, called "odd kind of sympathy" by Huygens, remained a mystery for centuries. Recently, two mathematicians Oliveira and Melo [6] calculated that, as pendulums move back and forth, sound pulses could travel through the wall from clock to clock. These pulses can interfere with the swings of the pendulums, eventually causing them to synchronize. Based on several experiments, Oliveira and Melo [6] have developed a model explaining the Huygens problem of synchronization between two clocks hanging from a wall. In their model, each element (i.e., clock) transmits once per cycle a sound pulse that is translated in a pendulum speed change. Today, because synchronization between two elements in a same environment (with the same constraints) is observed in a great number of areas, their model is used in several domains such as acoustics, cosmology, and mechanics. In other words, in physics, resonance occurs when the behaviors of two (or more) elements in a physical environment are synchronized by an autonomous (and unconscious) process of vibrating transmission between these elements.

B. Resonance in Psychology: Explanation of Imitation and Learning for Newborn

The young child's ability to imitate the actions of other human beings is an important mechanism for social learning and for acquiring new knowledge. Since the first study conducted by Meltzoff and Moore [7] who reported evidence that two- to three-week-old infants imitate the behaviors of an adult model, a lot of reports of newborn imitation have been cited to support hypotheses about the origins and nature of imitation, including the hypothesis that imitation is a unitary competency inherited as a unit and may be shared as a unit by species with common ancestry (e.g., [8][9]).

Several studies about newborn [10]–[13] imitation have also shown that a specialized neurological mechanism underlies imitative behavior in human infants and adults, and that this neurological mechanism is inherited. According to these authors, this neurological mechanism is a "mirror system". The idea of a mirror system specialized for imitation was initially suggested by the discovery of "mirror" neurons in monkeys [14][15]. Because mirror neurons appear to have both sensory and motor properties, nowadays researchers see in them the potential for a straightforward, automatic and heritable mechanism for imitation in humans [8]. The existence of this "mirror neurons" system for human has been demonstrated by using fMRI and was localized in the right inferior parietal lobe [16][17]. For human beings, the mirror system offers a way to make newborn imitation feasible: the "mirror-neuron" system appears to bypass the requirement for precocious knowledge and cognitive abilities in newborn infants who imitate because the system itself embodies that knowledge. The mirror system is thought to directly match visual input from an observed action with a stored motor program for the same behavior (e.g., [10][12][13]). If that motor program is then executed, the result is imitation.

Since ten years, the "mirror-neuron" system has received much interest in recent years because of its putative involvement in a range of important cognitive processes (for a synthesis, see [16]), from action understanding, observational learning, to socialization, theory of mind, and empathy. Moreover, dysfunction of the mirror system has been linked with some clinical disorders (e.g., in apraxia, autism,and schizophrenia, see [12]) and in social human behaviors, see [18].

The mirror-neuron system is the main biological support for resonance between individuals whatever the context (physical or social context): so, within natural social contexts, actions of individuals often imply interactions with others individuals by using the mirror-neuron system [19].

In other words, we assume that the mirror-neuron system is the physical/neurological support for the resonance in human behavior: newborn imitation is the result of a synchronization between behaviors issued from two elements in a same environment (i.e., the newborn and the adult). First, the adult initiates a behavior (e.g., tongue protrusion with mouth opening); Second, this external stimulus from the environment is processed by the newborn by perceptual/visual system to create internal representations, which "resonate with" memory to activate the relevant portion of memory automatically (Kitajima and Toyota (2012) [20]), and this initial activation triggers successive activation though its adjacent connected regions. The activated network at some time later defines what follows in the future, i.e., next behavior (i.e., tongue protrusion with mouth opening).

III. Resonance in Deterministic Chaos

If resonance is well-know in closed system from physicians and psychologists, the deterministic chaos is more relevant to understand it in our complex and open real systems.

A. The Deterministic Chaos: Generality

Classically, all physical laws are described by differential equations (e.g., [22]–[24]). Because initial state of elements present at the same time in a same physical environment, environmental constraint, and physical laws are known, it is possible to theoretically predict the future of the physical system (i.e., future states of elements) for all times. This is the deterministic view of nature. In other words, physics systems are deterministic because they obey deterministic differential equations. Because Wilhelm Wundt's background was in physiology, and this was reflected in the topics with which the Institute was concerned (e.g., the study of reaction times, sensory processes, and attention), this deterministic principle was used in the Institute for Experimental Psychology at the University of Leipzig in Germany in 1879, the first laboratory dedicated to psychology. This deterministic principle is one of the main principles of modern psychology and always used in experimental design in psychology.

As observed for many systems in physics, acoustics and mechanics, knowledge about the future state is limited by the precision with which the initial state can be measured [25][26]. That is, knowing the laws of nature is not enough to predict the future. There are deterministic systems whose time evolution has a very strong dependence on initial conditions. In other words, the differential equations that govern the evolution of the system are very sensitive to initial conditions. Usually, physicians and mathematicians say that even a tiny effect, such as a butterfly flying nearby, may be enough to vary the conditions such that the future is entirely different than what it might have been, not just a tiny bit different. In this way, measurements made on the state of a system at a given time may not allow us to predict the future situation even moderately far ahead, despite the fact that the governing equations are exactly known. By definition, these equations are named chaotic and that they predict a deterministic chaos (for a recent review: [27]). This difficulty to have a global and

TABLE I. NEWELL'S TIME SCALE OF HUMAN ACTION (ADAPTED FROM [21, PAGE 122, FIG. 3-3]), LEFT PORTION OF THE TABLE, ADDED WITH ASSOCIATED ACTIVITIES.

Scale (sec)	Time Units	System	World (Theory) BAND	Activity			
				Internal	Bodily Habitual	Organic Habitual	Organic Interactive
					System 2		
				System 1			
10^7	months						
10^6	weeks		SOCIAL				✓
10^5	days						
10^4	hours	Task					
10^3	10min	Task	RATIONAL			✓	✓
10^2	minutes	Task					
10^1	10sec	Unit Task					
10^0	1sec	Operations	COGNITIVE		✓	✓	
10^{-1}	100ms	Deliberate Act					
10^{-2}	10ms	Neural Circuit					
10^{-3}	1ms	Neuron	BIOLOGICAL	✓	✓		
10^{-4}	100μsec	Organelle					

perfect knowledge of the initial state of a human being is also a common characteristics in human and social sciences. In other words, as said Lorentz in 1963 [28], deterministic chaos can be used:

> When the present determines the future, but the approximate present does not approximately determine the future.

A deterministic chaos system has three characteristics that can be applied to human behavior:

(A) **Long term behavior is difficult or impossible to predict**: Even very accurate measurements of the current state of a chaotic system become useless indicators of where the system will be;

(B) **Sensitive dependence on initial conditions (a property noted by Poincare, Birkhoff, and even Turing)**: Starting from very close initial conditions a chaotic system very rapidly moves to different states;

(C) **Local instability versus global stability**: In order to have amplification of small errors and noise, the behavior must be locally unstable: over short times nearby states move away from each other. But for the system to consistently produce stable behavior, over long times the set of behaviors must fall back into itself, i.e., resilience.

So, deterministic chaos focuses on the behavior of dynamical systems that are highly sensitive to initial conditions but sustainable in the environment, that could change within a limited range, with a resilience mechanism.

B. The Deterministic Chaos in Human Action: Time Scale of Human Action

Human behavior can be best viewed as a composite of non-linearly connected four bands that are associated with different characteristic times, ranging from 10^{-4} sec to 10^7 sec as suggested by Newell [21, page 122, Fig. 3-3]. As shown by Table I, it identifies non-linearly connected four bands; SOCIAL, RATIONAL, COGNITIVE, and BIOLOGICAL BANDs. The claim that human action should be structured in terms of the discrete four bands suggests that it should be possible to build predictive and explanatory models for activities that happen within a single band, and at the same time, it should be impossible, or inappropriate, to build predictive models that include activities that happen in multiple bands with inter-band interactions. Impossibility of constructing predictive models for inter-band activities comes from the existence of non-linear connections between bands. This should make the models non-linear and even if they are deterministic they suffer from SEnsitive Dependence on Initial Condition (SEDIC), the primary feature of such a non-linear system and make them unpredictable.

C. The Resonance in Deterministic Chaos for Organizing Human Behavior

The majority of situations where an individual takes actions, such as walks, reads, stops, watching the other pedestrians' behavior in complex buildings or in street, etc., is performed in space-time environment where different factors and physical constraints exist. For example, as Hoogendoorns and Bovy [29] said, one of the most interesting and challenging theoretical and practical problems in describing/predicting pedestrians behavior are route choice and activity scheduling. The main reason is that, compared to other modes of transport, a characteristic feature of pedestrian route choice is that routes are continuous trajectories in time and space: since a pedestrian chooses a route from an infinite set of alternatives, dedicated theories and models describing pedestrian route choice are required. There exists several models describing and predicting pedestrians behavior, these models being mainly issued from mathematics, computer science, psychology, and sociology. Recently, Kitajima and Toyota [1] conceived an innovative model (called Model Human Processor with Real Time constraints (MHP/RT)) to describe and predict human behavior in dynamic and complex environments.

MHP/RT is directly inspired by models issued from physics and problem-solving cognitive processes, and simulates people's action selection as interactions between System 1 (uncon-

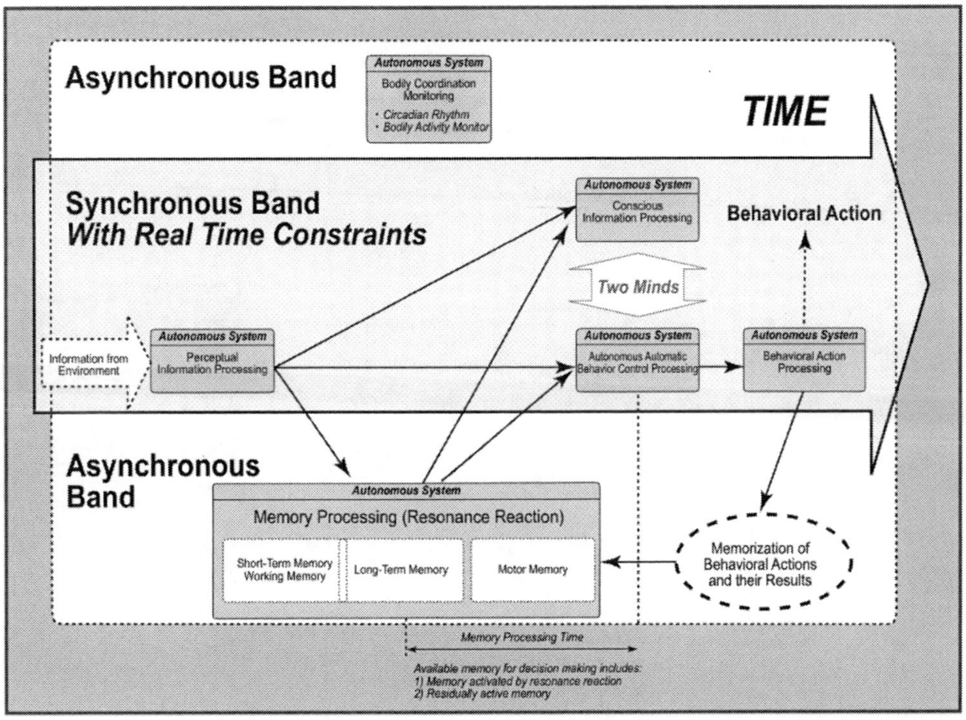

Figure 1. Outline of MHP/RT [1, Figure 4].

scious automatic fast processes carried out in the time range of < 100 msec in the BIOLOGICAL BAND) and System 2 (conscious deliberate slow processes which take seconds, minutes, and even much longer in the COGNITIVE, RATIONAL and SOCIAL BANDs) that make use of memory through the resonance mechanism. System 1 and System 2, otherwise called "Two Minds", are the terms used by Kahneman [30][31]. They constitute the basis of behavioral economics, which deals with decision making in human beings' economic activities. Figure 1 illustrates MHP/RT schematically. It operates in two bands, the asynchronous band and the synchronous band. The Bodily Coordination Monitoring System and the Memory Processing System operate in the asynchronous band. The Perceptual Information Processing System, Conscious Information Processing System, Autonomous Automatic Behavior Control Processing System, and Behavioral Action Processing System operate in the synchronous band. These systems work autonomously. System 1 of the Two Minds corresponds to the Autonomous Automatic Behavior Control Processing System, and System 2 corresponds to the Conscious Information Processing System.

Even if the human brain is not literally divided in a dual system, the distinction between the two systems (System 1 and System 2) is a useful analogy. Figure 2 illustrates how MHP/RT outlined by Figure 1 works while a person behaves in the real environment:

1) When a sensory input is extracted from the physical and/or social environment (e.g., visually and auditory information), System 1, System 2 and Long Term Memory (LTM) are activated by neural activation based on matching and mapping processes;
2) System 1 (biological band) thinking is automatic, quick, intuitive, emotional and reactive while System 2 thinking is conscious, effortful, logical, and deliberate. System 1 is driven by emotion and snap judgement, especially if we are time-pressed, multitasking or tired. Most of the time, most people function using their System 1 as it requires little effort. System 1 operates automatically and quickly, with little or no effort and no sense of voluntary control;
3) System 2 allocates attention to the effortful mental activities that demand it, including complex computations. The operations of System 2 are often associated with the subjective experience of agency, choice, and concentration;
4) Finally, a motor output (i.e., a behavior, an effective action) is produced on the basis of the mental representation elaborated;
5) In reality System 1 and 2 work in tandem, they complement each other: System 1 feeds relevant input into our System 2.

This dual-process approach posit that a lot of cognitive process – decision-making, emotion processing, memory formation, or even the manifestation of thought itself – can arise from one of two "pathways" (System 1 and System 2), and that those two pathways can operate relatively independently from one another. In other words, the MHP/RT model processes through a combination of Systems 1 (intuition or pattern-recognition) and Systems 2 (analytic) thinking.

Kitajima and Toyota [1] provided detailed explanations for the results of field study at train stations which focused on the

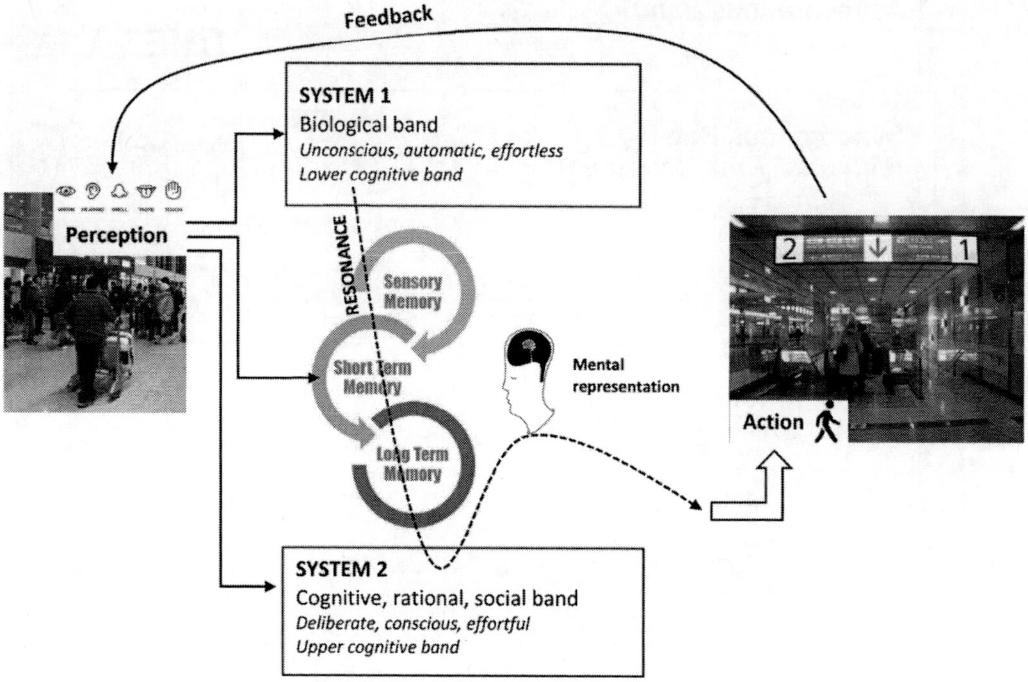

Figure 2. An illustration of MHP/RT's processes while a traveller tries to find his/her way at an airport.

characteristic behaviors of participants (or elderly passengers) who had deficit in one of three cognitive capabilities of attention, planning and working memory. The different operations can be described as follows:

- memory activation triggered by external/internal (bodily) stimuli starts in the lower BIOLOGICAL BAND, and it is kept activated in the lower BIOLOGICAL BAND;
- System 1 processes in the upper BIOLOGICAL BAND ($< 100 \sim 150$ msec) hook the part of activated memory to act in a feed-forward control, which we describe System 1 process uses the memory by resonance; because individual is arriving from Narita Airport by train and because s/he wants to go to visit the Imperial Palace in Tokyo, s/he has to go to the upper ground of the train station; so traffic signs about stairways and elevators are visually detected in surrounding environment;
- System 2 processes typically performed in COGNITIVE and RATIONAL BANDs hook the part of activated memory to act in a feed-back control, which we describe System 2 uses the memory by resonance; because many exits are possible from the upper ground of Tokyo train station, individual has to choose the most relevant; if s/he remembers that the Imperial Palace is located very closed to South exit, s/he has to choose the South exit; so s/he has to activate mental schema to find this relevant exit;
- System 1 and System 2 are synchronized occasionally to check if the feed-forward control works fine, – since System 1 and System 2 work in different BANDs, they may suffer from the features of deterministic chaos and cannot be connected linearly; if unfortunately, South exit is closed because works, individual has to choose another way; for instance, s/he can decide to go to the East exit then to take the way on the right side to access to the Imperial palace; or s/he can decide to follow other pedestrians who have map of the Imperial Palace in their hands because s/he can hypothesize that these other pedestrians want also to visit the same location;
- the memory activation that reflect directly the external and internal bodily situations which should represent "reality" is one part of resonance, and System 1 processes and System 2 processes for creating actions to interact with the environment and should cause changes that define the next situation for the behaving-self are the other part of resonance; several times during her/his movement, individual monitors and controls that s/he is on the good way;
- resonance is a mechanism for coordinating non-linearly connected BANDs to have the self behave in the ever-changing environment

IV. Conclusion

From a historical point of view, physics and psychology were strongly related. But nowadays, the distance between physics and psychology is very prominent. The main goal of this paper is to defend the necessity to (re-)create strong relationships between physics and psychology to better understand and predict human behaviors, especially in complex and dynamical environments where interactions between several bands and space-time constraints exist. And these situations are the majority of situations where an individual takes actions (such as walks, reads, stops, watching the other pedestrians' behavior in complex buildings or in street, etc.).

The modern MHP/RT elaborated by Kitajima and Toyota [1] is directly inspired by models issued from physics and problem-solving cognitive processes, and simulates people's action selection as interactions between System 1 (unconscious automatic fast processes carried out in the time range of $<$ 100 msec in the BIOLOGICAL BAND) and System 2 (conscious deliberate slow processes which take seconds, minutes, and even much longer in the COGNITIVE, RATIONAL and SOCIAL BANDs) that make use of memory through the resonance mechanism. Based on several notions issued from physics (deterministic chaos, resonance) and based on several concepts issued from psychology (long term memory, working memory, attention), we assume that this kind of model is a good example of models combining physics and psychology allowing to better describe human behaviors.

REFERENCES

[1] M. Kitajima and M. Toyota, "Simulating navigation behaviour based on the architecture model Model Human Processor with Real-Time Constraints (MHP/RT)," Behaviour & Information Technology, vol. 31, no. 1, 2012, pp. 41–58. [Online]. Available: https://doi.org/10.1080/0144929X.2011.602427 [retrieved: July, 2020]

[2] Y. Oleg, "Interdisciplinary Aspects of Learning: Physics and Psychology," Universal Journal of Educational Research, vol. 3, no. 11, 2015, pp. 810 – 814.

[3] L. I. Perlovsky, "Physics of the mind," Frontiers in Systems Neuroscience, vol. 10, article 84, 2016, pp. 1–12. [Online]. Available: https://www.frontiersin.org/article/10.3389/fnsys.2016.00084 [retrieved: July, 2020]

[4] C. Goodey, "Psychology: a physics of the soul?" Metascience, vol. 22, 2013, pp. 133 – 135.

[5] F. Vidal, The Sciences of the Soul: The Early Modern Origins of Psychology. University of Chicago Press, 2011.

[6] H. M. Oliveira and L. V. Melo, "Huygens synchronization of two clocks," Scientific Reports, vol. 5, no. 11548, 2015, pp. 1–12. [Online]. Available: https://doi.org/10.1038/srep11548 [retrieved: July, 2020]

[7] A. N. Meltzoff and M. K. Moore, "Imitation of facial and manual gestures by human neonates," Science, vol. 198, no. 4312, 1977, pp. 75–78. [Online]. Available: https://science.sciencemag.org/content/198/4312/75 [retrieved: July, 2020]

[8] S. S. Jones, "The development of imitation in infancy," Philosophical Transaction Royal Society London B, vol. 364, 2009, pp. 2325 – 2335.

[9] P. Ferrari et al., "Neonatal imitation in rhesus macaques," PLoS biology, vol. 4, 10 2006, p. e302.

[10] J. Decety, T. Chaminade, J. Grèzes, and A. Meltzoff, "A pet exploration of the neural mechanisms involved in reciprocal imitation," NeuroImage, vol. 15, no. 1, 2002, pp. 265 – 272. [Online]. Available: http://www.sciencedirect.com/science/article/pii/S1053811901909383 [retrieved: July, 2020]

[11] M. Iacoboni, "Neural mechanisms of imitation." Current Opinion in Neurobiology, vol. 15, no. 6, 2005, pp. 632–637.

[12] M. Iacoboni and M. Dapretto, "The mirror neuron system and the consequences of its dysfunction," Nature Reviews Neuroscience, vol. 7, no. 12, 2006, pp. 942–951. [Online]. Available: https://doi.org/10.1038/nrn2024 [retrieved: July, 2020]

[13] M. Iacoboni et al., "Cortical mechanisms of human imitation," Science, vol. 286, no. 5449, 1999, pp. 2526–2528. [Online]. Available: https://science.sciencemag.org/content/286/5449/2526 [retrieved: July, 2020]

[14] V. Gallese, L. Fadiga, L. Fogassi, and G. Rizzolatti, "Action recognition in the premotor cortex," Brain, vol. 119, no. 2, 04 1996, pp. 593–609. [Online]. Available: https://doi.org/10.1093/brain/119.2.593 [retrieved: July, 2020]

[15] M. Myowa-Yamakoshi, M. Tomonaga, M. Tanaka, and T. Matsuzawa, "Imitation in neonatal chimpanzees (pan troglodytes)," Developmental science, vol. 7, no. 4, September 2004, pp. 437–442. [Online]. Available: https://doi.org/10.1111/j.1467-7687.2004.00364.x [retrieved: July, 2020]

[16] T. Chong, R. Cunnington, M. Williams, N. Kanwisher, and J. Mattingley, "fmri adaptation reveals mirror neurons in human inferior parietal cortex," Current biology : CB, vol. 18, 11 2008, pp. 1576–80.

[17] G. Rizzolatti, "The mirror neuron system and its functions in humans," Anatomy and embryology, vol. 210, 01 2006, pp. 419–21.

[18] L. Oberman, J. Pineda, and V. Ramachandran, "The human mirror neuron system: A link between action observation and social skills," Social cognitive and affective neuroscience, vol. 2, 04 2007, pp. 62–6.

[19] L. Bonini and P. Ferrari, "Evolution of mirror systems: A simple mechanism for complex cognitive functions," Annals of the New York Academy of Sciences, vol. 1225, 04 2011, pp. 166–75.

[20] M. Kitajima and M. Toyota, "The role of memory in mhp/rt: Organization, function and operation," in Proceedings of the 11th International Conference on Cognitive Modeling, ICCM 2012, 04 2012, pp. 291 – 296.

[21] A. Newell, Unified Theories of Cognition (The William James Lectures, 1987). Cambridge, MA: Harvard University Press, 1990.

[22] H. Goldstein, Classical Mechanics. London: Addison-Wesley, 1959.

[23] J. Marion and S. Thornton, Classical Dynamics of Particles and Systems. Philadelphia: Saunders College Publishing, 1995.

[24] K. Symon, Mechanics. London: Addison-Wesley, 1957.

[25] K. Alligood, T. Sauer, and J. Yorke, Chaos: An Introduction to Dynamical Systems. London: Springer-Verlag, 1997.

[26] A. Lichtenberg and M. Lieberman, Regular and Stochastic Motion. London: Springer-Verlag, 1983.

[27] M. Cattani, I. Caldas, S. de Souza, and K. Iarosz, "Deterministic chaos theory: Basic concepts," Revista Brasileira de Ensino de Fisica, vol. 39, no. 1, e1309, 2017, pp. 1–13.

[28] E. N. Lorenz, "Deterministic nonperiodic flow," Journal of the Atmospheric Sciences, vol. 20, no. 2, 1963, pp. 130–141. [Online]. Available: https://doi.org/10.1175/1520-0469(1963)020<0130:DNF>2.0.CO;2 [retrieved: July, 2020]

[29] S. Hoogendoorn and P. Bovy, "Pedestrian route-choice and activity scheduling theory and models," Transportation Research Part B: Methodological, vol. 38, no. 2, 2004, pp. 169 – 190. [Online]. Available: http://www.sciencedirect.com/science/article/pii/S0191261503000079 [retrieved: July, 2020]

[30] D. Kahneman, "A perspective on judgment and choice," American Psychologist, vol. 58, no. 9, 2003, pp. 697–720.

[31] D. Kahneman, Thinking, Fast and Slow. New York, NY: Farrar, Straus and Giroux, 2011.

Cognitive Digital Twins for the Process Industry

Sailesh Abburu
SINTEF Industry, SINTEF AS
Trondheim, Norway
e-mail: sailesh.abburu@sintef.no

Arne J. Berre
SINTEF Digital, SINTEF AS
Oslo, Norway
e-mail: arne.berre@sintef.no

Michael Jacoby
Fraunhofer, IOSB
Karlsruhe, Germany
e-mail:
michael.jacoby@iosb.fraunhofer.de

Dumitru Roman
SINTEF Digital, SINTEF AS
Oslo, Norway
e-mail: dumitru.roman@sintef.no

Ljiljana Stojanovic
Fraunhofer, IOSB
Karlsruhe, Germany
e-mail:
ljiljana.stojanovic@iosb.fraunhofer.de

Nenad Stojanovic
Nissatech
Niš, Serbia
e-mail: nenad.stojanovic@nissatech.com

Abstract—**The concept of a Cognitive Digital Twin (abbreviated CT or CDT) is presented in this paper as an extension of Digital Twins (DTs) with cognitive capabilities in the context of the process industry. With cognitive capabilities, we foresee possibilities for the next level of automation in process control systems. This article proposes an architecture associated with a CT control system, exemplified in a process industry use case. The CT is therefore seen as a more comprehensive approach in comparison to a traditional DT.**

Keywords- Digital Twin; Cognitive Digital Twin; Cognitive Architecture; Cognitive Services; Process Industry, COGNITWIN.

I. INTRODUCTION

DTs are emerging nowadays as a popular technology approach in many industries. A DT is generally considered a digital replica of a physical system that captures attributes and behaviours of that system. The purpose of a DT is to enable measurements, simulations, and experimentations with the digital replica in order to gain understanding about its physical counterpart. A DT is typically materialized as a set of multiple isolated models that are either empirical or first-principles based.

In the context of the process industry (including sectors such as chemicals, ferrous and non-ferrous, ceramics, etc.), the existing automated systems, while performing well in predictable environments, require substantial human intervention when faced with unanticipated situations for which they weren't designed to handle. Such situations require perception, reasoning, decision making, learning – aspects usually associated with cognition and addressed in the area of cognitive computing.

Cognitive computing is the ability of machines to mimic human ability to sense, think, and make optimal decisions in a given situation. Although the journey to reaching fully cognitive systems is still in its infancy, there are several application areas where the technology has already been implemented (e.g., the use of chatbots by the service industry to provide optimal answers to customer feedback). The genesis of such cognitive systems in the process industry would be DTs where physical systems are represented by mathematical models. CTs can be seen as extensions of DTs where the semantic and cognitive aspects are also featured in the DTs.

For realizing CTs in the process industry, an essential aspect is to devise the architectural building blocks that can serve as a foundation for cognitive systems in this domain. In this paper, we present an architectural framework for CTs in the context of process industry. This work contributes to one of the fundamental challenges for building intelligent systems, where cognition plays an important role in the underlying infrastructure of such a system. A cognitive architecture should provide a blueprint, supporting a wide range of abilities similarly to human capabilities [9]. Indeed, the architecture proposed in this paper can be seen as a cognitive architecture for building CTs.

The rest of the paper is organized as follows. In Section II, we review the various definitions of the emerging concept of CTs. In Section III, we present our proposal for an architecture for CTs, including cognitive services and challenges for implementing the identified cognition services. In Section IV, we discuss a concrete use case from the process industry and the role of cognitive services in that particular use case. Section V summarizes the paper and outlines possible future work.

II. DEFINITIONS OF COGNITIVE DIGITAL TWIN

The concept of "Cognitive Digital Twin", often used in its shorter form "Cognitive Twin", has recently emerged in the context of DTs as a mean to expand their scope by encompassing cognitive capabilities.

The concept appears to be first introduced in the industry context. For example, El Adl [5] defined CT in 2016 as a "digital representation, augmentation, and intelligent companion of its physical twin as a whole, including its subsystems and across all of its life cycles and evolution phases" [5]. The "Cognitive Digital Twins" LinkedIn group, established in 2016, and administered by the same person, defined CTs as "highly interconnected distributed cognitive systems and in specific cases very large complex systems. They live in the digital space, span physical and virtual systems and will evolve over time as the Things they represent evolve. They should represent all the life cycle phases of Things. CTs should be able to interact and collaborate across domains, physical and virtual worlds, as well as evolve to be able to autonomously take smarter contextual decisions and execute complex tasks on behalf of the physical things or humans. In many cases, they will replace physical components with intelligent software components" [10]. Furthermore, the group identifies aspects needed in the definition and realization of CTs, such as categories of CTs, reference architectures, actions and interactions of CTs, artificial intelligence (AI) & machine learning (ML)/deep learning (DL) in the context of CTs, real world applications, CTs interaction to its physical body (machines), and cyber and physical security of CTs.

IBM has been active in the CT domain. In this context, Saračević [17] presented the CT concept in 2017 as a "virtual representation of a physical object or system across its lifecycle (design, build, operate) using real time data from IoT sensors and other sources to enable learning, reasoning and automatically adjusting for improved decision making" [14]. A similar definition is presented by Eran Gery who also presented a CDT architecture based on IBM technologies in the area of Cognitive Computing and Cognitive Sensing: "The Cognitive Digital Twin is the virtual, state-full representation of a physical object or system across its life-cycle (design, build, operate) using operational real-time data and other sources to enable understanding, learning, reasoning, and dynamically recalibrating for improved decision making" [7]. Mikell and Clark [12] discussed about the use of cognitive computing techniques such as natural language processing (NLP), ML, object/visual recognition, acoustic analytics, and signal processing in the context of DT: "using cognitive to improve testing a digital twin can determine which product tests should be run more frequently and which should be retired. Or cognitive sensing can improve what/when data from sensors is relevant for deeper analysis. Cognitive digital twins can take us beyond human intuition to design and refine future machines" [12].

Furthermore, in 2018, Miskinis [13] discussed about the possibility to manufacture DTs that have cognitive functions (together with the hidden dangers of CTs). CTs are introduced as DTs that execute conscious actions, for example, "by having the ability to execute cognitive tasks, a digital twin of a service fulfillment or product manufacturing process will be able to examine the current structure of a system or a process and give recommendations regarding what can be improved at the current moment" [13].

The CT concept also appeared in specific sectors. For example in the telemetry sector CT is introduced as an "artificially intelligent Digital Twin that has the potential to serve as an 'autonomous maintenance engineer'" [1].

More recently, the CT concept got traction in the scientific literature. For example, Fernández et al. [6] consider CT as a "digital expert or copilot, which can learn and evolve, and that integrates different sources of information for the considered purpose. The structure of a CT partially emulates the structure of the corresponding human mental models" and define an architecture for "Associative Cognitive Digital Twin". Lu et al. [11] consider CTs as "Digital Twins (DT) with augmented semantic capabilities for identifying the dynamics of virtual model evolution, promoting the understanding of interrelationships between virtual models and enhancing the decision-making based on DT". In our recent work [2], we introduced a layered framework of twins, consisting of three layers: DTs, Hybrid Twins (HTs), CTs, in which each higher layer is defined in terms of extensions to the lower levels. We thus defined a CT as "an extension of HT incorporating cognitive features that enable sensing complex and unpredicted behaviour and reason about dynamic strategies for process optimization, leading to a system that continuously evolve its own digital structure as well as its behaviour". Furthermore, Eirinakis et al. [4] proposed the concept of "Enhanced Cognitive Twin" (ECT) in the context of process industries, as a way to "introduce advanced cognitive capabilities to the DT artefact that enable supporting decisions, with the end goal to enable DTs to react to inner or outer stimuli. The ECT can be deployed at different hierarchical levels of the production process, i.e., at sensor-, machine-, process-, employee- or even factory-level, aggregated to allow both horizontal and vertical interplay" [4].

Finally, it is worth mentioning the CT concept appears also in non-engineering contexts. For example, Somers et al. discuss CT as a "digital reflection of the user, intended to make decisions and carry out tasks on the user's behalf", to "highlight the key role that cognitive mechanisms play in modeling human decision making in the IoT digital space" [16]. CT was applied to professional education, where a CT is "used by applications owned by an individual to identify knowledge obsolescence and gaps" [15]. Du et al. [3] introduces a personal DT model of information-driven cognition (Cog-DT). Cog-DT is a "digital replica of a person's cognitive process in relation to information processing", including a VR platform that collects information preference data during training, contains the modelling and optimization algorithm of DT modelling of human cognitions, and an adaptive UI design based on real-time cognitive load measures and Cog-DT models.

As can be seen from the above review of existing CT definitions, a common agreement appears to be that a CT is a DT extended with some forms of cognitive capabilities, however there is no widespread consensus on what kind of cognitive capabilities a CT should encompass. This is probably partly because the CT concept is still an emerging concept, and that various sectors may require various types of cognitive capabilities.

III. Cognitive Digital Twin Architecture

In this section, we provide the conceptualization of the cognition services, which are the main concept used for realizing human-like cognition on the top of DTs. As illustrated in Fig. 1, to cope with challenging industrial cases, we designed a hierarchy of twins (DT/HT/CT), whereas each layer provides a set of services required for realizing various operations on data and models, resulting in a cognition-based replica of a physical system. As presented in the figure, the architecture enables a control loop that supports a continuous adaptation of the real industry system (e.g. settings, reconfiguration). In this paper, we focus on the CT layer. Further details on the components of the DT and HT layers can be found in [2].

more connected view on the data and models. The key advantage is the introduction of new knowledge that should provide missing insights for resolving original cases, as illustrated in Fig. 2.

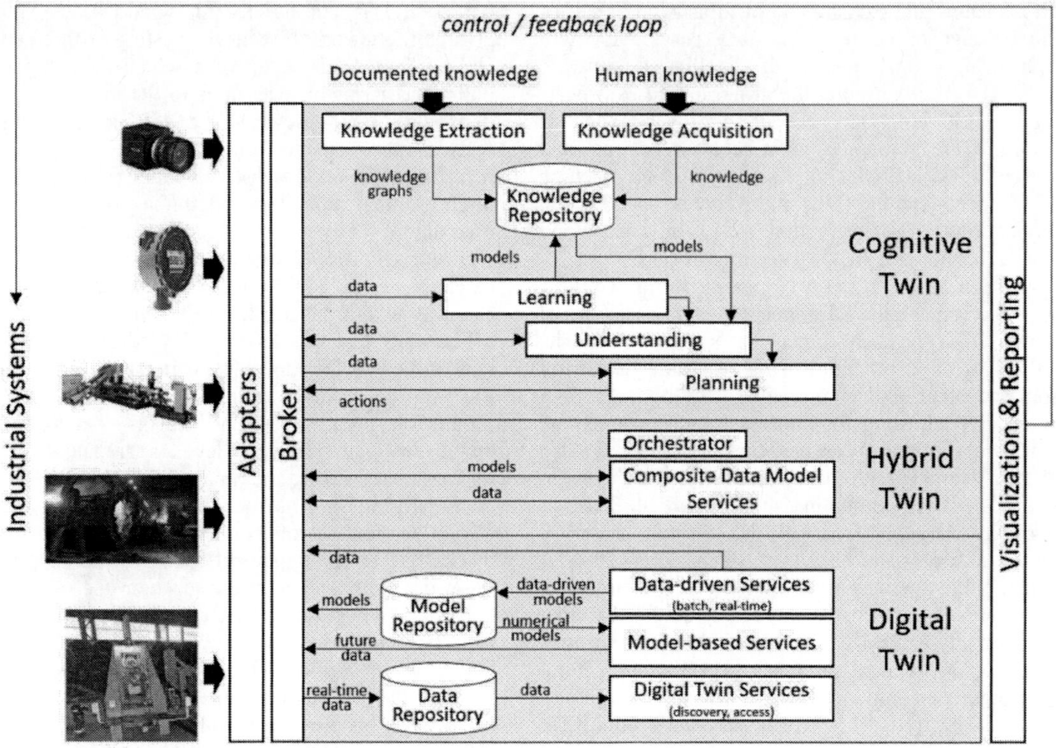

Figure 1. Conceptual architecture for CTs (based on [2]).

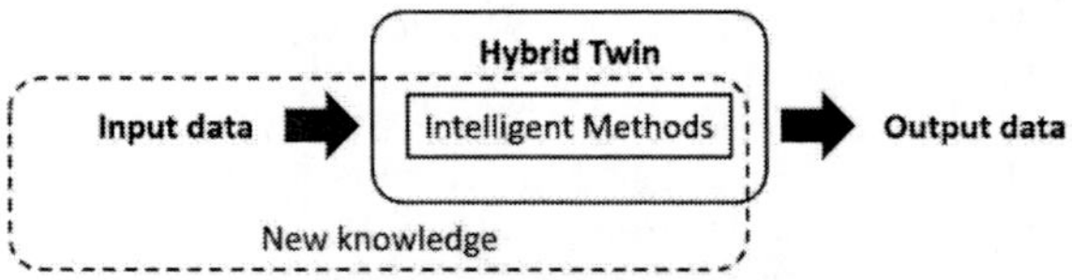

Figure 2. Cognition extending HT solution.

In order to facilitate the creation of such solutions for the industry, in the context of the H2020 COGNITWIN project we are currently developing the COGNITWIN Toolbox (CTT), which represents a set of technological components that can be used to build DTs, HTs, and CTs. Fig. 1 represents the conceptual architecture of a solution created by the application of the CTT.

A. *Cognitive Twin Layer*

There are many definitions of the cognition, but for this paper, we focus on that derived from the cognitive computing domain, which is related to reasoning and understanding at a higher level, in a manner that is analogous to human cognition [8]. We specialize this view for the complex cases where there are many uncertainties inherent in the available data and models. We expect that a human-cognition-like approach will enable a broader, as well as a more connected view on the data and models.

As presented in the figure, we assume that "intelligent methods", which can be a part of Hybrid Twin (see [9]), supports the development of a solution that "maps" inputs into outputs. However, the solution might be missing a high accuracy, due to not having enough data in the training set. As illustrated, cognition supports augmenting the input data, as well as intelligent methods with new knowledge (gathered directly from experts or other sources), with the goal to generate new outputs (with a higher accuracy). Therefore, we argue that the uncertainty inherited in the problem (e.g., missing data or models) can be resolved by augmenting data and intelligent methods to compensate missing information. Notice that this process is not about getting new data, but rather new insights about existing data (through cognition).

Therefore, the main role of cognition services is to enable understanding of the behaviour of the monitored system under various types of uncertainties/unknowns, to support reliable decision making (by human experts) or control (in autonomous systems). Uncertainties can be of different types, but we focus on two most important types from the DT point of view: lack of data and unavailability of models regarding the current system behavior. Other types of uncertainty can be related to the uncertainty in the data values and the precision of available models. For our approach, it means that the current system behaviour cannot be understood neither by analysing past data, since the relevant data is missing, nor by simulations of numerical models, since these do not exist (or are not accurate enough). In such cases, it is important to compensate these unknowns by introducing new processing steps that will gradually improve the understanding of the system behaviour, until this understanding is enough for the desired action. This process we consider as cognition, where the processing steps are part of cognition services.

The main challenge is that real-time data is not enough for understanding the current situation (regarding the underlying problem). The main goal of the cognition service is to enable resolution of the original problem by introducing new knowledge that provides new insights for the model learning/creation processes, e.g., introduction of some constraints in the interpretation of originally collected data. Therefore, cognition is working on the top of existing models, which can be derived using AI methods, extending the intelligence with deep understanding and reasoning strategies.

We can materialize this general process through following four steps:

1. Inserting new knowledge (relevant for the problem).
2. Learning models that are more accurate by applying new knowledge.
3. Better situational understanding (e.g., lower interpretation uncertainty), by applying new models.
4. Planning actions for resolving the problem, based on improved situational understanding. We describe these steps as follows:
   a. Knowledge extraction and knowledge acquisition, for gathering knowledge from the existing data sources (e.g., unstructured and semi-structured content) and from experts, respectively. The goal is to collect knowledge, which is related to the uncertainties in data and models. Since the process is related to supporting human-like understanding, it is important that the process is driven by well-defined knowledge structures (like knowledge graphs) which provide a general description of the domain. Indeed, one of the main characteristics of the human cognition is a very fast discovery of hidden connections between arbitrary information items, which is based on large memory maps.
   b. Learning, which encompasses applying new knowledge on the existing data, models, and methods, with the goal of learning more accurate models (from existing datasets). There are three main activities:
      - Transforming existing datasets into anomaly free ones, which can be used for learning models that are more accurate.
      - Improving used learning methods by introducing some knowledge-driven constraints in the learning process.
      - Adding new methods that can complement existing ones in the context of the above-mentioned uncertainties.
   c. Understanding, which is related to applying new models on real-time data for getting a better interpretation of the situations of interests (e.g., problem/anomaly detection). We assume that, as in the human-like cognition, this process can be iterative, i.e., understanding a process can generate data, which can be used for improving the learning process (like in reinforcement learning).
   d. Planning, for defining optimal actions based on system behaviour understanding.

B. Challenges for Cognition

There are several challenges to be addressed in order to realize the vision of CTs, with the most important ones discussed in the following.

1) Knowledge representation challenge

The first question to be clarified is how knowledge can be formally represented to enable the fact that a DT learns from experience and behaves intelligently, like a human. All cognitive services mentioned above heavily depend on this decision.

The more complex the representation of knowledge, the more difficult it is to acquire this knowledge automatically. However, more advanced reasoning services can be offered. Our goal is not only to support the decision-making process, but also to increase its accuracy and human-acceptance. Thus, both declarative and procedural knowledge is needed, as questions such as 'what?', 'how?', 'when?', 'in what context?', 'what-if?', etc., should be answered.

Several knowledge representation formalisms seem to be suitable for CTs. To clearly separate general knowledge from specific knowledge, it makes sense to structure the knowledge into two parts: ontologies for representing the domain knowledge and rules for representing the problem-solving knowledge.

To better understand a current situation (i.e., the asset itself, the context in which it is used, its environment, etc.), we consider using ontologies. They are a knowledge representation method that is on one hand expressive enough and on the other hand extensible. They could be used to:

- Represent the domain knowledge which includes the vocabulary domain-experts apply (e.g., brick wall, types of bricks like red shale or clay bricks, the features of bricks like thermal shock resistance or mechanical strength, etc.) as well as the constraints (e.g., temperature threshold at which the stone is unusable).
- Take into account existing standards for the domain (e.g., standards from the steel process industry for the use case described in Section IV).
- Support collaboration between DTs, e.g., for cooperative execution of complex tasks.

Although simple constraints (e.g., temperature of a ladle must not exceed a certain threshold) can be modelled by using ontologies, there are many scenarios where complex (functional or behavioural) constraints should be considered (e.g., calculations that include results of different physics-based/AI/statistic-based models).

To mimic the reasoning of human expert in solving knowledge intensive problems, there is a need to use rules (e.g., event condition action rules). Rules should be used even in the present of incomplete and/or uncertain information to (i) focus the attention to the most important aspects and (ii) collect additional, goal-oriented information relevant for a given context. This can be done by mapping of raw sensor data and/or outputs of different DT models to actions (such as control decisions or recommendations for human operators).

2) Knowledge acquisition challenge

The second challenge is collecting knowledge which is not only spread in different documents (e.g., excel tables) and software systems (e.g., error reports in MES systems), but could be also implicit as it is based on personal experience that is even more difficult to express. To make the tacit knowledge explicit and machine-understandable and machine-processable, different cognitive technologies could be used such as NLP, speech recognition, etc. For example, one possibility is to apply a speech-to-knowledge approach, as speech is relevant for the shop floor workers for short information interchange allowing hands-free conversations. Since in recent years the multilingual speech functionality has become a commodity available on smart speakers, mobile phones, and computers, the pre-existing solutions could be reused and added to the CT to enable speech communication channels with human operators. Ontologies can help achieving higher accuracy of resulting rules, as synonyms, multilingual aspects, context, etc., can be taken into account. In this way, the domain and problem-solving knowledge will be connected.

3) Knowledge update challenge

In addition to collecting knowledge, the ability to learn, to unlearn and continuously update knowledge is crucial for CTs to create competitive advantage. Knowledge update is however a complex process, which includes knowledge extension (e.g., adding a new entity in the ontology for new types of bricks), knowledge forgetting (removing an ontology entity representing material not used anymore for bricks) and knowledge evolution (e.g., changing a max temperature of a ladle). The similar strategies can be applied on the problem-solving rules. The challenge lies not only in ensuring the consistency after applying a change, but also more importantly in discovering the need for a change. This can be done by applying usage-driven strategies (e.g., by monitoring whether the proposed decisions were accepted by domain experts) or by using structure-driven methods (e.g., by using ontology-based reasoning to discover conflicting rules or generalized/specialized rules).

IV. Cognitive Digital Twin Use Case From the Process Industry

To illustrate the concept and role of CTs in process industry, a discussion on an application of such an approach to a real-world problem from steel production process industry is presented in this section. The use case shows how various hurdles concerning asset maintenance and predictive controls from the process industry can be further improved from its current state.

The steel production process typically has three stages. First, the scrap steel is collected and melted in an electric arc furnace. In the second stage, the molten melt is transferred to the ladles for secondary metallurgy. In the third and final step, the casting process, the molten steel is moulded to a desired shape. In the secondary metallurgy process, the molten metal is mixed with several substances (or impurities are removed) to produce the specific grades of steel depending upon the customer requirements. This process is carried out in specially developed ladles that are designed to withstand such extreme temperatures and condition for a sustained period. The inner walls of the ladles are lined with magnesium oxide bricks and carbon, which is worn out little by little with every heat. After a certain number of heats, typically ranging anywhere from 50 to 100 heats, these brick walls are so thinned down that the brick lining needs to be completely demolished, and a fresh batch of bricks are placed along the inner walls. The challenge here is that the decision about when/whether or not the bricks need to replaced is taken by a technician or an engineer by visually inspecting the brick conditions and also taking a look at the process parameters. If the brick linings are not sufficiently thick enough, molten steel in the ladle can leak from the ladle and flow into the factory floor potentially causing accidents. Due to the enormous risk to the health and safety of the workers in the production plant, the technician usually makes the decision about whether or not to re-line with fresh batch of bricks based on the "better safe than sorry" philosophy. The drawback of this approach is that if the bricks are replaced even if they really do not need to be replaced, it results in increased production overheads and costs for the company.

If one were to address this problem using DTs, a mathematical model that simulates the behaviour and degradation mechanism of the bricks in the ladle would be an obvious starting point. By developing advanced ML algorithms, it may be possible to develop programs that can predict when the bricks need to be replaced. In addition, it is possible to develop physics-based models that simulate the brick wall conditions when subjected to severe mechanical and thermal stresses, which can further improve the ML-based models to create a HT of the process. The CTs on the other hand will include the human intelligence factor in the models to deal with the uncertainty inherent in the process. One of the main challenges for resolving this problem is the lack of sufficient data, given that the process is rather complex. Ideally, it would help to detect false negatives; meaning decisions to replace the brick lining were taken even if it was not required. This however is not always available due to practical reasons. The models in the CTs would include instances that were exceptional and rare scenarios and decisions taken by the manual intervention to best suggest whether the bricks in the ladle will need be replaced or repaired.

V. Conclusion and Future Work

In this paper, we introduced the concept of CTs in the context of the process industry and proposed a CT architecture a baseline for building CTs. Despite recent attempts in defining CTs, the concept is still emerging; with various aspects and perspectives presented in the literature and no shared agreement on the scope of CT, other than extension of DTs with cognition elements. We reviewed the relevant definitions in the literature and provided our architectural perspective on the type of cognitive services needed for CTs in the context of process industry, identified the challenges for realizing the proposed cognitive services, and discussed their role in the context of a concrete use case in the process industry. Progress on cognitive architectures is seen through the development of hybrid representations that combine symbolic and numeric content, mechanisms for learning procedural and control knowledge, incorporation of large-scale knowledge structures, construction of embodied and interactive agents, and support for both declarative and episodic memories [9].

Less progress has been made in areas such as abductive understanding, dynamic memories that acquire new conceptual structures, creative aspects of problem solving, emotional processing, agent personality, along with plausibly related topics of metacognition and goal reasoning [9].

We plan to apply the CT approach in a set of use cases as follows:

- Operational optimization of gas treatment centre (GTC) in aluminium production, where CT of the GTC recommends optimal operating parameters for adsorption based on real-time data gathered about conditions such as the pressure, temperature, humidity, etc., from sensors.
- Minimize health & safety risks and maximize the metallic yield in Silicon (Si) production to provide best estimates of when the furnace can be emptied to the ladle for further operations.
- Real-time monitoring of finished steel products for operational efficiency with an ability to react on its own to situations requiring an intervention, thus stabilizing the production process further.
- Improving heat exchanger efficiency by predicting the deposition of unburnt fuel mixtures, ash and other particles on the heat-exchanger tubes based on both historical practices and real-time process.

As part of future work, we plan to validate the proposed cognitive services architecture in all these use cases.

Acknowledgment

The work in this paper is partly funded by the H2020 project COGNITWIN (grant number 870130, https://cognitwin.eu/). We thank the COGNITWIN consortium partners for fruitful discussions related to CT and the use case presented in this paper.

References

[1] "5 Trends that will influence the Telemetry Sector in 2020," [Online]. Available from: https://www.servelectechnologies.com/servelec-technologies/news/news-events/5-trends-that-will-influence-the-telemetry-sector-in-2020. [retrieved 2020.07.17].

[2] S. Abburu et al., "COGNITWIN – Hybrid and Cognitive Digital Twins for the Process Industry," IEEE International Conference on Engineering, Technology and Innovation (ICE/ITMC), 2020.

[3] J. Du et al., "Cognition digital twins for personalized information systems of smart cities: Proof of concept," Journal of Management in Engineering, vol. 36, no. 2, p. 04019052, 2020.

[4] P. Eirinakis et al., "Enhancing Cognition for Digital Twins," IEEE International Conference on Engineering, Technology and Innovation (ICE/ITMC), 2020, in press.

[5] A. El Adl, "Cognitive Digital Twins" [Online]. Talk at GE Predix IIOT Platform and Cognitive Digital Twins, 2016. Available from: https://www.slideshare.net/slideshow/embed_code/key/JB60Xqcn7QVyjb. [retrieved 2020.07.17].

[6] F. Fernández, Á. Sánchez, J. F. Vélez, and A. B. Moreno, "Symbiotic Autonomous Systems with Consciousness Using Digital Twins," International Work-Conference on the Interplay Between Natural and Artificial Computation, pp. 23-32, 05/2019.

[7] E. Gery, "Industry Transformation with IBM Digital Twin," [Online]. Available from: https://www-01.ibm.com/events/wwe/grp/grp309.nsf/vLookupPDFs/am2%20%20IBM%20Eran%20Gery%20%20CE%20strategy/%24file/am2%20%20IBM%20Eran%20Gery%20%20CE%20strategy.pdf. [retrieved 2020.07.17].

[8] N. Joshi, "AI and cognitive computing: are they different?" [Online]. Available from: https://www.allerin.com/blog/ai-and-cognitive-computing-are-they-different. [retrieved 2020.07.17].

[9] P. Langley, "Progress and Challenges in Research on Cognitive Architectures," AAAI'17: Proceedings of the Thirty-First AAAI Conference on Artificial Intelligence, February 2017, Pages 4870–4876.

[10] "LinkedIn Group: Cognitive Digital Twins," [Online]. Available from: https://www.linkedin.com/groups/8561450. [retrieved 2020.07.17].

[11] J. Lu, X. Zheng, A.Gharaei, K. Kalaboukas, D. Kiritsis "Cognitive Twins for Supporting Decision-Makings of Internet of Things Systems," Proceedings of 5th International Conference on the Industry 4.0 Model for Advanced Manufacturing. Springer, pp. 105-115, 2020.

[12] M. Mikell, and J. Clark, "Cheat sheet: What is Digital Twin?" [Online]. Available from: https://www.ibm.com/blogs/internet-of-things/iot-cheat-sheet-digital-twin. [retrieved 2020.07.17].

[13] C. Miskinis, "Is it possible to manufacture a digital twin that has cognitive functions," [Online]. Available from: https://www.challenge.org/insights/cognitive-digital-twins/. [retrieved 2020.07.17].

[14] F. Saračević, "Slideshare: Cognitive Digital Twin by Fariz Saračević," [Online]. Available from: https://de.slideshare.net/BosniaAgile/cognitive-digital-twin-by-fariz-saraevi. [retrieved 2020.07.17].

[15] R. Saracco, "Digital Twins: Bridging Physical Space and Cyberspace," IEEE Computer, vol. 52, no. 12, pp. 58-64, 2019.

[16] S. Somers, A. Oltramari, and C. Lebiere, "Cognitive Twin: A Cognitive Approach to Personalized Assistants," AAAI Spring Symposium: Combining Machine Learning with Knowledge Engineering, 2020.

A Hybrid Model Applied to the Vehicles Routing Problem With Simultaneous Pickups and Deliveries – VRPSPD

Pedro Pablo Ballesteros Silva
Facultad de Tecnología
Universidad Tecnológica de Pereira - UTP
Pereira, Colombia
e-mail: ppbs@utp.edu.co

Diana Paola Ballesteros Riveros
Centro de Comercio y Servicio
Servicio Nacional de Aprendizaje - SENA
Pereira, Colombia
e-mail: dipballesteros@sena.edu.co

Yanci Viviana Castro Bermudez
Facultad de Ingeniería Industrial
Universidad Tecnológica de Pereira - UTP
Pereira, Colombia
e-mail: yvcastro@utp.edu.co

Abstract— **Since many decades ago, one of the topics of greatest interest in research is that one related with the vehicle routing problem, present in many organizations. This, which is a transport problem, has multiple implications of economic, social, technological, and environmental order, when there is a provision of services to customers in the development and implementation of production processes, in the provisioning and distribution of goods and services, including carrying people within a determined time frame, with an adequate quality level. This paper presents a methodology to solve the homogeneous vehicles routing problem with simultaneous pickups and deliveries (VRPSPD) using matheuristics formed by the specialized genetic algorithm's Chu-Beasley and exact techniques of mixed integer linear programming, based on the Branch-and-Bound procedure. The VRPSPD problem considers a set of customers, whose demands of pick-up and delivery of products or people are known, and whose objective is to get the set of routes of minimal cost, which permit to satisfy the demand of the customers, considering the respective constraints of the system and the vehicles necessary for the completion of the same. Two new algorithms designed by the authors are implemented, which have been coded in C ++, obtaining good results in relatively short computing times, depending on the characteristics of the computers used.**

Keywords-constructive heuristic; exact techniques; genetic algorithm's Chu-Beasley; matheuristics.

I. Introduction

The issue related with the vehicles routing problem (VRP) constitutes a set of possibilities, which range from simple situations to high complexity problems that are currently subject of important research. The solution of VRP in practical terms consists of the identification of a series of routes of a set of vehicles to provide service to customers in the best way possible, in the development and implementation of the distribution and provisioning processes.

In its structure, the problem is oriented to the search of a set of optimal solutions, or solutions obtained through heuristics, metaheuristics or matheuristics, which are affected by diverse constraints related to the quantity of vehicles, their capacity, destination and demand sites, pick-up and delivery times, duration of routes, use of multiple depots, fleets of vehicles, among others.

The tours established in all the solutions start and finish in a depot, and the loading of the vehicles used is made up of the merchandise to be delivered and the merchandise which is simultaneously picked up from each customer, and in the combinatorial optimization, where many variables are considered with a good amount of parameters and the majority of their versions are of the NP-Hard class, as in their solving process the polynomial time is not worked.

One of the first researches concerning the vehicles routing problem with simultaneous pick-up and delivery (VRPSPD) arises by the year 1989, with the work carried out by Min [15], who developed a heuristic of three stages for a case study of a distribution system for the Franklin county public library, Ohio, where an important saving in time and distance was achieved through the application of a mathematical model.

The following is a list of the most important variants that this problem has presented from 1989 to 2019:

- Routing problems of multiple vehicles with simultaneous pick-up and delivery [15].
- Pick-up and delivery applying time windows [6].
- Pick-up and delivery systems [18].
- Routing problems with simple and multiple vehicles with simultaneous pick-up and delivery [12].
- Routing problems of multiple vehicles with pick-ups fractioning [13].
- Pick-up and delivery applying time windows and waiting times [7].
- Routing problems of a single vehicle with selective pick-up and delivery [11].

• Routing problems of multiple vehicles with load fractioning for pick up and deliveries [17].

• Routing problems of a single vehicle with pick-up and delivery based on customer satisfaction [8].

Vehicle routing problem with load fractioning for pick up and deliveries, applying time windows [1].

Flexible pick-up and delivery, applying time windows [23]

• Vehicles routing problems with pick-up and delivery VRPPD applying transport routes VRPPDSR [14].

Multiproduct inventory routing problem with transfer option and green approach IRP [25].

VRP with pick-up and delivery and transfer problem PDPT [26].

VRP with pick-up and delivery, time windows and contamination TWPDPRP [27].

• Oil routing and programming problems with fractioned pick-up and delivery GPDP [28].

VRP with synchronized pick-up and delivery SPD [29].

• VRP with pick-up and delivery with full loads FTPDP [30].

• VRP with simultaneous pick-up and delivery with constrained time [31].

VRP with pick-up and delivery, time windows and multiple products stacks PDPTWMS [32].

VRP with simultaneous pick-up and delivery and bi-dimensional loading constrains VRP2LSPD [33].

• Traveling Salesman problem with multi-product pick-up and delivery m-PDTSP [34].

• VRP with pick-up and delivery, time Windows, benefits and reserve requests PDPTWPR [35].

Other authors like [20] make a proposal of a general scheme of classification of the problems of delivery and pick up with their corresponding characteristics. The classification presents three groups:

• The first group is formed by the graph "many to many problems", where any vertex can be used as a source or as a destination. Its structure is similar to that of the Vehicle Routing Problem with simultaneous pick-up and delivery VRPDPD.

• The second group includes the problems of "one to many to one". Its equivalent is the Mixed Vehicle Routing Problem (MVRP). It is inferred here that the customer requests exclusively one of the services.

• The third group is formed by the one-to-one routing problems where each product is considered as a request coming from an origin and having a defined destination. An example of this case is the messenger operations and the door-to-door transport service.

On the other hand, it should be kept in mind that the application of exact methods for the solution of VRPSPD has had difficulties concerning the use and consideration of many variables and restrictions [5] [24]. This situation is easily overcome with the use of matheuristics, getting good solutions, very close to optimal in relatively short computing times, depending on the characteristics of the computers used.

Many of the applications of VRPSPD are found in the different processes of inverse logistics, where the enterprises should carry out activities of inverse flux management both for finished products and raw materials. Examples of these operations are found in the beer or soft drink's bottling plants, when customers are visited to whom bottles full of the product are delivered and from whom empty bottles are picked up, guaranteeing the synchronization of deliveries and pick-ups, accomplishing the customer's satisfaction, and getting the optimal route with the minimal impact in costs in the supply chain.

Another application of the VRPSPD is observed in the transport of passengers when they are moved and picked up in different locations; in the home delivery service, where goods or documents are delivered and picked up, or where money is picked up; in data transmission and reception; in electric energy transmission and reception; in production systems when raw materials are delivered and finished or semi-finished products are picked up. It is important to consider that VRPSPD is also applied when new products are delivered and outdated or obsolete products are picked up, in order to give them an appropriate final deposition.

In practice, these processes are carried out mostly in empirical form, incurring in high transportation costs, in strong environmental impact, and in a questionable level of service to the final customer. Therefore, the efforts leading to the improvement and scientific solution of this situation are another of the contributions and objectives of this work.

In addition to the introduction, this article includes the following parts: 2. Description of the problem. 3. Formulation of the mathematical model. 4. Description of the implementation of the genetic algorithm of Chu-Beasley to solve the VRPSPD problem. 5. Experimental results of the matheuristics, where the genetic algorithm of Chu-Beasley and exact techniques for a depot, 50 clients and 4 vehicles are applied. 6. Analysis of sensibility of the genetic algorithm of Chu-Beasley, with variation of the size of the population. 7. Conclusions, with a final relationship of the consulted references.

II. DESCRIPTION OF THE PROBLEM

The Vehicle Routing Problem Pickup and Delivery (VRPPD) has been considered as an extension of the Vehicle Routing Problem -VRP), where each vehicle that visits each customer only once.

Once on the road, one must not only deliver, but also pickup certain products with a 100% service level (Full service). Vehicles of the project considers several scenarios: a depot, a vehicle and several clients; a depot, several vehicles and many clients; several depots, several vehicles and must exit and arrive at a depot or distribution center.

The scope many clients incorporating environmental effects in this last variant. In practical terms, it consists of identifying a series of routes for a set of vehicles to provide delivery and pickup services to customers in the most appropriate way possible, in the development and execution of the supply and distribution processes.

The VRPSPD problem claims towards the search for a set of optimal solutions, or solutions obtained through heuristics (a procedure based on rules developed to determine a good quality solution to a specific problem), which are affected by different restrictions related to the number of vehicles, their capacity, places of destination and demand, delivery and pickup times, duration of the route, use of multiple depots, mixed vehicle fleet, among others.

The situations dealing with the pick-up and delivery of goods or people who must be transported between one origin and a destination, constitute a sort of vehicle routing problem, which must fulfill certain constrain of capability. Starting from the bibliographical revision made for this type of problem, it was found that there are three important groups, the description of which is presented below:

- Vehicle Routing Problem with Backhauls VRPBH. The situation outlined points out first to attend customers to whom merchandise is delivered and then from whom it is picked up [7].
- Mixed Vehicle Routing Problem MVRP. In this case, the customers require exclusively one of the services [15].
- Vehicle Routing Problem with Simultaneous Pickup and Delivery – VRPSPD. Here, the customers need the two services: deliver and pick up the merchandise or personnel, with a 100% service level, using one vehicle in one visit [2] [3] [24] [4].

In this work, we focus on this last group, where a deposit is considered: two sets, one of homogeneous capacity vehicles and another of customers whose delivery and pickup
demands of merchandise or people must be attended simultaneously, with a 100% service level. The objective of the solution is to find the set of routes that guarantee the fulfillment of the restrictions shown below:

- The defined routes must start and end in the deposit.
- The requirements of all the customers must be satisfied at the 100% of the service level.
- Each customer can be visited just on time in the selected route.
- In each of the customers or nodes of the route, the total of the load transported by the vehicles should not exceed its capacity. That is, situations of no feasibility are not accepted.

Figure 1 shows the graphic configuration of the VRPSPD for three vehicles with their respective routes.

III. FORMULATION OF THE MATHEMATICAL MODEL

The feasibility of the problem VRPSPD depends on the sequence of the found route to visit the customers, and it is determined when upon verification of the customer's demand, this does not exceed the capacity of the vehicles.

Below is the description of the formulation of the mathematical model, proposed by Dell'Amico et al [4], applied by [21], with the following notation:

A = set of arcs which consist of the pairs (i, j) e (j, i) for each edge $\{i, j\}$ ε E_k.

G = (V_k, E_k) = complete graph with vertexes V= {0, 1, 2… n}, where the vertex 0 represents the depot and the rest corresponds to the customers. Each edge $\{i, j\}$ ε E_k has a non-negative cost and each customer i ε V'=V-{0} = {1, 2, 3…... n}.

d_i = amount of merchandise or product that has to be delivered to the customer i.

p_i = amount of merchandise or product that has to be picked up from customer i.

c_{ij} = matrix of travelling costs or distances, i, j ε V.

C = {1, 2… m} = set of m homogeneous vehicles with capacity Q.

E_k = subset of $Vk*Vk$ that comprises all the possible arcs.

Decision variables:

x_{ij} { 1, if the k vehicle travels the arc (i, j) ε V of the selected route
0, in any other case.

D_{ij} = amount of products or merchandise pending to be delivered, which is transported in the arc (i, j).

Q = capacity of the homogeneous vehicles.

P_{ij} = amount of products or merchandise pending to be picked up, which is transported in the arc (i, j)

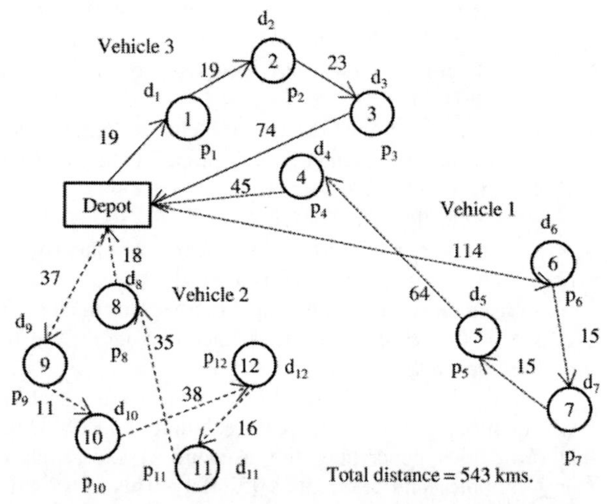

Figure 1. Graphic structure of the VRPSD for three vehicles.

The objective function and the constraints are presented below:

$$Z_{min}= \min \sum_{i\in V}\sum_{j\in V} c_{ij}x_{ij} \tag{1}$$

$$Z_{min}= \min \sum_{i\in V}\sum_{j\in V} c_{ij}x_{ij} \tag{2}$$

$$\sum_{j\in V} x_{ji} = 1 \quad \forall i \in V' \tag{3}$$

$$\sum_{j\in V'} x_{0j} \le m \tag{4}$$

$$\sum_{j\in V} D_{ji} - \sum_{j\in V} D_{ij} = d_i \quad \forall i \in V' \tag{5}$$

$$\sum_{j\in V} P_{ij} - \sum_{j\in V} P_{ji} = p_i \quad \forall i \in V' \tag{6}$$

$$D_{ij} + P_{ij} \le Qx_{ij} \quad \forall (i,j)\in A \tag{7}$$

$$D_{ij} \ge 0 \qquad \forall (i,j)\in A \tag{8}$$

$$P_{ij} \ge 0 \quad \forall (i,j)\in A \tag{9}$$

$$x_{ij} \in \{0,1\} \quad \forall (i,j)\in A \tag{10}$$

$$d_j x_{ij} \le D_{ij} \le (Q-d_i)x_{ij} \quad \forall (i,j)\in A \tag{11}$$

$$p_i x_{ij} \le P_{ij} \le (Q-p_j)x_{ij} \quad \forall (i,j)\in A \tag{12}$$

$$D_{ij} + P_{ij} \le (Q-\max\{0, p_j - d_j, d_i - p_i\})x_{ij} \quad \forall (i,j)\in A \tag{13}$$

$$x_{ij} + x_{ji} \le 1 \qquad \forall i,j,i<j,\in V' \tag{14}$$

The objective function (1) minimizes the addition of the travelling costs or travelled distances in the selected route. With the constraint (2), there is a guarantee for each customer to be visited just once in the selected route. The constraint (3) makes each vehicle to leave each node or customer once in the route. With constraint (4) it is assured that, each vehicle is used once at the most. The expressions (5), (6) and (7) are constraints that guarantee the conservation of the flow of the delivered and picked up products in the established routes.

The nature of the variables of decision and the conditions of non-negativity are presented in the restrictions (8), (9), and (10).

If there is an attempt to get a stronger inequality for the non-negativity of the constraint (8), this can be substituted for inequality (11), as Gouveia holds in his work published [10], whose characteristic is the use of narrower limits.

Following the same strategy presented before of using stronger inequalities for P_{ij}, constraint (9) can be substituted for (12) and (7) for (13). With inequality (14), we get that each edge non-adjacent to the depot travels once as a maximum.

IV. Description of the Implementation of the Chu-Beasley Genetic Algorithm for the Solution of VRPSPD.

One of the reasons to apply the diverse techniques to the exact methods in the solution of NP-Hard problems, to which the VRPSPD belong, is that they require a lot of computation time as the size of the population or customers increases, since it is necessary to keep in mind a great number of variables and constraints. The application of metaheuristics like the Chu-Beasley genetic algorithm has generated good answers in relatively short computation times in comparison with the exact methods.

As shown in [36], the Chu-Beasley genetic algorithm has some features that make it more efficient as the following: It uses the objective function to identify the value of the best quality solution and considers the no feasibility in the process of substitution of one solution generated in the implementation of the algorithm; it just substitutes one individual at a time in each generational cycle; to avoid the premature convergence to optimal local solutions, each individual that joins the population has to be different to all those who make up the current population; it includes an aspiration criteria, though the new individual does not meet the requisite of controlled diversity; it incorporates an stage of improvement, after the recombination, that from certain intra-route and inter-route strategies there is an evaluation of a feasible solution before deciding if it makes part of the current population.

The implementation of the Chu-Beasley genetic algorithm includes the following stages:

A. *Construction of the Initial Population*

It can be constituted by two components: a first component is the configurations of the routes obtained from some constructive heuristics, and a second component is the configurations of the routes obtained I a controlled randomly way. For each configuration, there is an evaluation of the objective function (fitness) and the no feasibility associated to the load of each vehicle in the routes. The presentation of a configuration or solution of the VRPSPD for 20 nodes or customers and their codification is shown in Figure 2.

The length of the configuration or solution remains defined by the quantity of customers or nodes attended by the vehicles. It is important to note that the routes are determined by the capacities of the vehicles and by the

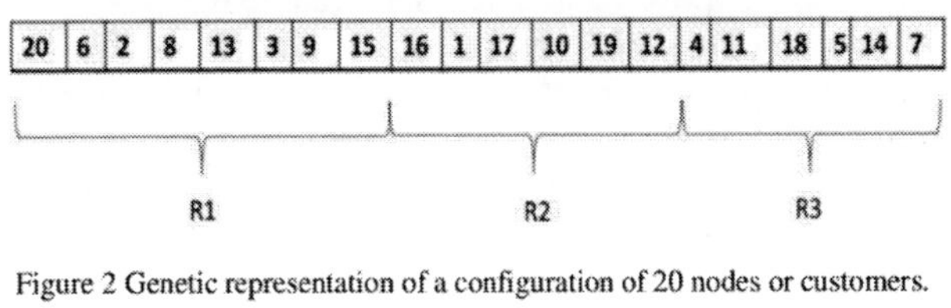

Figure 2 Genetic representation of a configuration of 20 nodes or customers.

quantities of the products that have to be delivered and picked up from each customer.

The input data are the matrix of costs or distances c_{ij}; the quantity of products to deliver d_i; the amount of products to pick up p_i; the amount of vehicles k with homogeneous capacity Q.

The parameters of the Chu-Beasley genetic algorithm: recombination rate = 0.80; mutation rate= 0.05.

In each configuration generated from the Chu-Beasley genetic algorithm, we get the value of the objective function (fitness), showing the feasibility or no feasibility of the route and the load of each vehicle assigned in the different subroutes or vehicles of the configuration. From the values of the objective function and the feasibility of the configurations or individuals, the genetic operators described in item *B* are used.

B. Genetic Operators

Three genetic operators are used in this work: Selection, recombination and mutation, whose procedures are detailed below.

1) Selection

In this stage, we use the method of selection by tournament. Two tournaments are carried out with the participation of all individuals of the current population k individuals are selected randomly, among whom the values of their objective functions and their no feasibilities are compared, selecting that who has the best value of the objective function if the k individuals are feasibility, or selecting that who has the least no feasibility if the k individuals are no feasibility. In the case of the presence of feasibility and no feasibility individuals, the feasibility individual with better objective function is selected. Two parents are left from these two tournaments, which pass on to the stage of recombination.

2) Recombination

This operator facilitates the exchange of information present in the two parents, and generates two descendants who own genetic material from parent 1 and parent 2. In this algorithm, which is elitist, just one of the children passes on to the current population. There are several techniques for the recombination, as: single-point crossover, two-point crossover, uniform crossover, partially mapped crossover (PMX), order-based crossover (OBX), Cycle crossover (CX), multi-parents crossover (MPX), longest common subsequence crossover (LCSX), among others. In this work, several forms of recombination are applied which explain the so-called PMX method, whose procedure is:

- Starting from the two parents P_1 and P_2 a common random segment is selected and copied in the child from P_1. From the first crossover point, elements i of this segment that have not been copied are sought in P_2. Para each element of these elements i, it is sought what elements j have been copied in its position from P_1.
- To place i in the taken position j from P_2, results in finding that said element is not there, since it has been copied before. If the place taken by j in P_2 has already been filled in the child k, i is placed in the position taken by k in P_2. The remaining elements are obtained from P_2, ending the process (See Figure 3).

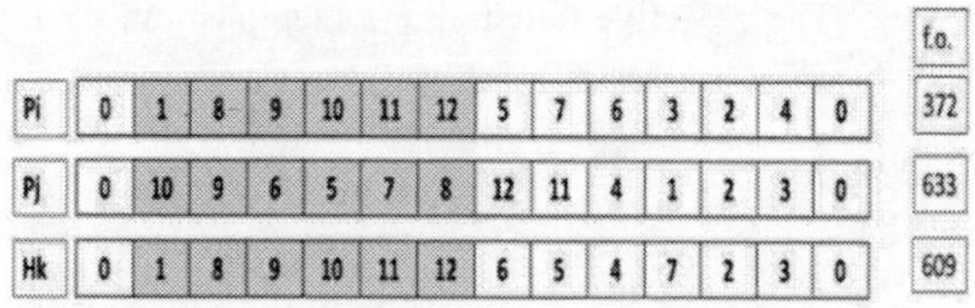

Figure 3 Application of the recombination PMX in a configuration of twelve customers. P_i, P_j are parents and H_k is the child resulting from the recombination.

Several recombination rates were used, 0.8 being the one with the best results.

3) Mutation

With this operator, some changes are made or parts of the resulting solution in the recombination are altered. This mechanism has the capacity to modify the current solution, applying small alterations. The mutation rate applied in this work is 0.05. There are several strategies that can help in this stage, like:

- Inter-routes local search through the shift (1, 0), shift (2, 0), shift (3, 0) strategy, with which 1, 2, 3 customers are transferred from one route to another.
- Inter-routes local search through the swaft (1, 1), swaft (2, 1), swap (2, 2), which facilitates the exchange of 1, 2 or 3 customers from one route to another.

Intra-routes local search. In this case, neighboring criteria from the customers are considered in order to make movements in the same route.

The strategies that can be applied are Rotation and 2-Opt. This is a local search algorithm proposed by Croes in 1958 to solve the problem of the travel agent. The idea is to consider a route that crosses over itself and reorder it to avoid such crossover.

In this work, several exchange strategies were used, and a swap (1, 1) application is described, for example, in order to exchange customer 3 of the route 3 for customer 4 of the route 1 of the next configuration, as it is shown in Figure 4.

As it can be observed, with the applied swap (1, 1) strategy in the mutation we find a configuration with an incumbent, which passes on to the process of improvement.

C. Process of improvement of an individual

After the selection, of the recombination and mutation, each configuration is subject to a stage of local improvement,

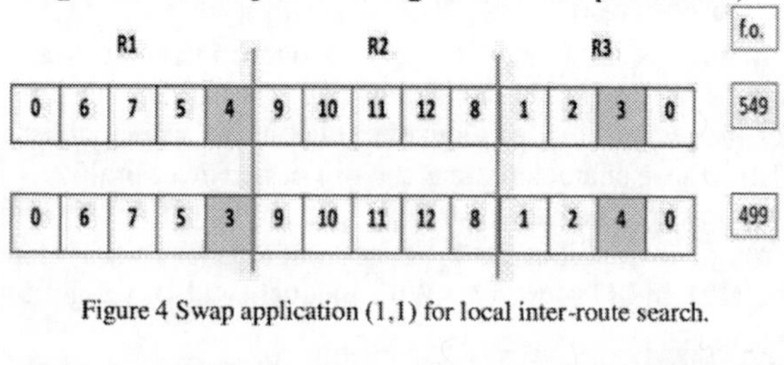

Figure 4 Swap application (1,1) for local inter-route search.

which consists of separating the routes individually and constructing sub-problems of a single route each one, and a deposit, with fewer customers that the complete problem, which are solved using the branch-and-cut exact technique, and the partial routes are constructed through optimal solutions. The resulting configuration passes on to the replacement stage.

D. Replacement stage

Here, there is a comparison of the resulting configurations of the previous stages with the individuals of the current population. A replacement is made for one of the individuals of the population, privileging the feasibility over the no feasibility and objective function when feasible solutions are compared.

V. EXPERIMENTAL RESULTS OF THE MATHEURISTICS WHERE THE CHU- BEASLEY GENETIC ALGORITHM AND EXACT TECHNIQUES ARE APPLIED FOR A DEPOT, 50 CUSTOMERS AND 4 VEHICLES.

In the literature associated to the VRPSPD three types of testing problems are known: Dethloff proposed 40 reference instances with 50 customers and the quantity of vehicles was 4,9 and 10 [5], Salhi and Nagy worked 14 instances, the quantity of customer was in the range of 50-199 and the vehicles used were 3,4,5,6,7 and 10 [19], and Montané and Galvão used 12 instances with 100-200 customers and the quantity of vehicles were 3,5,9, 10,12,16,23, and 28 [16]. The experimental tests were carried out with some of the instances proposed by Dethloff and the solutions with the best optimal limits have been published in the specialized literature [22] [9].

The applied methodology is, consequently, a hybrid of the Chu-Beasley genetic algorithm and mixed integer linear programming. The respective computing results are presented in Table I, using the Dethloff CON 3-8 instance. As can be observed in the Table I, out of 24 experiments, two configurations with values of the objective function of **537.63** and **537.36** were obtained, which compared with **523.05** that is the reported value by [20] as the optimal value of the instance, show good results in relatively short computing times (13.77 min and 14.45 min respectively) against the 32.05 minutes requires in [20]. Then, starting from the configuration obtained applying the Chu-Beasley genetic algorithm with the value of the objective function of 537, 36, the four routes travelled by the four vehicles are considered.

Each route is treated as a small linear programming problem, which may be solved easily with the corresponding mathematical model. In other words, we are applying the matheuristics, which supported by a good configuration produced by the Chu-Beasley genetic algorithm, with two constructive algorithms designed by the authors.

TABLE I. COMPUTATIONAL RESULTS IN THE IMPLEMENTATION OF THE CHU-BEASLEY GENETIC ALGORITHM USING THE CON3-8 INSTANCE OF DETHLOFF

Number of experiments	Population size	Last generation in which the best objective function was maintained	A	B	C(s)
1	200	9,546,568	539.28	539.22	826.58
2	200	169,195,900	631.47	634.56	6022.13
3	200	14,797,376	604.41	606.86	621.71
4	200	18,281,904	601.59	604.66	865.83
5	200	25,751,135	566.4	569.15	1296.69
6	200	3,875,938	618.01	620.88	272.66
7	200	21,615,848	606.92	608.98	750.13
8	200	13,634,095	538.78	543.38	612.28
9	200	6,847,952	543.45	545.59	413.04
10	200	2,136,193	690.19	692.52	196.78
11	200	1,557,888	601.54	604.33	101.57
12	200	1,795,437	610.41	614.69	107.84
13	200	139,029	676.67	701.18	51.40
14	200	7,860,846	612.69	613.77	216.72
15	200	6,991,854	546.82	550.75	411.33
16	200	594,774	605.87	609.91	134.55
17	200	16,078,477	644.01	646.70	523.78
18	200	41,765,529	593.76	597.38	1131.61
19	200	44,159,790	551.33	553.53	1378.16
20	200	12,396,611	584.14	586.64	803.85
21	200	17,381,286	537.36	541.40	866.87
22	200	19,271,996	602.20	604.85	851.25
23	200	105,346,307	567.76	579.51	4786.89
24	200	50,972,211	571.41	573.79	1836.32

A: Best value of the objective function in the respective generation,
B: Worst value of the objective function in the respective generation.
C: Computation time for the related number of generations (seconds).

The first algorithm generates the traveling matrices and the amount of the products to be delivered and picked up from each customer (node) of each of the routes. The second algorithm permits the control of the load for each route, data necessary for the mixed integer linear mathematical programming model to be applied. The resulting solutions in this case for the four routes are observed in Table II.

Next, the description of the matrix generator called array generation algorithm and clustering algorithm are presented.

A. Array generator algorithm

This algorithm is applied to the best configuration or the incumbent configuration obtained from the AGCB. Its description is:

- Start: the best configuration of the AGCB is taken.
- Considering the capacity of each vehicle, customers are assigned sequentially until their capacity is exhausted.
- The previous action is repeated for the rest of the vehicles until the last customer of the AGCB configuration.
- The configurations established for each vehicle are the basis for generating the distance matrices and the quantities to be delivered and collected in each sequence.
- Once the matrices for each vehicle have been generated, they become small problems to which the mathematical model encoded in GAMS is applied separately, obtaining the optimal solution for each vehicle.

• With the integration of the solutions for each vehicle, a new configuration.

B. Clustering algorithm

This algorithm is applied before using the Chu - Beasley AGCB genetic algorithm). It consists of the following phases:

Phase 1:

• Be based on known instances for multiple depots. If the instances are given in coordinates, the distance between customers and between them and the depot is calculated.
• The closest neighbor heuristic is applied, assigning the closest customers to each depot, regardless of their capacity.

Phase 2:

• With the previous result, the capacity of each depot is evaluated taking into account the assigned customers. That is, if depots are overloaded, the difference between the current depot and the other depots is calculated.

• Determine if there are reassignable depots. If the answer is affirmative, the depot with the shortest distance is chosen and it is analyzed whether said depot has the capacity to receive one or more clients.

• If the answer is affirmative, the client (s) are reassigned to said depot, considering the capacity of the depot.

• The previous action is repeated until all clients are assigned to depots without exceeding their capacity.

• Each depot remains with its respective clients, obtaining feasible assignments. Once the allocation for each depot is known with its respective clients, the AGCB is applied for each depot.

TABLE II. SOLUTIONS OBTAINED WITH MIXED INTEGER LINEAR PROGRAMMING.

Routes	Sequence of the routes	Solution	Best possible solution
Route vehicle 1	dep 25 27 42 36 37 24 4 9 2 43 50 31 29 39 dep	194.71	190.26
Route vehicle 2	dep 14 21 22 12 6 41 18 15 26 19 48 49 3 dep	128.74	116.52
Route vehicle 3	dep 35 45 16 5 10 30 1 13 17 32 44 28 33 7 46 20 47 8 11 dep	183.73	183.73
Route vehicle 4	dep 40 23 38 34 dep	31.30	31.30
	Total distance traveled	**538.48**	
	Total distance from Chu Beasley	**539.28**	
	Optimal solution according to Subramanian (20)	**523.05**	

VI. Analysis of Sensibility of the Chu-Beasley Genetic Algorithm Varying the Size of Population

The analysis of sensibility may be made for different scenarios. For example, it can be made for evaluating the performance of the algorithm varying the recombination rate, the mutation rate, modifying the techniques for selection of parents for the recombination, or varying the size of the population.

In this research for reasons of space in this paper, the analysis is done to evaluate the performance of the algorithm by varying the size of the population. In Table IV shows the results of several generations with their corresponding objective function (fitness) for three population sizes: 100, 200 and 300 configurations.

It can be observed both in Table III and in Figure 5 concerning the results of the evolutionary process in these tests or experiments that for the size of the population of 300 the value of the objective function differs significantly from the values for the other two sizes.

Between the size of 200 and 100 the incumbent (best solution accomplished in the process) is obtained for the size of 200, result which gets stable starting from 6.000.000 generations, placing itself with likelihood in a local optimal solution (537,36) which at any rate is very close to the optimal solution found by [20].

The implementation of the Chu-Beasley genetic algorithm was made in C++ from the configurations obtained with the best objective functions, each of the routes defined in the solution was considered as a sub-problem which was solved by the exact method, using the CPLEX Optimization Studio software, version 12.4, and was run in

TABLE III. ANALYSIS OF SENSIBILITY FOR DIFFERENT POPULATION SIZES IN MULTIPLE GENERATIONS IN THE IMPLEMENTATION OF THE CHU – BEASLEY ALGORITHM USING THE DETHLOFF CON 3-8 INSTANCE.

Population size			Generation of evolutive process	Objetive function . OF (100)	Objetive function . OF (200)	Objetive function . OF (300)
100	200	300	500,000	668,06	670,73	677,91
100	200	300	1,000,000	594,55	591,68	665,57
100	200	300	1,500,000	589,76	589,35	658,70
100	200	300	2,000,000	555,06	589,35	652,20
100	200	300	2,500,000	550,81	589,35	651,09
100	200	300	3,000,000	550,82	586,48	651,09
100	200	300	3,500,000	550,83	579,25	650,88
100	200	300	4,000,000	550,84	572,81	650,88
100	200	300	4,500,000	550,85	571,37	650,17
100	200	300	5,000,000	550,86	555,82	650,17
100	200	300	5,500,000	550,87	547,78	650,17
100	200	300	6,000,000	550,88	537,36	650,17
100	200	300	6,500,000	550,89	537,36	650,17
100	200	300	7,000,000	550,90	537,36	650,17
100	200	300	7,500,000	550,91	537,36	650,17
100	200	300	8,000,000	537,36	537,36	650,17
100	200	300	8,500,000	537,37	537,36	650,17
100	200	300	9,000,000	537,38	537,36	650,17

TABLE IV: CHARACTERISTICS OF THE COMPUTERS USE

Lenovo B40 Laptop	Dell Latitude E6500 Laptop	Lenovo Personal Computer
Intel processor core (TM) 1.70 GHz – 2.40 GHz x4.	Intel processor core (TM)2 Duo 2.80 GHz – 2.80 GHz.	Intel Processor Core (TM) 3.00 GHz – 3.00 GHz x4.
RAM memory: 4.00 GB	RAM memory: 4.00 GB	RAM memory: 8.00 GB
64 bits OS.	64 bits OS.	64 bits OS.

three computers with the following characteristics. (See Table IV).

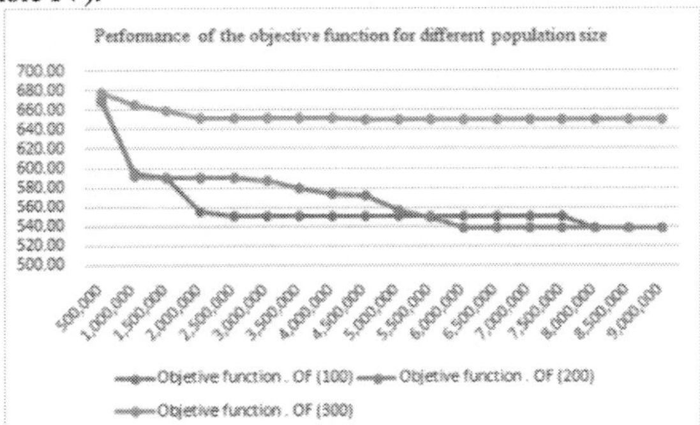

Figure 5 Performance of the objective function for different population size

VII. CONCLUSIONS

The proposed matheuristic and applied in this research, which combined the Chu - Beasley genetic algorithm and the exact technique based on the Branch and Cut algorithm, incorporated in the GAMS software, was a very good alternative to solve the VRPSPD for large sizes of clients or nodes with a single depot or multiple depots, where due to the nature of NP-Hard problems, mixed linear integer programming (MILP) does not solve them within an acceptable time frame. One of the critical stages in the implementation of the genetic algorithm of Chu & Beasley [20] was the synchronization of the parameters used.

With the two-phase methodology (genetic algorithm of Chu & Beasley [20] with the exact technique based on linear programming) and the incorporation of constructive heuristic algorithms, provided by the author for the generation of routes from the configuration with the incumbent of Chu & Beasley [20], the route matrices were obtained with the determination of the number of customers per route from the load control per vehicle. This methodology considerably facilitated the application of the matheuristic proposed in this research and allowed through certain sensitivity analyzes the evaluation of the performance of the algorithm used, being able to verify that its implementation was efficient and worked well.

It should be taken into account that the mathematical statistics do not guarantee the obtaining of an optimal global solution of the problems, but they did generate good solutions in very reasonable computation times, depending on the characteristics of the computer equipment used.

This research showed a classification of the VRPSPD, according to some of its variants and applied solution methods. As the complexity of the problem increases, the interest of researchers to apply metaheuristics or hybrid methods in its solution grows, including, as in this case, the proposed matheuristic.

The vast majority of the articles reviewed referred to real situations, which makes the application of solution techniques more interesting.

The trend of heuristics for the VRPSPD allowed the development of new algorithms with a good level of performance that, in general, required significant computation times in their processes.

The proposed matheuristic considered the costs of the routes (measured in distances) and their environmental impact (CO_2 generation), from which it was deduced that the amount of fuel used depends on the number of depots and vehicles used in the execution of deliveries and pickups.

The results achieved with the applied matheuristic can become a starting point for new research, since at present there are no known research that include the proposed matheuristic.

In its objectives, this research contributed to knowledge through the discovery of new contributions, also in the application of existing knowledge to new situations, or the connection of previously unrelated events in the specialized literature, and with it important contributions were made, which were described in this document.

REFERENCES

[1] P. Belfiorea and H. Yoshizaki. "Heuristic methods for the fleet size and mix vehicle routing problem with time windows and split deliveries". *European Journal of Operational Research-ELSEVIER.* Part B 40. pp. 589-601, 2013.

[2] N. Bianchessi and G. Righini. "Heuristic algorithms for the vehicle routing problem with simultaneous pickup and delivery" [Journal] // *Computer and Operation Research Elsevier*, vol.36 (12), pp.3215-3223, 2007.

[3] E. Cao and M. Lai.2009. "An improved differential evolution algorithm for the vehicle routing problem with simultaneous pickups and deliveries and time windows". *European Journal of Operational Research-ELSEVIER. Engineering Applications of Artificial Intelligence*, pp. 188-195, 2009.

[4] M. Dell'Amico, G. Righini, and M. Salani. "A branch-and-price approach to the vehicle routing problem with simultaneous distribution and collection". *Transportation Science*, 40(2), pp. 235–247, 2006.

[5] J. Dethloff. "Vehicle routing problem and reverse logistics: the vehicle routing problem with simultaneous delivery and pick-up" [Journal]. - Springer Berlin: *Operation Research Spectrum*, vol. 23, pp.79 -96, 2001.

[6] Y. Dumas, J. Desrosiers and F. Soumis. "The pickup and delivery problem with time windows". *European Journal of Operational Research-ELSEVIER.* Vol. 54, pp. 7-22, 1991.

[7] A. Fabri and P. Recht. "On dynamic pickup and delivery vehicle routing with several time windows and waiting times". *European Journal of Operational Research-ELSEVIER.* Part B 40. pp. 335–350, 2006.
[8] J. Fan. "The vehicle routing problem with simultaneous pickup and delivery based on customer satisfaction". *European Journal of Operational Research-ELSEVIER*, pp. 5284- 5289, 2011.
[9] Y. Gajpal and P. Abad. "An ant colony system (acs) for vehicle routing problem with simultaneous delivery and pickup". Computers & Operations Research, vol. 36 (12), pp. 3215–3223, 2009.
[10] L. Gouveia. "A result on projection for the vehicle routing problem". *European Journal of Operational Research*, pp. 610–624, 1995.
[11] I. Gribkovskaiaa, G. Laporte and A. Shyshou, "The single vehicle routing problem with deliveries and selective pickups". *European Journal of Operational Research-ELSEVIER.* Part B 40. pp. 2908-2924, 2008.
[12] I. Karaoglan, F. Altiparmak, I. Kara, I., & Dengiz, B. "A branch and cut algorithm for the location routing problem with simultaneous pickup and delivery. *European Journal of Operational Research-ELSEVIER.* pp. 318-332, 2011.
[13] C. G. Lee, M. A. Epelman, C. C. White III and Y. A. Bozer. "A shortest path approach to the multiple-vehicle routing problem with split pickups". *European Journal of Operational Research-ELSEVIER.* Part B 40. pp. 265-284, 2006.
[14] R. Masson, S. Ropke, F. Lehuédé and O. Péton. "A branch, cut, and price approach for the pickup and delivery problem with shuttle routes". *European Journal of Operational Research-ELSEVIER*, vol. 236, Issue 3, pp. 849-862, 2014.
[15] H. Min. "The multiple vehicle routing problem with simultaneous delivery and pick up points". *Transportation Research*. Vol. 23. No. 5, pp. 377-386, 1989.
[16] F.A.T Montané and R.D Galvao. "A tabu search algorithm for vehicle routing problem with simultaneous pickup and delivery services". *European Journal of Operational Research, 33, 3 // Computers and Operation Research Elsevier*, pp. 595 -619, 2006.
[17] M. Nowak, O. Ergun and C. White III Chelsea. "An empirical study on the benefit of split loads with the pickup and delivery problem". *European Journal of Operational Research-ELSEVIER.* Part B 40, pp. 734-740, 2009.
[18] S. N. Parragh, K. F. Doerner, R. F. Hartl. "A survey on pickup and delivery problems" Part II: Transportation between pickup and delivery locations. *Institut fur Betriebswirtschaftslehre*, Universitat Wien Brunnerstr. 72, 1210 Wien, Austria, 2008.
[19] S. Salhi and G. A. Nagy. "A cluster insertion heuristic for single and multiple depot vehicle routing problems with backhauling" [Journal]. - [s.l.]: *Journal of the Operational Research Society*, Vol. 50, no. 10, pp. 1034 – 1042, 1999.
[20] A. Subramanian. (2012) "Heuristics exact and hybrid approaches for vehicle routing problems". Universidade Federal Fluminense. Tesis Doctoral. Niteroi. pp. 13, 17, 19.
[21] A. Subramanian, L. Satoru, E. Uchoa. "New Lower Bounds for the Vehicle Routing Problem with Simultaneous Pickup and Delivery". *9th International Symposium, SEA* Ischia Island, Napoles, Italy, may 20/22, pp. 276-287, 2010.
[22] A. Subramanian, L. M. A. Drummond, C. Bentes, L. S. Ochi, and R. Farias. "A parallel heuristic for the vehicle routing problem with simultaneous pickup and delivery". *Computers & Operations Research*, Vol. 37, Issue 11, pp. 1899-1911, 2010.
[23] H. Wang and Y. Chen. "A coevolutionary algorithm for the flexible delivery and pickup problem with time windows". *European Journal of Operational Research-ELSEVIER.* International Journal of Production Economics. pp. 4-13, 2013.
[24] E. Zachariadis, C. Tarantilis and C. Kiranoudis. "A hybrid methaheuristic algorithm for the vehicle routing problem with simultaneous delivery and pick - up service" [Journal]. - [s.l.]: *Expert System with Aplications*, Vol. 36, Issue 2, part 1, pp. 1070 -1081, 2009.
[25] E. Zachariadis, C. D. Tarantilis, and C.T. Kiranoudisb, "The vehicle routing problem with simultaneous pickups and deliveries and two dimensional loading constraints", *European Journal of Operational Research – ELSEVIER*, vol. 251, pp. 369-386, 2016.
[26] A. Subramanian, E. Uchoa, A. Alves Pessoa, and L. Satoru Ochi, "Branch and cut with lazy separation for the vehicle routing problem with simultaneous pickup and delivery". *European Journal of Operational Research-ELSEVIER,* vol. 39, Issue 5, pp. 338-341, 2011.
[27] Y. Li, H. Chen, and C. Prins, "Adaptive large neighborhood search for the pickup and delivery problem with time windows, profits, and reserved requests", *European Journal of Operational Research – ELSEVIER,* vol. 252, pp. 27-38, 2016.
[28] F. Hennig, B. Nygreena, K. C. Furmanb, and J. Song, "Alternative approaches to the crude oil tanker routing and scheduling problem with split pickup and split delivery", *European Journal of Operational Research – ELSEVIER*, vol. 243, pp.41-51, 2015.
[29] T. Gschwind, "A comparison of column generation approaches to the synchronized pickup and delivery problem", European Journal of Operational Research – ELSEVIER, vol. 247, pp. 60-71, 2015.
[30] M. Gendreaua, J. Nossackb, and E. Pesch, "Mathematical formulations for a 1- full truckload pickup and delivery problem". *European Journal of Operational Research – ELSEVIER*, vol. 242, pp. 1008-1016, 2015.
[31] O. Polata, C. B. Kalaycia, O. Kulaka, and H. Otto, "A perturbation based variable neighborhood search heuristic for solving the vehicle routing problem with simultaneous pickup and delivery with time limit", *European Journal of Operational Research - ELSEVIER*, vol. 242, pp. 369-382, 2015.
[32] M. Cherkesly, G. Desaulniers, S. Irnich, and G. Laporte, "Branch price and cut algorithms for the pickup and delivery problem with time windows and multiple stacks", *European Journal of Operational Research – ELSEVIER*, vol. 250, pp. 782-793, 2016.
[33] E. Zachariadis, C. D. Tarantilis, and C.T. Kiranoudisb, "The vehicle routing problem with simultaneous pickups and deliveries and two dimensional loading constraints", *European Journal of Operational Research – ELSEVIER*, vol. 251, pp. 369-386, 2016.
[34] H. Hernández, I. Rodríguez, and J. J. Salazar, "A hybrid heuristic approach for the multi-commodity pickup and delivery traveling salesman problem", *European Journal of*

Operational Research – ELSEVIER, vol. 251, pp. 44-52, 2016.

[35] Y. Li, H. Chen, and C. Prins, "Adaptive large neighborhood search for the pickup and delivery problem with time windows, profits, and reserved requests", *European Journal of Operational Research – ELSEVIER*, vol. 252, pp. 27-38, 2016.

[36] R. Gallego, E. Toro y A. Escobar, "Técnicas Heurísticas y Metaheurísticas", *Colección de trabajos de Investigación Editorial UTP*, pp.158-162, 2015.

The Dictionary Game: Toward a Characterization of Lexical Primitives Using Graph Theory and Relational Concept Analysis

Mickaël Wajnberg, Jean-Marie Poulin, Alexandre Blondin Massé and Petko Valtchev

Département d'informatique, Université du Québec à Montréal, Montreal, Quebec, Canada H3C 3P8
Emails: wajnberg.mickael@courrier.uqam.ca poulinjm@gmail.com
blondin_masse.alexandre@uqam.ca valtchev.petko@uqam.ca

***Abstract*—In language theory and cognition, the search for a minimal set of language primitives from which every other concept could be defined is an ever-recurring topic. In order to help identify such primitives, a serious game was designed, where the player has to produce a meaningful lexicon as small as possible, starting by defining a single word and, recursively, all those appearing in any definition. Using simple graph theory and relational concept analysis (RCA), we extracted association rules from feature tables while putting in common the newly discovered abstractions into the overall knowledge data discovery process. The utility of the mined rules has been validated by the success in linking the dictionaries structural attributes to the psycholinguistics characteristics of the words they contain.**

***Keywords*–Lexicon; Dictionary; Relational concept analysis; Cicularity; Association rule; Serious game.**

I. Introduction

If someone is trying to learn a new language using only a dictionary, he must first identify a set of words in the foreign language's dictionary that he can relate to words in his mother tongue. one must also ensure that this set of words covers the lexical primitives (assuming that they exist) of the foreign language, *i.e.*, a set of "indecomposable" words sufficiently large to span all the other words of the language. The process of acquiring the first words of the foreign dictionary is addressed by the so-called *symbol grounding problem*, which was formalized in 1990 [1]. The task is all the more difficult when the alphabets do not match, like Mandarin or Arabic. It is nevertheless achievable, and even characteristic of the work of palaeographers aiming to understand extinct languages.

To identify such lexical primitives of a language, some authors put forward the concept of *minimal grounding sets* (MGS) of dictionaries, *i.e.*, minimum size sets of dictionary words from which one can define all the other words in a dictionary [2][3]. To properly characterize these MGS, it is necessary to understand both their structural aspect and their description from a psycholinguistic point of view [3].

By means of *association rules*, we analyze in this article a body of small dictionaries produced by human players as an artefact of a serious game called "Dictionary Game". These association rules are derived using a mathematical procedure known as *Relational Concept Analysis* (RCA) [4], an extension of *Formal Concept Analysis* (FCA) [5]. First, in Section II, we detail the context of the study. Section III introduces the formalization of a dictionary. Next, in Section IV, we describe in more detail "The Dictionary Game", which supplies our datasets. Finally, Section V is devoted to the description of the characteristics of the data set and the experiment carried out.

II. Symbol Grounding and Lexical Primitives

In language theory, as well as in cognitive science, the search for lexical primitives has been a very active subject for several decades [6][7]. These primitives form a set of lexical units, such that any word in a language can be defined from them. In theory, we can integrate in an iterative way this collection to eventually define all the words of a dictionary. To be really helpful in this purpose, a valuable set of lexical primitives should both contain as few words as possible and be as expressive as possible.

One of the famous first attempt to identify a minimum set of lexical primitives was made in 1930 by Ogden [8]. Although he did not succeed in constructing a universal language, one can still retrieve his word list [9]. Emphasizing the timeless aspect of this line of research, the graph structure of Ogden's Basic English Word List was even recently studied [10].

In 1972, Wierzbicka introduced a group of 14 semantic primitives, which she considers to be universal *Semantic Primitives* [11]. Pursuing this line of research for two decades, she extended her list of words to more than 50 semantic primitives and has shown that they can be translated into a large number of languages [12]. Not long ago, Browne et *al.* have constructed several "general" lists of words, such as the *New General Service List* [13][14]. These word lists, carefully chosen to meet the requirements of lexical primitives, have been used primarily for teaching English, but have also been used in other contexts [15]. More recently, Goddard proposed a *Minimal English* based on Wierzbicka's theory [16]. It aims to manually build a set of basic English words which allow to describe a large number of more complex words, which are translatable into many different languages [16]. Its main goal is to provide a basic language as an effective entry point for learning English as a secondary language.

Although useful in practice, all these approaches start by proposing a set of primitives and try, from these, to construct as many concepts as possible. However, the authors of these methods emphasize that they should not be considered as complete and definitive [17]. Even the notion of "indecomposability" is not obvious: Wierzbicka's list of 65 primitives includes the concepts NOT, GOOD and BAD; however, one could argue that among the concepts GOOD and BAD, at least one of them could be removed, since each can be defined by combining the other with the negation concept NOT, *i.e.*, GOOD = NOT BAD and BAD = NOT GOOD.

Still in response to the problem of symbol grounding, a complementary approach was developed by Blondin Massé et al. [2]. As an alternative to a fixed set of word primitives, the authors propose to calculate the MGS for dictionaries, *i.e.*, identify in a dictionary a minimum set of words which allow to define in an iterative manner all the other words. Although the number of MGS for a dictionary can be exponential with respect to its number of words, all MGS seem to share common psycholinguistic characteristics [3]. Indeed, it has been shown that these words tend to be used more frequently, learned younger and are more concrete [3]. For these psycholinguistic variables (age of acquisition, frequency, concreteness), one can also note a difference, depending on the part of the dictionary in which a word is found.

When taking a closer look at several MGS, other interesting features have been observed. Indeed, the authors of [3] focused on the largest strongly component connected (SCC), called the *core* of a dictionary, and compared it to the smallest remaining SCC, called the *satellites*. They found out that, when partitionning the MGS into two parts, one in the core and the other in the satellites, the words in the core are more frequent, more abstract and learned earlier, unlike those found in the satellites [3]. Thus, the core seems to mirror some abstraction occurring in the mental lexicon.

III. PRELIMINARIES

We now recall the terminology about lexicons and graphs. Formalism on lexicons is adaptated from [18].

Definition 1. [18] A *complete disambiguated lexicon* is a quadruple $X = (\mathcal{A}, \mathcal{P}, \mathcal{L}, \mathcal{D})$ where

- $\mathcal{A}$ is a finite *alphabet*, whose elements are *letters*;
- $\mathcal{P}$ is a finite set whose elements are *part-of-speech (POS)*;
- $\mathcal{L}$ is a finite set of triples of the form $\ell = (w, i, p)$, called *lexemes*, denoted by $\ell = w_p^i$, where $w \in A^*$ is a word, $i \geq 1$ is an integer and $p \in P$. The triple (w, i, p) is called the *i-th sense* of the *POS-tagged* ordered pair (w, p)
- $\mathcal{D}$ is a partial application associating with a lexeme $\ell \in \mathcal{L}$ a finite non empty sequence $D(\ell) = (\ell_1, \ell_2, \ldots, \ell_k)$, where for each i, $d_i \in \mathcal{L}$. Such a sequence is called the *definition* of ℓ.

The quadruple must satisfy the following constraints:

stop lexeme The set $\mathcal{P}$ contains a special element S, identifying the *stop lexemes*;

completeness For each triple $(w, i, p) \in \mathcal{L}$, if $p \neq S$, then $\mathcal{D}(w, i, p)$ is well-defined;

consistent numbering of lexemes If $(w, i, p) \in \mathcal{L}$ and $i > 1$, then $(w, i-1, p) \in \mathcal{L}$.

If for each triple $(w, i, p) \in \mathcal{L}$, we have $i = 1$, then the lexicon $X = (\mathcal{A}, \mathcal{P}, \mathcal{L}, \mathcal{D})$ is called *monosemic*. In that case, we write w_p instead of w_p^i.

TABLE I. A COMPLETE DISAMBIGUATED LEXICON.

ℓ	$D(\ell)$
BIG$_A$	(NOT$_S$, SMALL$_A$)
HUGE$_A$	(VERY$_S$, BIG$_A$)
SMALL$_A$	(NOT$_S$, BIG$_A$)

Roughly speaking, a complete disambiguated lexicon is a list of lexemes that are all defined, except the stop lexemes, and such that each definition is disambiguated.

Example 1. Let $X = (\mathcal{A}, \mathcal{P}, \mathcal{L}, \mathcal{D})$, where $\mathcal{A} = \{a, b, \ldots, z\}$, $\mathcal{P} = \{A, S\}$ (N = name, A = adjective, S = stop) and $\mathcal{L}$, $\mathcal{D}$ are defined in Table I. Each lexeme used in a definition is itself defined, except the stop lexemes NOT$_S$ and VERY$_S$. Hence, the lexicon X is complete and disambiguated.

In practice, words tagged with S are words playing mostly a syntactic role and whose semantic value is poor (such as *no*, *the*, *a*). However, any word can be placed in that category whenever its sense is not pertinent for a given study. From now on, we assume that $\mathcal{P} = \{N, V, A, R, S\}$, denoting respectively the POS *name*, *verb*, *adjective*, *adverb* and *stop*.

A *directed graph* is an ordered pair $G = (V, A)$, where V is a finite set whose elements are called *vertices* and $A \subseteq V \times V$ is a finite set whose elements are called *arcs*. The *density* of G, denoted by density(G), is the ratio of the number of arcs belonging to the graph over the number of possible arcs, *i.e.*, $\text{density(G)} = |A|/|V|^2$.

Let $G = (V, A)$ be a graph, $u, v \in V$ and k be a positive integer. We say that $p = (v_1, v_2, \ldots, v_k)$ is a *(directed) uv-path* of G if $u = v_1$, $v = v_k$ and $(v_i, v_{i+1}) \in E$ for $i = 1, 2, \ldots, k-1$. In particular, if $u = v$, the path p is called a *circuit* of G. Let $u, v \in V$. We write $u \rightarrow_G v$ whenever there exists a uv-path in G, or simply $u \rightarrow v$ if the graph G is clear from the context. Also, we write $u \leftrightarrow v$ if and only if $u \rightarrow v$ and $v \rightarrow u$. It is easy to verify that $\leftrightarrow$ is an equivalence relation. Hence, an equivalence class of the relation $\leftrightarrow$ is called *strongly connected component (SCC)* of $G = (V, A)$. In other words, two vertices belong to the same SCC if there exist directed paths connecting the first one to the second one and vice-versa. SCC can be computed in linear time by different algorithms, such as Tarjan's [19].

When computing statistics about directed graphs, it is often convenient to consider their undirected version. Given two vertices u, v of a directed graph $G = (V, A)$ and a positive integer k, we say that $p = (v_1, v_2, \ldots, v_k)$ is a *uv-chain* of G if $u = v_1$, $v = v_k$ and, for each $i = 1, 2, \ldots, k-1$, we have $(v_i, v_{i+1}) \in E$ or $(v_{i+1}, v_i) \in E$. The *length* of a uv-chain, denoted by $|p|$, is the number $k - 1$, *i.e.*, the number of arcs traveled by p. The *distance between u and v*, denoted by $\text{dist}(u, v)$, is the length of a shortest chain between u and v, *i.e.*,

$$\text{dist}(u, v) = \min\{|p| : p \text{ is a } uv\text{-chain}\}.$$

From these definitions, we can derive structural statistics for a given graph G. For instance, the *diameter of G*, denoted by $\text{diam}(G)$, is the maximal distance between two vertices of G:

$$\text{diam}(G) = \max\{\text{dist}(u, v) : u, v \in V\}.$$

Finally, the *characteristic path length (CPL)* of G is the average length of a shortest path between two vertices. It is denoted by $\mathrm{CPL}(G)$ and defined by

$$\mathrm{CPL}(G) = \sum_{u,v \in V} \frac{\mathrm{dist}(u,v)}{|V|(|V|-1)}.$$

If $X = (\mathcal{A}, \mathcal{P}, \mathcal{L}, \mathcal{D})$ is a complete disambiguated lexicon, then the *graph* of X is the directed graph $\mathrm{Graph}(X) = (\mathcal{L}, A)$, such that $(\ell_1, \ell_2) \in A$ if and only if the lexeme ℓ_1 appears in the définition $\mathcal{D}(\ell_2)$ of lexeme ℓ_2.

IV. The Dictionary Game

The "Dictionary Game" is a web-based, crowdsourced game, whose purpose is to create small but complete micro dictionaries of tractable size [3][20].

The reader can take a look at the game's web site for a more complete description of the game and even get down to build a new dictionary of one's own [21]. At the outset of the game, the player has to pick a "seed word" and provide a definition for it. After that, the words used in this first definition must in turn be defined. The game continues in the same manner, new definitions being created, new words being added and defined using existing or new words. The goal of the game is to "complete" the dictionary so that all the words used in definitions are themselves defined. Thus, the dictionary obtained at the end verifies all criteria of a complete lexicon according to Definition 1. To improve the expressiveness of the resulting dictionary, the player must also ensure that all the definitions provided contain at least three non stop lexemes. An error message is displayed if this constraint is not satisfied, inviting the player to improve the definition. Example 2 shows the written representation of the first words and definitions of a dictionary built using the seed word *horse*.

Example 2. Using the seed word *horse*:

- *horse*: animal on which one human rides
- *animal*: organism that belongs to the living kingdom
- *human*: animal species that possess reason
- etc.

Also, a graphical representation of the graph associated with a dictionary produced from the seed word *clock* is depicted in Figure 1.

Some additional data representation aspects must be taken into account to prepare the output of the "Dictionary Game" for further analysis.

1) Seed Words: As mentioned just before, game dictionaries are built using seed words. In the current version of the game, one can choose between 4 different seed words. We can see in the first columns of Table V these seed words along with the number of dictionaries built for each of them.

2) Graph Characteristics: The dictionaries produced by the players are converted to directed graphs, using the natural transformation described in Section III. To get an overview of the underlying structure, we computed several classic measures on the resulting graphs, summarized in Table II.

3) Words Psycholinguistic Properties: In order to portray the words used to build the game lexicons, we used external norms to tag them according to their psycholinguistic properties. Table III shows a few sample words along with their associated psycholinguistic properties:

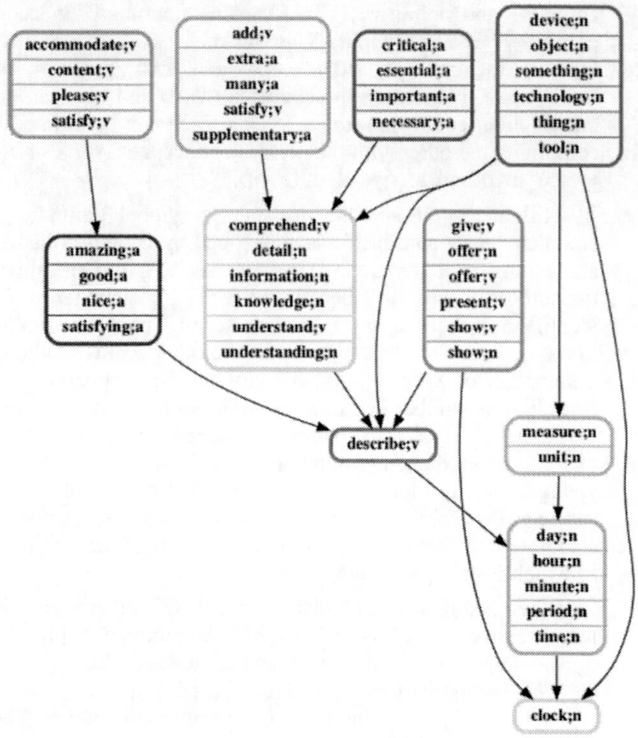

Figure 1. A dictionary produced by a player in the game, represented as a so-called "condensed" graph. Each SCC has been merged into a single meta-vertex containing equivalent words with respect to the relation $\leftrightarrow$.

TABLE II. Statistical properties of graph characteristics for all game dictionaries: *numV*: number of vertices, *numE*: number of edges, *nSCC*: number of Strongly Connected Components, *CPL*: characteristic path length, *dens*: density, *diam*: diameter.

	numV	*numE*	*nSCC*	*CPL*	*dens*	*diam*
Mean	124.0	436.1	7.0	4.8	0.038	13.1
Std	73.9	272.7	11.2	1.5	0.022	4.7
Min	35	120	1	0.87	0.008	3
Max	433	1558	88	11.4	0.108	35

Age of Acquisition: The variables AOAB and AOAC both represent estimations of the age at which a word is supposed to have been learned. They were sourced from psycholinguistic norms, [22] and [23], respectively.

Concreteness: The variable *Conc* is an evaluation, on a 1 to 5 scale, of whether a word is abstract or concrete [24].

Frequency: *FreqP* – [25] is a measure of the relative occurrence rate of words in the $\mathrm{SUBTLEX}_{US}$ corpus, while

TABLE III. A sample of words and their psycholinguistic properties. A missing value is written as a dash.

	AOAB	AOAC	*Conc*	*FreqP*	*FreqL*
abandon	8.32	—	2.54	8.10	1
abide	9.50	4.00	1.68	2.71	1
ability	8.84	—	1.81	19.22	38
able	7.79	4.77	2.38	159.90	39
absence	7.70	—	2.31	6.31	5
absent	6.50	8.28	2.70	2.57	1
...					

FreqL is a measure of the words' frequency in the corpus formed by collecting all the words from the game dictionaries definitions.

V. Experiments

We now describe the experiment we conducted, the resulting observations, and end with a short discussion.

A. Objectives and Method

The goal of this study is to understand the underlying structure of the game produced dictionaries. Specifically, since the game asks the players to construct dictionaries with a minimal number of words, we focused on the "winning" strategies. To provide such insights, we aim to extract co-occurrences between psycholinguistic and structural features in the dictionaries. To present these co-occurrences we use a dedicated formalism, the *association rules* [26]. Such rules are pairs $Y \rightarrow Z$, where Y and Z are sets of features respectively called *antecedent* and *consequent*, and state that any object presenting all the Y features, has also all the Z features. Associations are typically assessed by metrics, such as the *rules support* (proportion of objects incident to $Y \cup Z$) and *confidence* (proportion of objects with Z among those with Y). For clarity, we also provide the *antecedent support*, the proportion of objects presenting all the antecedent features. For instance, Rule #4 in the Table VII states that 35% objects (dictionaries) are $numV(lo)$ (low number of vertices), 29% objects are $numV(lo)$ and $dens(hi)$ (high density), and finally, 84% objects that are $numV(lo)$ are also $dens(hi)$.

To limit redundancy and maximize informativity, we focus on associations of a special form, called *concise association*. Such association are written $Y \rightarrow Z - Y$, where $Y \subseteq Z$ and there is no sets of features U, V such as $U \subseteq Y$, $Z \subseteq V$, where the rule $U \rightarrow V$ has the same support or confidence than $Y \rightarrow Z - Y$ [27]. To produce these specific associations rules, we use *RCA* [4]. FCA is a method that reveals the concise association rules of objects × attributes datasets (called *formal context*), such as the table *dict* in Figure 2, by expliciting, in a lattice, the hidden conceptual structure [5]. RCA extends FCA to the case where relations exists between objects, such as described in Example 3. The input of RCA is called a *Relational Context Family* (RCF), *i.e.*, a pair composed of a set of contexts and a set of binary relations between these concepts.

Example 3. Consider Figure 2. The *dict* table depicts a set of the dictionaries 1 to 5 with 6 features : three levels of vertices number $numV(lo)$, $numV(med)$ and $numV(hi)$ along with three seed words $horse$, $clock$ and $person$. Crosses indicate that the object has the given attribute, so dictionary 1 has many vertices and has been started with the seed word $clock$. Such a table, composed with a set of *objects* (the dictionaries), a set of *attributes* (the features) and an *incidence relation* (the set of couples represented by the crosses) is called a *formal context*. The *wd* table presents the *formal context* of words A to D with the attributes "young Brisbaert age of acquisition", "high concretude" and "lowest P-frequency". These two contexts can both be analyzed separately through FCA. RCA enrich each context with the use of *relations*, such as the one represented by the *ct* table (*ct* stands for "contains"), linking the dictionaries to the words by specifying which word exists in which dictionary.

dict	*numV*(hi)	*numV*(med)	*numV*(lo)	horse	clock	person
1	×				×	
2			×		×	
3			×			×
4	×			×		
5		×			×	

ct	*A*	*B*	*C*	*D*
1	×		×	×
2		×	×	
3				×
4	×	×	×	×
5	×		×	

wd	AOAB(young)	Conc(hi)	FrP(q_1)
A	×		
B	×	×	
C		×	
D	×		×

Figure 2. A sample RCF drawn from the dictionary game dataset.

TABLE IV. Extended problem context.

$dict{+}$	1	2	3	4	5
$\forall\exists ct$: (⊤)	×	×	×	×	×
$\exists_{60\%} ct$: (AOA(young))	×		×	×	
$\forall\exists ct$: (AOA(young), *FrP*(q_1))			×		
$\forall\exists ct$: (Conc(hi))		×			
$\forall\exists ct$: (AOA(young), Conc(hi))					

On such data, RCA iteratively performs multiple FCA tasks, one per context in the RCF. In doing that, relational links between objects are translated into special type of attributes, called *relational*, by a dedicated *propositionalization* mechanism [28]. It applies a variety of *scaling operators* mimicking role restrictions from description logics thus yielding attributes of the shape $q\ r : (Y)$ where q is the operator (*e.g.*, $\exists$, $\forall$, $\forall\exists$), r is a relation name (*e.g.*, *ct*) and Y is a set of attributes from the range context of r (*wd* for r =*ct* in our RCF). To avoid circularity and reduce redundancy, only maximal sets of attributes computed in anterior RCA iteration are considered, as suggested in [29]. An attribute $q\ r\ :\ (Y)$ refines the descriptions of the objects from the domain context of r (*dict* for *ct*), *i.e.*, it becomes an additional column in the ×-table, whereby its incidence to an object o is function of object's image, $r(o) = \{\bar{o} | (o, \bar{o}) \in r\}$, and the objects having the attributes Y in the range context. The exact function is defined by the operator q, *e.g.*, $\forall\exists$ tests $r(o) \neq \emptyset$ and if every objects of $r(o)$ has Y while $\cap_{\geq 60\%}$ checks if at least 60% objects of $r(o)$ has Y. Table IV presents some of the attributes generated by scaling upon *ct* with operators $\forall\exists$ and $\cap_{60\%}$.

As a result of the scaling, dictionary descriptions is refined with respect to the properties of the words they comprise, *e.g.*, 2 and 3 are both small-sized, yet 2 contains only highly concrete words which is not true for 3. When RCA terminates, a last FCA task is launched to generate the association rules from the final and extended contexts.

B. Model

As presented, RCA allows association rules extraction on a ×-table dataset. Therefore, dictionaries and words attributes need to be discretized into categorical attributes to enable the use of this method. For example, we can observe in Table V the

TABLE V. EXAMPLE OF DISCRETIZATION FOR THE *numV*GRAPH CHARACTERISTIC: *Seed*: SEED WORD USED TO BUILD THE DICTIONNARY, *NbDicts*: NUMBER OF DICTIONARIES BUILT USING THE SEED WORD, *Lo/Med/Hi* UPPER/LOWER LIMITS USED TO ESTABLISH THE CATEGORY

Seed	NbDicts	Lo	Med	Hi
clock	47	[39, 71]	[72, 111]	[112, 433]
horse	24	[40, 107]	[108, 136]	[137, 407]
person	13	[40, 108]	[109, 158]	[159, 243]
thing	10	[35, 103]	[104, 162]	[163, 288]

TABLE VI. DISCRETIZATION OF PSYCHOLINGUISTIC VARIABLES

	Words	
Property	Range	Category
AOAB	[2.3, 6.6]	young
	[6.7, 9.2]	middle
	[9.3, 16.2]	older
AOAC	[1.3, 3.74]	young
	[3.75, 4.70]	middle
	[4.71, 11.0]	older
CONC	[1.1, 2.3]	lo
	[2.4, 3.6]	med
	[3.7, 5.0]	hi
FREQP	[0.02, 3.56]	lo
	[3.57, 25.52]	med
	[25.53, 6161.41]	hi
FREQL	[0, 1]	Q1
	[2, 3]	Q2
	[4, 8]	Q3
	[9, 87]	Q4

minimum and maximum values for discrete categories for the *numV* property which equates to the number of vertices. For the *clock* seed word, the dictionaries whose *numV* is less than 72 are assigned to category *lo*, to category *med* if it is 72 or more but less than 111, and to category *hi* if it is 112 or more. We proceeded in a similar manner to subdivide the words into categories according to the value of their psycholinguistic properties, as shown in Table VI.

Using this discretization, we designed an RCF such as the one presented in Figure 3. The *words* formal context describes the words present in at least one of the dictionary with the discretized attributes presented in Table VI. The *dict* formal context describes the dictionaries using the seed words and the discretization, as shown in Table V, of every structural variable presented in Table II. Along with these two contexts, we use the relations *contains* (ct) that specify which words a dictionary contains and the inverse relation *in* that indicates in which dictionary a word is. An excerpt is presented in Figure 2.

To highlight special word classes, the relation *in* is scaled with the propositionnalization operator $\forall\exists$. A word having an attribute $\forall\exists in : (Y)$ can be interpreted as being used exclusively in dictionaries presenting all the features of Y. On the other side, the relation the relation *in* is scaled with the propositionnalization operators $\cap_{\geq p\%}$ for $p \in \{40, 50, 60, 70, 80, 90, 100\}$. A dictionary having an attribute $\cap_{\geq p\%}$ can be interpreted as being composed of at least $p\%$ words presenting all the features of Y. Note that $\cap_{\geq 100\%} = \forall\exists$. This choice is done because a granularity of 0.1 seems sufficient and below 40% an attribute does not present relevant information (characterizing a dictionary that has at least one word learned at young age does not bring substantial information).

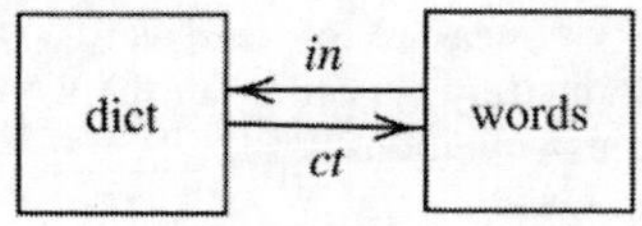

Figure 3. RCF schema used in our experiment

TABLE VII. SOME ASSOCIATION RULES PRODUCED BY THE RCF OF FIGURE 3

#	Antecedent	Consequent	Antecedent Support	Rule Support	Confidence
1	$\cap_{>60\%}$ *ct* : *FrL*(q_4)	$\forall\exists$ *ct* : ($\top$)	65%	65%	100%
2	$\forall\exists$ *ct* : ($\top$)	$\cap_{>40\%}$ *ct* : *FrL*(q_4)	100%	96%	96%
3	*numV(lo)*	$\cap_{\geq 60\%}$ *ct* : *FrL*(q_4)	35%	27%	79%
4	*numV(lo)*	*dens(hi)*	35%	29%	84%
5	*dens(hi)*	*numV(lo)*	32%	30%	93%
6	*dens(lo)*	*numV(hi)*	35%	31%	88%
7	*numV(hi)*	$\cap_{\geq 40\%}$ *ct* : *FrL*(q_4)	33%	31%	94%
8	*lSCC(lo)*	$\cap_{\geq 50\%}$ *ct* : *FrL*(q_4)	35%	35%	100%
9	*lSCC(lo)*	$\cap_{>60\%}$ *ct* : *FrL*(q_4)	35%	27%	79%
10	*lSCC(lo)*	*numV(lo)*	35%	32%	94%
11	$\forall\exists$*in* : (*numV(hi)*)	*FrL(q1)*	37%	27%	76%
12	*FrL(q1)*	$\forall\exists$*in* : (*numV(hi)*)	47%	28%	59%
13	$\forall\exists$*in* : (*numV(lo)*)	*FrL(q1)*	6.5%	6.2%	94%
14	*FrL(q1)*	$\forall\exists$*in* : (*numV(lo)*)	47%	6%	13%

C. Results

We now present the result of our experiment. They are summarized by association rules extracted by RCA.

Based on RCA's results after one iteration, we discovered interesting rules on the words (24 954 rules) as well as on the dictionaries (206 476 rules). Some of these rules are presented in Table VII. The rules are indexed in the first column. Other columns are described at the beginning of subsection V-A.

It is worth mentioning that we focused our rules extraction on the those related to the size of the dictionary (*numV*). Rules found in Table VII can be interpreted as follows:

#1 65% of the dictionaries contain more than 60% of words frequently used by the players (FrL(q_4)).

#2 96% of the dictionaries contain more than 40% of frequently used words (FrL(q_4))

Already, those two first rules suggest that players tend to use a significant set of common words.

#3 79% of the small dictionaries (*numV(lo)*) contain more than 60% of frequently used words (FrL(q_4)).

#4 85% of small dictionaries (*numV(lo)*) are dense (*dens(hi)*).

#5 93% of dense (*dens(hi)*) dictionaries are small (*numV(lo)*).

On one hand, these three rules show that, among the dense dictionaries, the probability of having 60% of frequent word (*FrL*(q_4)) increase when compared to the same probability for all dictionaries (79% against 65%). Moreover, there is a strong correlation between small and dense dictionaries.

#6 88% of sparse dictionaries (*dens*(lo)) are large (*numV*(hi)) and contain more than 60% words frequently used (*FrL*(q_4)).

#7 94% of large dictionaries (*numV(hi)*) contain more than 40% of frequently used words ($FrL(q_4)$).

Conversely, large dictionaries are sparse. Moreover, since there is no rule of the form $numV(hi) \rightarrow \cap_{>50\%}\ ct : FrL(q_4)$ is produced, we can state that 94% of large dictionaries contain more than 40% , but less than 50% of frequent words.

#8 All dictionaries having a small largest SCC (*lSCC(lo)*) have at least half of their words frequently used ($FrL(q_4)$).

#9 79% of dictionaries having a small largest SCC (*lSCC(lo)*) have at least 60% of words frequently used ($FrL(q_4)$).

#10 94% of dictionaries having a small largest SCC (*lSCC(lo)*) are small (*numV(lo)*).

Roughly speaking, a small largest SCC signifies that used words are more frequent and smaller.

#11 76% of words used only in large dictionaries (*numV(hi)*) are unfrequent (*FrL(lo)*).

#12 59% of rarely used words (*FrL(lo)*) are exclusively used in large dictionaries (*numV*(hi)).

#13 94% of words used exclusively in small dictionaries (*numV(lo)*) are unfrequent.

#14 13% of words unfrequent (*FrL(lo)*) words are exclusively used in small dictionaries (*numV(lo)*).

Hence, words exclusive to large dictionaries are unfrequent, and so are those exclusive to small dictionaries. However, unfrequent words are more characteristic to large dictionaries.

VI. Discussion and Concluding Remarks

From those observations, it seems that the following latent scenario is followed. For a given seed word, there are ideal sets of words that should be chosen. These ideal sets form a dictionary by minimizing the number of words, by exploiting a stronger density and, in particular, the density of the largest strongly connected component. However, players sometimes have difficulty to formulate those more complex definitions, and then diverge from these ideal sets of words. Two tendencies seem to prevail. In most of the cases, when a player hesitates over a definition, this definition loses concision and several definitions must be produced to compensate. There is no special reason to expect these divergences on the same words for different players. Words exclusive to small dictionaries suggest the existence of another answer from the players when facing more complex definitions: the players fall back on synonymy (see Figure 1) to avoid providing a complete and unambiguous definition.

One surprising discovery we made in the experiment was the absence of significant association rules related to the two other psycholinguistic variables (age of acquisition and concreteness). Almost all extracted rules have either weak antecedent support or weak rule support. It is also important to mention some limits of our experiments. First, the variable *numV* seems to be a rough and convenient statistic to measure the quality of a strategy for the dictionary game. However, it does not take into account the concision, the precision and the pertinence of the definitions. Moreover, the seed word seems to play a significant role in the observations. Consequently, in a future experiment, we intend to normalize the frequencies with respect to their seed words. In the same spirit, we plan to verify if the seed word is, by itself, important, or if it is only its psycholinguistic category that impacts the dictionary structure.

References

[1] S. Harnad, "The symbol grounding problem," Physica D: Nonlinear Phenomena, vol. 42, no. 1-3, 1990, pp. 335–346.

[2] A. Blondin Massé et al., "How is meaning grounded in dictionary definitions?" in Proceedings of the 3rd Textgraphs Workshop on Graph-Based Algorithms for Natural Language Processing, 2008.

[3] P. Vincent-Lamarre et al., "The latent structure of dictionaries," Topics in cognitive science, 2016.

[4] M. Rouane-Hacene et al., "Relational concept analysis: mining concept lattices from multi-relational data," AMAI, 2013.

[5] B. Ganter and R. Wille, Formal concept analysis: mathematical foundations, 1999.

[6] C. Goddard et al., "Introducing lexical primitives," Semantic and Lexical Universals. Theory and Empirical Findings, 1994.

[7] M. Taddeo et al., "Solving the symbol grounding problem: a critical review of fifteen years of research," Journal of Experimental & Theoretical AI, 2005.

[8] C. K. Ogden, "Basic English: A general introduction with rules and grammar, paul treber & co," Ltd. London, vol. 1940, 1930.

[9] ——, "Ogden's basic english," 2018. [Online]. Available: http://ogden.basic-english.org/wordmenu.html

[10] C. Garrido et al., "Dictionaries as networks: Identifying the graph structure of ogden's basic english," in Proceedings of COLING, 2016.

[11] A. Wierzbicka, Semantic Primitives. (Frankfurt/M.)Athenäum-Verl., 1972.

[12] ——, Semantics: Primes and universals: Primes and universals. Oxford University Press, UK, 1996.

[13] C. Browne, "The new general service list: A core vocabulary for EFL students & teachers," 2013.

[14] ——, "A new general service list: The better mousetrap we've been looking for," Vocabulary Learning and Instruction, vol. 3, 2014.

[15] C. Browne et al., "The new general service list: Celebrating 60 years of vocabulary learning," The Language Teacher, 2013.

[16] C. Goddard, Minimal English for a global world. Springer, 2018.

[17] A. Wierzbicka, "Natural semantic metalanguage," 2020. [Online]. Available: https://intranet.secure.griffith.edu.au/schools-departments/natural-semantic-metalanguage/what-is-nsm

[18] J.-M. Poulin et al., "Strategies for learning lexemes efficiently: A graph-based approach," in COGNITIVE 2018: The Tenth International Conference on Advanced Cognitive Technologies and Applications, 2018.

[19] R. Tarjan, "Depth-first search and linear graph algorithms," SIAM journal on computing, vol. 1, no. 2, 1972, pp. 146–160.

[20] O. Picard et al., "Hidden structure and function in the lexicon," arXiv preprint arXiv:1308.2428, 2013.

[21] P. Vincent-Lamarre et al., "The dictionary game," 2017. [Online]. Available: http://lexis.uqam.ca:8080/dictGame/index.jsp

[22] V. Kuperman et al., "Age-of-acquisition ratings for 30,000 english words," Behavior Research Methods, 2012.

[23] B. MacWhinney, The CHILDES Project: Tools for Analyzing Talk. Mahwah, NJ: Lawrence Erlbaum Associates, third edition, 2000.

[24] M. Brysbaert et al., "Concreteness ratings for 40 thousand generally known english word lemmas," Behavior research methods, 2014.

[25] M. Brysbaert and B. New, "Moving beyond kučera and francis: A critical evaluation of current word frequency norms and the introduction of a new and improved word frequency measure for american english," Behavior research methods, vol. 41, no. 4, 2009, pp. 977–990.

[26] R. Agrawal et al., "Fast discovery of association rules." Advances in knowledge discovery and data mining, vol. 12, no. 1, 1996.

[27] M. Kryszkiewicz, "Concise Representations of Association Rules," in Pattern Detection and Discovery. Springer, 2002, vol. 2447.

[28] S. Kramer et al., "Propositionalization approaches to relational data mining," in Relational Data Mining, 2001, pp. 262–291.

[29] M. Wajnberg et al., "Concept analysis-based association mining from linked data: A case in industrial decision making," JOWO, 2019.

International Academy, Research, and Industry Association (IARIA)
412 Derby Way
Wilmington, DE 19810

ISBN 978-1-7138-2166-3

9 781713 821663

CURRAN ASSOCIATES INC.
proceedings
.com

Eighth International Conference on Advances in Vehicular Systems, Technologies and Applications (VEHICULAR 2019)

Held at InfoWare 2019

Rome, Italy
30 June – 4 July 2019

IARIA